Reading Researchers
in Search of
Common Ground

Rona F. Flippo, Editor
Fitchburg State College
Fitchburg, Massachusetts, USA

INTERNATIONAL
Reading
Association

800 Barksdale Road, PO Box 8139
Newark, Delaware 19714-8139, USA
www.reading.org

The International Reading Association attempts, through its publications, to provide a forum for a wide spectrum of opinions on reading. This policy permits divergent viewpoints without implying the endorsement of the Association.

Director of Publications   Joan M. Irwin
Editorial Director, Books and Special Projects   Matthew W. Baker
Special Projects Editor   Tori Mello Bachman
Permissions Editor   Janet S. Parrack
Associate Editor   Jeanine K. McGann
Production Editor   Shannon Benner
Editorial Assistant   Tyanna L. Collins
Publications Manager   Beth Doughty
Production Department Manager   Iona Sauscermen
Art Director   Boni Nash
Supervisor, Electronic Publishing   Anette Schütz-Ruff
Senior Electronic Publishing Specialist   Cheryl J. Strum
Electronic Publishing Specialist   Lynn Harrison

Project Editor   Shannon Benner

Copyright 2001 by the International Reading Association, Inc.
All rights reserved. No part of this publication may be reproduced or transmitted in any form or by any means, electronic or mechanical, including photocopy, or any information storage and retrieval system, without permission from the publisher.

Library of Congress Cataloging-in-Publication Data
    Reading researchers in search of common ground / [edited by] Rona F. Flippo.
        p.   cm.
    Includes bibliographical references and index.
ISBN 0-87207-275-4
    1. Reading (Elementary) 2. Children—Books and reading. I. Flippo, Rona F.
LB1573 .R2799 2001
372.4—dc21   00-011703

For Tyler, Tara, and Todd

CONTENTS

PART II
MAKING SENSE OF LITERACY   99

FOREWORD

Our profession is indebted to Rona F. Flippo for conceptualizing an important investigation that has the potential to help us move forward as reading professionals. More than a decade ago, Rona set out to find common ground among experts in the much-fragmented field of reading research. Over a 10-year period, she conducted her groundbreaking "Expert Study," investigating what 11 eminent literacy scholars with diverse philosophies could agree to regarding contexts and practices for teaching reading. *Reading Researchers in Search of Common Ground* follows up and expands on the Expert Study, reinforcing and supplementing the evidence of common ground in the reading profession.

I'm pleased to see in Chapter 1 a reprint of the 1998 article "Points of Agreement: A Display of Professional Unity in Our Field" (originally published in *The Reading Teacher*), which provides background information and the basis for the remaining 18 chapters in this volume. Another thing that pleases me about this book is the quality of the professionals who responded so thoughtfully to their assigned tasks. These professionals are scholars; moreover, I know many of them personally, and they are also teachers. They possess a strong commitment to strengthening the quality of reading instruction.

Rona set out to find common ground, and she has. Comprehensive analyses of these findings and their implications are shared in *Reading Researchers in Search of Common Ground*, an invaluable resource for the entire literacy community.

I hope our profession heeds Rona's "real" common ground: Reading is not simple, and there are no simple answers or solutions that can be applied to all children and situations. This statement reflects the essence of a recent position statement of the International Reading Association titled *Making a Difference Means Making It Different*. I believe this statement and Rona's edited volume have the potential to empower teachers to plan and carry out instruction that is responsive to students' needs. Dedication to such instruction would be a huge step forward.

Jerry L. Johns
Distinguished Teaching Professor Emeritus
Northern Illinois University
DeKalb, Illinois, USA
Vice President, International Reading Association, 2000–2001

PREFACE

When people outside the reading field ask me about the research related to the "Expert Study" discussed throughout this volume, I always try to avoid the inevitable question that often follows: "But what approach to teaching reading works best?" If I do get cornered at some social event by someone who insists on asking this question, my response is typically, "For whom? For what? Why? When? And where?" Of course, this never satisfies the questioner, but without the answers to all of these questions, how could anyone suggest the "how"?

In this volume, no one will attempt to tell you "how." Instead, many notable scholars of reading and literacy research with diverse perspectives will try to help you better understand the need for these many questions. These same scholars will do so by reflecting on their own research and understandings and the findings from the Expert Study.

The Expert Study resulted from my interest in finding out what a group of eminent, highly respected reading experts, representative of various and diverse philosophies and orientations, could agree to regarding contexts and practices for teaching reading. I asked them each to respond with their ideas and to review each other's responses. This study took place over a 10-year period—neither the experts involved nor I had any idea that it would take so long, but once we got started, it became clear that *it was not as simple as one might think*. In Chapter 1, I share the findings of the study as well as provide the details on how it was conducted.

In addition to the beginning evidence of common ground that I reveal in Chapter 1, you will see more threads of it in Part I, "The Study, Findings, and Experts' Points of View." As you will note, the format of the chapters in Part I is as diverse as the experts themselves and often their points of view. Many have been written by the actual experts who took part in the study, while several were written by other scholars acting as biographers or voices for some of the experts. These scholars—Linda Fielding for Richard Anderson, Diane DeFord for Jerome Harste, and Robert Rude for Wayne Otto—were former doctoral students and have remained close associates of these experts, and Richard Robinson, both a scholar of the history of reading and an admirer of George Spache, does an excellent job conveying George's views based on his work and well-known publications. Although each author was given an identical set of specifications as to what to include in his or her chapter, true to their diversity, they approached the task by different paths. Even though the formats, writing styles, and content of these chapters, not to mention the authors, are diverse, readers of this volume are asked to keep in mind that *all of the experts agreed to all of the findings of the Expert Study*, as shared in Chapter 1.

In Part I, you will be enlightened by each of their points of view, and you will probably be amazed that they were able to reach agreements, sharing some common ground, even if it took 10 years to evolve.

Next, in Parts II and III, yet more evidence of this common ground appears in the discussions prepared by additional distinguished literacy scholars. In Part II, "Making Sense of Literacy," I asked literacy scholars with particular expertise in the areas of multicultural education and students of diverse backgrounds (Kathryn Au), struggling readers (Victoria Purcell-Gates), and motivation and reading (Linda Gambrell) to review the literature and research in these areas, and to discuss to what extent these might support the findings from the Expert Study.

Then, in Part III, "Toward a Common Ground," other scholars with specialized experiences and vantage points from which to view the Expert Study were invited to review the findings reported in Chapter 1 and share their insights. Jay Campbell, first author of the 1994 National Assessment of Educational Progress (NAEP), discusses the NAEP data and the findings of the Expert Study. Timothy Rasinski, former coeditor of the International Reading Association (IRA) journal *The Reading Teacher* and a spokesperson for parent education and involvement, discusses his views and concerns. Richard Vacca, former IRA president, discusses the media, the policies, and his own experiences with these as president of IRA, offering suggestions regarding use of the Expert Study findings. Finally, in Chapter 19, I pull together the threads of common ground that I see and share them: Although some of the experts involved in my study may still be somewhat in denial of any real common ground, and one of them has actually explained why (see remarks by Scott Paris in Chapter 9), *I really do see common ground throughout this volume* and in this final chapter, I point it out.

A project of the magnitude of this volume certainly involved a major amount of my time and energy, but it could not have been completed without the help and encouragement of many others. I especially want to acknowledge my husband, Tyler Fox, for the many hours he spent with me discussing, agonizing over, and analyzing the "politics" outside as well as inside the field of literacy education, and for his encouragement and helpful suggestions throughout this entire project. Also, my daughter, Tara Flippo, whose unwavering love, support, and interest in my work have always sustained me. Additionally, special recognition must go to Sherri Borreson, a classroom teacher and graduate student at Fitchburg State College, who worked with me "behind the scenes" throughout this endeavor. Sherri helped prepare innumerable letters and proposals to everyone involved with this project, and she assisted me during the editing stages that followed. Ron Elbert, my typist, deserves acknowledgment for his hard work and advice. Richard Robinson provided encouragement throughout. He helped me pull things together with his excellent insight and graciously authored the part introductions. Matt Baker, IRA's Editorial Director of Books and Special Projects, with his wisdom and understanding of the complexities involved, facilitated closure to this project. And Shannon Benner, IRA's Production Editor, must be thanked for her hard work and assistance in getting this book to press.

I must finally acknowledge and thank the many experts who contributed to this volume—both the experts involved in my study and the other experts, also distinguished scholars in the field of reading and literacy, who contributed the point of view and discussant chapters. Thank you all for your insightful contributions.

Rona F. Flippo

BIOGRAPHIES

The Editor

Rona F. Flippo, Professor of Education at Fitchburg State College, Fitchburg, Massachusetts, USA, is the researcher and author of the Expert Study reported in this volume, and author of several related publications, including *What Do the Experts Say? Helping Children Learn to Read* (1999). Her Expert Study has been the subject of an educational television series, broadcast internationally, featuring Rona and many of the contributors to this book. Rona is also known for her many other publications on reading assessment, reading education, reading tests, and study and test-taking strategies for students at all levels, as well as teacher certification testing issues. Her strong interest in policy and the politics affecting education have led her toward research and writing for a broad audience, including the general public.

The Experts

Richard C. Anderson, Professor of Education and Psychology and Director of the Center for the Study of Reading at the University of Illinois, Champaign, Illinois, USA, is first author of the U.S. national report and best-selling book *Becoming a Nation of Readers* (1985). He was Chair of the National Academy of Education–National Institute of Education Commission on Reading 1983–1984, served as President of the American Educational Research Association in 1983, and was elected to the Reading Hall of Fame in 1991.

Brian Cambourne, Associate Professor and Head of the Centre for Studies in Literacy at the University of Wollongong, New South Wales, Australia, authored the internationally recognized Conditions for Learning model to explain how literacy learning occurs. He was featured in *The Reading Teacher* Distinguished Educator Series in November 1995 and was elected to the Reading Hall of Fame in 1998.

Edward B. Fry, Professor Emeritus at Rutgers University, New Brunswick, New Jersey, USA, is author of the Fry Readability Graph, used worldwide by publishers, test developers, and educators; he is also known for his Instant Word List. He was President of the National Reading Conference 1974–1976 and was elected to the Reading Hall of Fame in 1993.

Yetta M. Goodman, Regents Professor of Education at the University of Arizona, Tucson, Arizona, USA, is author of the Reading Miscue Inventory, as well as numerous publications on this and other topics. Her research on early literacy resulted in the concept of "kidwatching." She was President of the National Council of Teachers of English 1979–1980 and on the International Reading Association's Board of Directors 1994–1997. She was featured in *The Reading Teacher* Distinguished Educator Series in May 1996 and was elected to the Reading Hall of Fame in 1994.

Jane Hansen, Professor in the McGuffey Reading Center at Curry School of Education, University of Virginia, Charlottesville, Virginia, USA, was co-originator of the Author's Chair, a procedure for sharing writing and literature that is used by teachers and children in classrooms all over the world. She was President of the National Reading Conference 1994–1995 and was featured in *The Reading Teacher* Distinguished Educator Series in November 1996.

Jerome C. Harste, Professor in the Department of Language Education at Indiana University, Bloomington, Indiana, USA, is author of several books on whole language. He was President of the National Reading Conference 1986–1987, the National Council of Teachers of English 1999–2000, and on the International Reading Association's Board of Directors 1989–1991. He was featured in *The Reading Teacher* Distinguished Educator Series in 1994 and was elected to the Reading Hall of Fame in 1997.

Wayne R. Otto, Professor Emeritus in the Department of Curriculum and Instruction at the University of Wisconsin-Madison, Madison, Wisconsin, USA, was the principal investigator for the Wisconsin Design for Reading Skill Development—a plan used throughout the United States for managing classroom reading instruction with a focus on specific skill development. He served on the boards of directors of the National Reading Conference (1975–1977) and the American Reading Forum (1980–1984), and was elected to the Reading Hall of Fame in 1992.

Scott G. Paris, Professor of Psychology and Education at the University of Michigan/Center for the Improvement of Early Reading Achievement, Ann Arbor, Michigan, USA, is the author of many publications on authentic reading assessment and the development of reading strategies. Additionally, he has researched the effects of different assessments, such as standardized tests and portfolios, on students, teachers, and parents. He is 2000–2001 Chair of the International Reading Association Issues in Literacy Assessment Committee.

P. David Pearson, Hannah Distinguished Professor of Education and Codirector of the Center for the Improvement of Early Reading Achievement at Michigan State University, East Lansing, Michigan, USA, was first editor of the *Handbook of Reading Research* in 1984 and coeditor of two subsequent volumes. He codirected the original "Standards Project for English Language Arts" (1992–1994), was President of the National Reading Conference 1985–1986, and was on the International Reading Association's Board of Directors 1984–1988. In 1990 he was elected to the Reading Hall of Fame.

George D. Spache, former Professor Emeritus at the University of Florida, Gainesville, Florida, USA, authored the Diagnostic Reading Scales, a widely used reading test originally published in 1963. His research on vision and reading led to his development of the Binocular Reading Test. He served as President of the International Reading Association 1958–1959, President of the National Reading Conference 1962–1964, and was on the American Reading Forum Board of Directors from its founding in 1980 through 1984. He was elected to the Reading Hall of Fame in 1974.

Rand J. Spiro, Professor of Educational Psychology and a researcher at the Center for the Improvement of Early Reading Achievement at Michigan State University, East Lansing, Michigan, USA, is the author and editor of many research books and articles on reading comprehension, text processing, schema theory, learning in complex domains, and hypertext. He is also the originator of Cognitive Flexibility Theory.

Other Contributors

Kathryn H. Au, Professor of Education at the University of Hawaii, Honolulu, Hawaii, USA, is known for her research on multicultural literacy and students of diverse backgrounds and languages. Kathryn has been Vice President of the

American Educational Research Association (1992–1994), President of the National Reading Conference (1996–1997), and an International Reading Association Board member (1998–2001). She was elected to the Reading Hall of Fame in 1999.

Jay R. Campbell, Director of Reporting for the National Assessment of Educational Progress (NAEP) at Educational Testing Service, Princeton, New Jersey, USA, is an educational psychologist with an expertise in large-scale educational assessment. He was the coordinator of the NAEP reading assessment and first author of the 1994 NAEP Reading Report Card, one of the catalysts for the so-called Reading Wars; additionally, Jay has been a researcher and coauthor of various NAEP reports from 1992 to the present.

Diane E. DeFord, Professor of Education at The Ohio State University, Columbus, Ohio, USA, was one of Jerome Harste's graduate students, and she had the opportunity to work with him during both her master's and doctoral programs. Her own research, which has led to assessing teachers' beliefs about literacy, and her additional success as an author of books for children are known widely.

Linda G. Fielding, Associate Professor of Education at the University of Iowa, Iowa City, Iowa, USA, was one of Richard Anderson's doctoral students and his research assistant when Anderson was doing much of his research and reporting for *Becoming a Nation of Readers*. Linda also conducted research with Anderson related to children's voluntary reading; her own research has focused on literacy instruction for struggling readers and writers in regular classrooms.

Linda B. Gambrell, Professor and Director of the School of Education at Clemson University, Clemson, South Carolina, USA, is known for her studies related to motivation and reading performance. Linda was President of the National Reading Conference (1998–1999), President of the College Reading Association (1981–1982), and an International Reading Association Board member (1992–1995).

Victoria Purcell-Gates, Professor of Education at Michigan State University, East Lansing, Michigan, USA, researches literacy acquisition and has considerable experience working with struggling readers of all ages. She is Program Chair for the American Educational Research Association (2001) and is a member of the National Reading Conference Board of Directors (2000–2002). Her award-winning book, *In Other People's Words: The Cycle of Low Literacy* (1997), chronicles her successful work with a nonliterate family.

Timothy V. Rasinski, Professor of Education at Kent State University, Kent, Ohio, USA, is known for his interest in and work with parents and families of school-aged children. He was Coeditor of the International Reading Association's *The Reading Teacher* (1992–1999) and served as President of the College Reading Association 1997–1998.

Richard D. Robinson, Professor of Education at the University of Missouri-Columbia, Columbia, Missouri, USA, is known for his studies of the history of reading and as a commentator regarding the reading debates of recent years. He has studied and admired the works of George Spache and has authored publications on content area reading and issues and trends in literacy education.

Robert T. Rude, Professor of Elementary Education at Rhode Island College, Providence, Rhode Island, USA, was one of Wayne Otto's doctoral students during and immediately following the time when Wayne and his colleagues created the Wisconsin Design for Reading Skill Development. Subsequently Robert's own research has focused on teacher training and directing Rhode Island College's literacy clinic.

Richard T. Vacca, Professor and Program Coordinator of Curriculum and Instruction at Kent State University, Kent, Ohio, USA, was President of the International Reading Association from 1996–1997, while the so-called Reading Wars were getting constant media attention. He also served on the Board of Directors of the College Reading Association 1985–1988, and is known for his expertise and books on content area reading for middle and high school students.

PART I

THE STUDY, FINDINGS, AND EXPERTS' POINTS OF VIEW

Literacy education has a long history of a seemingly never-ending search for the best method of teaching reading. At almost any point in this history there have been struggles, both philosophical and pedagogical, between various positions on what constitutes effective reading instruction. Recent controversies in the teaching of reading have included whole language, phonics, and the basal reader. In each of these examples, advocates of a particular position, skill, or reading approach believed that their ideas and beliefs were so unique and of such significant difference from all previous systems of reading instruction to mark them as indispensable. Thus, we have had a "pendulum of change" in reading education that has been characterized by methods and approaches extending from one extreme to another (Robinson, Baker, & Clegg, 1998).

One recurring theme throughout these extremes in reading education has been the belief that one approach to reading instruction was better than another; however, the First-Grade Studies (see Bond & Dykstra, 1967), perhaps the most extensive evaluation of various approaches to the teaching of reading, proved that belief wrong. This U.S. Office of Education–sponsored research was based on a comparison of 27 different classroom reading programs. Of the many findings of this work, the most important for this discussion was that while there were significant differences within a particular approach, this was not also true for differences between approaches or individual reading programs. As noted by Bond and Dykstra (1967), "There is supporting evidence that greater variation is found within any method than between the methods" (p. 8).

The other recurring theme has been the belief that there are few, if any, commonalities between the understandings of those representing various philosophies and approaches in the field of reading; however, the Expert Study described and discussed in this volume (Flippo, 1998; refer to Chapter 1 in this book) has proved that belief wrong, too. It was the purpose of the Expert Study to search for common understandings and beliefs in the teaching of reading. While in one sense this has been an interesting academic question, it also has profound implications for classroom reading instruction.

The search for agreements and common ground in reading education is of utmost importance. If we hope to positively influence classroom instruction, we need to recognize and build on what are generally considered by diverse reading experts to be effective reading development contexts and practices, and we need to be aware of the practices that diverse reading experts agree are not generally effective with most children and in most situations. A basic canon of these understandings in reading education should be part of the foundation against which new developments in the field can be measured in determining potential effectiveness and impact on children and their learning. Without an acute awareness of these common agreements in reading education we are destined for additional non-productive pendulum swings and meaningless searches for a one best approach.

In Part I, the diverse reading experts who took part in the Expert Study identify their views and discuss their individual beliefs about reading and learning as well as provide readers with the opportunity to see some of the commonalities in their thinking. The authors each describe their personal views regarding literacy in reference to their own unique belief systems and research concerning reading education. While there are many differences between these experts' views, there are also surprising similarities.

Flippo sets the stage for this discussion in the opening chapter, where she describes the basic research design and procedures she used to identify the common agreements that became evident from her study. As she explains, these statements of agreement include both those practices that tend to facilitate learning to read as well as those that can make learning to read difficult.

The first viewpoint article, written by Linda Fielding, details the point of view of reading expert Richard Anderson. The theme of this chapter is the influence of research and its implications for effective reading instruction. Anderson's well-known report, *Becoming A Nation of Readers* (1985), details many of his views on the reading process, supported by his and others' extensive research. These views support the common agreements of the reading experts in the Expert Study.

Brian Cambourne traces his own development in the last decade or so as a literacy researcher and teacher. In particular, he notes how his experiences during this time period have shaped and at times changed some of his beliefs concerning reading education. Of particular note is his continued realization of the complexity of the reading process and how this learning process frequently is not taken into account in many research studies.

Next, Edward Fry focuses on his beliefs and research on testing, readability, word frequency, phonics, and diacritical markings. He discusses his own participation in the First-Grade Studies (see Bond & Dykstra, 1967) and emphasizes the conclusion that the results show there was not a great difference in students' learning between any of the methods of teaching reading. Even though he still strongly believes in the importance of readability, phonics, and testing students, he makes it clear that he does agree with all the items on the agreement lists of the Expert Study. He explains how he would add other things to these agreements as well if it were solely up to him.

The importance of the classroom setting and the role of the classroom teacher in literacy education are fundamental themes in Yetta Goodman's chapter. She clearly illustrates her growth and development as a teacher, a teacher of teachers, and a researcher in her understanding of the reading process. Each of these educational experiences has enriched her basic understanding of the complexities of the classroom and, in turn, has provided deep insights into how the agreements of the reading experts in this study can potentially have a significant impact on school literacy instruction.

Jane Hansen describes her past and current development as a teacher of reading through her experiences as a graduate student, a classroom teacher, and a university professor. Each of these aspects of her professional life have added significantly to her current belief system about reading education, which is reflected in the points of agreement among the experts in this study.

The expert viewpoint of Jerome Harste, written by Diane DeFord, describes Harste's basic beliefs as they relate to the reading process. Of particular importance in this discussion is Harste's sense of the importance of community as a foundation for putting basic literacy theory into practice in the classroom setting.

The expert viewpoint piece on Wayne Otto, written by Robert Rude, traces the development and implementation of the *Wisconsin Design for Reading Skill Development* (1970). He notes the strengths and the weaknesses of this view or philosophy of the reading process, especially in relation to current practices in reading education.

Scott Paris describes his background in education, especially his insightful work with classroom teachers. It was through these experiences that he began to develop a belief system as to how to influence classroom instruction and learning. Throughout his chapter he notes how his current beliefs interact with what the other reading experts in this study consider important in the facilitation or limiting of students' learning to read.

P. David Pearson defends his position as one who takes the middle ground in relation to various reading paradigms and practices. He carefully details his reasons for taking this philosophical as well as practical position by explaining in seven tenets or premises his basic beliefs concerning the reading process. It is important to note how closely many of these concepts relate to the common agreements of all the reading experts in this study.

The expert viewpoint of George Spache, written by Richard Robinson, builds on Spache's rich and varied lifelong experience as a reading researcher, as a teacher trainer in reading education, and as a director of one of the first reading clinics in the United States. Noted are how many of the fundamental beliefs in reading education have remained remarkably constant throughout much of the history of the teaching of reading. This is an important conclusion in the face of the seeming constant change in the fads and foibles of reading instruction. Spache's work clearly supports the collective agreements of the experts in this study, through support of the relevant research literature and classroom practices in this area.

Finally, Rand Spiro discusses his own research and understandings of reading and other cognitive processes. His extensive research led him to the agreements that have been documented in Flippo's Expert Study. He explains the coordination of multiple theoretical perspectives into actual practice and how this involves principled pluralism and its relationship to the need for adaptive flexibility in teaching reading and all other learnings. Spiro lays out these ideas as important "next generation" research questions, challenges, and frontiers.

Richard D. Robinson

REFERENCES

Anderson, R.C., Hiebert, E.H., Scott, J.A., & Wilkinson, I.A.G. (1985). *Becoming a nation of readers.* Washington, DC: National Institute of Education.

Bond, G.L., & Dykstra, R. (1967). Interpreting the first-grade reading studies. In R.G. Stauffer (Ed.), *The first grade reading studies: Findings of individual investigations* (pp. 1–9). Newark, DE: International Reading Association.

Flippo, R.F. (1998). Points of agreement: A display of professional unity in our field. *The Reading Teacher, 52,* 30–40.

Robinson, R.D., Baker, E., & Clegg, L. (1998). Literacy and the pendulum of change: Lessons for the 21st century. *Peabody Journal of Education, 73,* 15–30.

Wisconsin Research and Development Center for Cognitive Learning. (1970). *Wisconsin Design for Reading Skill Development.* Minneapolis, MN: National Computer Systems.

CHAPTER 1

About the Expert Study: Report and Findings

Rona F. Flippo

C all me an optimist, but I have always believed that most people, whoever they are, share something in common—some common denominator that makes them human, that allows them to reason, to share, to discuss, and then to reason some more—*to search for their common understandings, beliefs, and goals.* That is probably why I was so interested in beginning, in 1986, what has come to be known as the "Expert Study."

I believed then, and I still believe now, that despite their many and obvious differences and orientations, reading experts with very diverse philosophies and experiences do share some common ground. I set out to find it, and I believe I have.

The remainder of this first chapter reviews the background, rationale, procedures, and findings of the Expert Study. With the permission of the International Reading Association, my article "Points of Agreement: A Display of Professional Unity in Our Field" (Flippo, 1998b) has been reprinted in this chapter to provide the necessary details and information. In the chapters that follow, contributors to this volume reflect on the clustered summary agreements displayed in Figures 3 and 4 (pages 12 and 14). The experts involved in this study are themselves each briefly described in Figure 2 (page 10), and in Figure 5 (page 17) they each present their personal definitions and philosophy statements regarding education and literacy development.

I do want to emphasize that these agreements, both the lists of contexts and practices that "would make learning to read difficult" and those that "would facilitate learning to read" (see Figures 3 and 4), are the very carefully agreed-upon wording of the experts—all 11 of them who took part in my study. These are not my words or ideas: The ownership of these agreements rests with the experts you will hear from in the remaining chapters of Part I. Also, it should be understood that these agreements are not ordered in any way (e.g., from most important to least important), nor do they represent all that is important to reading development.

Finally, it is essential to understand that these agreements are *not* about approaches or methods of teaching reading. The experts *have clearly not* endorsed any particular approach. They have instead developed and agreed on certain contexts and practices that they collectively believe would *tend* to facilitate reading and others that they believe would *tend* to make reading more difficult *for most children*. However, they would all quickly point out that teachers' decisions need to be both child- and situation-specific. *There are no absolutes.*

For those readers who are interested in reading some of the other publications I have authored pertaining to this study, and also more about the politics I see surrounding the so-called "Reading Wars," see Flippo, 1997, 1998a, and 1999a. For the complete original listings of expert agreements—as well as a look at what classroom teachers, experts in their own right, think about these findings and how these findings relate to actual classroom situations—refer additionally to Flippo, 1999b.

REFERENCES

Flippo, R.F. (1997). Sensationalism, politics, and literacy: What's going on? *Phi Delta Kappan, 79*, 301–304.

Flippo, R.F. (1998a). Finding common ground: A review of the Expert Study. In E.G. Sturtevant, J. Dugan, P. Linder, & W.M. Linek (Eds.), *Literacy and community: Twentieth yearbook of the College Reading Association* (pp. 31–38). Carrollton, GA: College Reading Association.

Flippo, R.F. (1998b). Points of agreement: A display of professional unity in our field. *The Reading Teacher, 52*, 30–40.

Flippo, R.F. (1999a). Redefining the Reading Wars: The war against reading researchers. *Educational Leadership, 57*, 38–41.

Flippo, R.F. (1999b). *What do the experts say? Helping children learn to read.* Portsmouth, NH: Heinemann.

Reprinted from *The Reading Teacher*, 52, 30–40, September 1998.

Points of Agreement: A Display of Professional Unity in Our Field

Rona F. Flippo

A headline from a recent article in *Parents Magazine* (Levine, 1996) graphically illustrates a growing misperception that poses a serious dilemma for the literacy education community: "Parents report on America's reading crisis: Why the whole-language approach to teaching has failed millions of children" (p. 63). How does this affect our field? Looking a little further, we read:

> Concerns are being echoed nationwide by thousands of parents, who have been fighting for more skills instruction in schools. Parents have pressed at least 15 state legislatures to pass pro-phonics legislation. And many parents have had to hire private tutors to teach the reading skills their schools ignored. (p. 64)

A spirit of divisiveness about reading instruction now exists that is causing a tangle of problems for communities, schools, teachers, and children and their families. This divisiveness has led to misunderstandings of the issues, discrediting of teachers and schools, misinformation being disseminated to parents and families, searches for simplistic solutions, and, not least, to the media and politicians "stepping in" to exploit these concerns. (See Flippo, 1997, for some examples of what has been going on.)

The media, politicians, and general public believe that the field of literacy is so divided that we do not agree on anything. Therefore, they take it upon themselves to seek solutions and make decisions without regard to the informed opinion of the literacy education community.

But are we as a field really that divided? The study reported in this article explored the idea that, as a field, even within a continuum of very divergent beliefs and philosophies, there must be some things that most of us really do agree on. Public misperceptions of intractable divisions within the field of literacy education need not persist. We do have many common agreements about contexts for learning and instruction in classrooms, as this study shows.

The Study

In 1973 Frank Smith, a leader in the psycholinguistic movement, published a list of practices that he felt would impede children's reading development. Smith's list of statements has been cited fairly often in the literature, and it seemed to furnish an adequate starting point on which to stimulate interest and discussion, to identify what might be the areas of agreement among acknowledged experts in an often contentious field. Beginning in 1986 I contacted leading experts in the field of reading to arrange a meeting of the minds on Smith's statements. The question was how to conduct the discussion, and I decided to use the Delphi technique.

Linstone and Turoff (1975) define the Delphi "as a method for structuring a group communication process so that the process is effective in allowing a group of individuals, as a whole, to deal with a complex problem" (p. 3). The problem in my study was "What can you agree to regarding contexts and practices for teaching reading?" Linstone and Turoff suggest there are no hard and fast rules for conducting a Delphi technique study—which endows it with a flexibility that actually enhances the problem-solving process. The Delphi technique thus provided an opportunity for structured communication, by which expert panel members could provide feedback, revise judgments, and contribute to the development of agreed-upon practices—all with complete anonymity.

Through the use of this technique, the selected group of reading experts responded to Smith's 1973 list individually, each expert agreeing or disagreeing with each of the statements. The items on the Smith list that they all agreed would make learning to read difficult I have indicated with an asterisk (see Figure 1). Then, over a period of 10 years (which was unplanned but necessary to effectively complete the procedure), they each generated their own items that they believed would make learning to read difficult for children and a separate listing of items they believed would facilitate learning to read. During this time, each of the participants anonymously reviewed items generated by the others to thus produce lists of items most of them agreed with.

Each time we communicated, I reminded the experts to accept, modify, or reject any of the suggested items. All changed items were added to the suggested list to be scrutinized by the others. None of the participants directly communicated any of the items to any of the other participants—they did so only to me as the researcher, during follow-up interviews, when clarification seemed necessary. If at any time more than two experts disagreed with the idea or wording of an item, it was dropped from the lists. This procedure continued for the duration of the study.

I wanted the 11 participating experts selected to represent the broad and diverse range of research, beliefs, and philosophies regarding reading instruction. I did not choose participants at random. When I planned the study, I generated listings of the names of leading representatives of each of the three most prevalent

---

Figure 1
Twelve Easy Ways to Make Learning to Read Difficult

---

1. Aim for early mastery of the rules of reading.
2. Ensure that phonic skills are learned and used.
*3. Teach letters and words one at a time, making sure that each new letter or word is learned before moving on.
*4. Make word-perfect reading the prime objective.
5. Discourage guessing; be sure the children read carefully.
6. Encourage the avoidance of errors.
7. Provide immediate feedback.
*8. Detect and correct inappropriate eye movements.
9. Identify and give special attention to problem readers as soon as possible.
10. Make sure children understand the importance of reading and the seriousness of falling behind.
11. Take the opportunity during reading instruction to improve spelling and written expression, and also insist on the best possible spoken English.
12. If the method you are using is unsatisfactory, try another. Always be alert for new materials and techniques.

Note: We had total agreement on each of Smith's (1973) items noted with an asterisk (*).

---

philosophies (*traditional, whole language,* and *interactive*). I sought experts who had achieved wide recognition from their peers for their publications and leadership in the field of reading and literacy, and whose contributions teachers, administrators, and politicians would respect. P. David Pearson, who edited the first *Handbook of Reading Research* (1984), which surveyed the entire field, reviewed the list of those who had accepted the invitation and confirmed that, in his opinion, the list was balanced and representative of all the major philosophies.

Figure 2 presents a listing of these experts and what they are each generally most known for in reading and literacy. Of the 11 experts, 4 have been featured in *The Reading Teacher* (3 in its Distinguished Educator Series), and 8 have been elected to the Reading Hall of Fame. All have published seminal works or designed widely accepted theories, models, strategies, and assessments/tests affecting the field of reading education.

About halfway through the study, I again asked Pearson to confirm my list, to determine whether he still felt it struck a representative balance among the current major perspectives. Finally, at the conclusion of the study, I called on an outside panel of six reading educators, all familiar with the past research and publications of the 11 experts, especially their best known works, to each independently evaluate the list's representativeness in regard to the three main (and notably divergent) philosophies in contemporary literacy education.

Figure 2
Expert Participants: Who Are They? Why Are They Important?

Richard Anderson — Coauthor of the national report *Becoming a Nation of Readers* (Anderson, Hiebert, Scott, & Wilkinson, 1985), and elected to the Reading Hall of Fame in 1991.

Brian Cambourne — Australian author of the Conditions for Learning model (see Cambourne, 1988), featured in *The Reading Teacher* Distinguished Educator Series (November 1995), and elected to the Reading Hall of Fame in 1998.

Edward Fry — Author of the Fry Readability Graph (see Fry, 1977), and elected to the Reading Hall of Fame in 1993.

Yetta Goodman — Author of the Reading Miscue Inventory (see Goodman, Watson, & Burke, 1987), known as the original "kidwatcher," featured in *The Reading Teacher* Distinguished Educator Series (May 1996), and elected to the Reading Hall of Fame in 1994.

Jane Hansen — One of the conceivers of the Author's Chair concept (Graves & Hansen, 1983) and featured in *The Reading Teacher* Distinguished Educator Series (November 1996).

Jerry Harste — Author of whole language books (e.g., Short & Harste, 1996), featured in *The Reading Teacher* (Monson & Monson, 1994), and elected to the Reading Hall of Fame in 1997.

Wayne Otto — Author of "The Wisconsin Design" (Otto, 1977)—a plan that was used throughout the U.S. for managing classroom reading instruction with a focus on specific skill development. Authored the "Views and Reviews" column in the *Journal of Reading* for over 10 years and was elected to the Reading Hall of Fame in 1992.

Scott Paris — Author of many publications on authentic/portfolio assessment and the development of reading strategies (e.g., Paris & Ayres, 1994; Turner & Paris, 1995).

P. David Pearson — Editor of the *Handbook of Reading Research* (1984), codirector of the original "Standards Project for English Language Arts" (1992–1994), and elected to the Reading Hall of Fame in 1990.

George Spache — Author of the *Diagnostic Reading Scales* (1981)—a widely used reading test originally published in 1963, past President of IRA (1958–1959), and elected to the Reading Hall of Fame in 1974.

Rand Spiro — Author and editor of many research books and articles on reading comprehension, text processing, and schema theory (e.g., Spiro, 1980; Spiro, Coulson, Feltovich, & Anderson, 1994).

Although these experts would not want to be "labeled" in any simplistic way, the works that they are each most known for often put them into one of the three main camps or positions: the *traditional* perspective, also known as the "text-based," "specific skills," or "bottom-up" perspective of how text is processed by readers; the *whole language* perspective, also known as the "reader-based," "holistic," or "top-down" perspective of how readers process text; and the *interactive* perspective, also known as the "integrated" perspective of text processing, which employs both text-based and reader-based processing.

All too often in recent years, the misleading and false issue of "phonics *or* whole language" has been raised by media, politicians, and special interest groups. (In this debate the "phonics" side is usually attributed to those who represent a *traditional* position.) This type of public debate and posturing renders it all the more vital that this study should represent all sides, not forgetting the middle, on its panel of experts. Although the debates about reading instruction go much deeper and broader than discussions about how readers process text, these text-processing designations (*traditional, interactive,* and *whole language*) have come to represent a range of ideas in the field of reading that for most of us express the much larger viewpoints. Thus I sought to ensure that all of these "camps" would be represented.

The Findings

The experts, as it turned out, unanimously agreed on a whole range of contexts and practices that would make learning to read difficult for children and many other practices that would facilitate learning to read. In order to organize the items into a more usable and readable form, I reviewed and sorted the items into natural categories. Figures 3 and 4 present clustered summary lists of these points of agreement.

The agreements from each of the original lists are sorted into five clusters: "Combining Reading With Other Language Processes," "Contexts, Environment, and Purposes for Reading," "Developing (or Shaping) Students' Perceptions and Expectations," "Materials," and "Reading Instruction." Some items clearly fit into more than one cluster. When this was the case, I included the items in as many clusters as I conceptualized them to fit. My choice of cluster categories and my arranging of the agreements into these categories are unique to my conceptualizations and purposes. Others, of course, might choose other descriptors or categories for their purposes.

In order to make this information more useful to classroom teachers and other practitioners, I also eliminated or collapsed many of the more redundant points of agreement from the original lists and edited them for clarity. The original list of contexts and practices the experts totally agreed would "Make Learning to Read Difficult" shrank from 33 to 29, and the number of nonredundant contexts and practices they unanimously agreed would "Facilitate Learning to Read" fell from 15 to 12 when combined or eliminated. The experts subsequently reviewed and approved these edits and cluster categories.

The items listed under these categories are not all equally significant or equally central to reading. Many are clearly more important than others.

Additionally, these items are not inclusive of or representative of every aspect or dimension of reading. However, these are the summary items on which the experts agreed, and they are important because they are the beginning of an opportunity for public pronouncements of some agreements in our field regarding contexts and practices for reading instruction in the classroom.

This is not to say, of course, that the experts agree on everything. We all know they do not, nor would agreement even be desirable, since without differences and discourse in the field there would not be growth. Differences extend our understandings. But where there is some agreement, it is important that such agreements be shared with all concerned.

Figures 3 and 4 show contexts and practices on which the participating experts unanimously agreed; however, there were several other items they felt it was important to qualify and share with teachers and other classroom decision makers. These items on which there was near total agreement among the

---

Figure 3
Clustered Summary Agreements: Contexts and Practices That "Would Make Learning to Read Difficult"

Combining Reading With Other Language Processes
• Teach reading as something separate from writing, talking, and listening.
• Require children to write book reviews of every book they read.

Contexts, Environment, and Purposes for Reading
• Make sure kids do it correctly or not at all.
• Avoid reading for your own enjoyment or personal purposes in front of the students.
• Encourage competitive reading.
• Expect pupils to be able to spell all the words they can read.
• Focus on the single best answer.
• Make a practice of not reading aloud very often to children.
• Select all the stories that children read.
• Stop reading aloud to children as soon as they get through the primer level.
• Reading correctly or pronouncing words "exactly right" should be a prime objective of your classroom reading program.

Developing (or Shaping) Students' Perceptions and Expectations
• If students are weak in reading, let them know that reading is a difficult and complex process and that you do not expect them to be able to do the more difficult reading work.
• Avoid reading for your own enjoyment or personal purposes in front of the students.
• Expect pupils to be able to spell all the words they can read.
• Focus on the single best answer.
• Make sure children understand the seriousness of falling behind.
• Remove the freedom to make decisions about reading from the learner.

(continued)

Figure 3 (continued)
Clustered Summary Agreements: Contexts and Practices
That "Would Make Learning to Read Difficult"

Materials
- Follow your basal's teaching procedures as detailed without making any modifications.
- Use workbooks with every reading lesson.
- If a child is not "getting it," assign a few more skill sheets to remedy the problem.
- Select all the stories children read.
- Have kids read short, snappy texts rather than whole stories.
- Drill children on isolated letters and sounds using flashcards, chalk or magnetic boards, computers, or worksheets.
- Never give children books in which some of the words are unknown (i.e., words that you haven't previously taught or exposed them to in some way).

Reading Instruction
- Teach the children in your classroom letters and words one at a time, making sure each new letter or word is learned before moving on to the next letter or word.
- Detect and correct all inappropriate or incorrect eye movements you observe as you watch children in your classroom during silent reading.
- Emphasize only phonics instruction.
- Make sure kids do "it" correctly or not at all.
- Teach reading as something separate from writing, talking, and listening.
- Follow your basal reading program's teaching procedures as detailed without making any modifications.
- Use workbooks with every reading lesson.
- Focus on kids learning the skills rather than on interpretation and comprehension.
- If a child is not "getting it," assign a few more skill sheets to remedy the problem.
- Focus on the single best answer.
- Group readers according to ability.
- Have the children do oral reading exclusively.
- In small groups, have children orally read a story, allowing one sentence or paragraph at a time for each child, and going around the group in either a clockwise or counter-clockwise rotation.
- Drill children on isolated letters and sounds using flashcards, chalk or magnetic boards, computers, or worksheets.
- Test children with paper and pencil tests whenever they complete a new story in their basal, and each time you have finished teaching a new skill.
- Be sure that you provide lots of training on all the reading skills prior to letting children read a story silently. Even if there isn't much time left for actual reading, you have to focus first on skill training.
- Reading correctly or pronouncing words "exactly right" should be a prime objective of your classroom reading program.

Note: We had total agreement on all of the items listed. Items on which we had near total agreement are considered separately elsewhere in this article. ("Near" total agreement means that only one, or possibly two, expert(s) found fault with the item, or qualified the item.)

Figure 4
Clustered Summary Agreements: Contexts and Practices
That "Would Facilitate Learning to Read"

Combining Reading With Other Language Processes
- Use every opportunity to bring reading/writing/talking/listening together so that each feeds off and feeds into the other.
- Instead of deliberately separating reading from writing, plan instruction and individual activities so that, most of the time, students engage in purposeful reading and writing.
- Encourage children to talk about and share the different kinds of reading they do in a variety of ways with many others.

Contexts, Environment, and Purposes for Reading
- Focus on using reading as a tool for learning.
- Make reading functional.
- Give your students lots of time and opportunity to read real books (both narrative and expository) as well as time and opportunity to write creatively and for purposeful school assignments (e.g., to do research on a topic, to pursue an interest).
- Create environments, contexts in which the children become convinced that reading does further the purposes of their lives.
- Encourage children to talk about and share the different kinds of reading they do in a variety of ways with many others.
- Use silent reading whenever possible, if appropriate to the purpose.

Developing (or Shaping) Students' Perceptions and Expectations
- Develop positive self-perceptions and expectations.
- Create environments, contexts in which the children become convinced that reading does further the purposes of their lives.

Materials
- Use a broad spectrum of sources for student reading materials.
- Include a variety of printed material and literature in your classroom so that students are exposed to the different functions of numerous types of printed materials (e.g., newspapers, magazines, journals, textbooks, research books, trade books, library books, menus, directions).
- Give your students lots of time and opportunity to read real books (both narrative and expository) as well as to write creatively and for purposeful school assignments (e.g., to do research on a topic, to pursue an interest).

Reading Instruction
- Provide multiple, repeated demonstrations of how reading is done or used.
- Instead of deliberately separating reading from writing, plan instruction and individual activities so that, most of the time, students engage in purposeful reading and writing.
- Use silent reading whenever possible, if appropriate to the purpose.

Note: We had total agreement on all of the items listed. Items on which we had near total agreement are considered separately elsewhere in this article. ("Near" total agreement means that only one, or possibly two, expert(s) found fault with the item, or qualified the item.)

experts on contexts and practices that "would make learning to read difficult" included *Encourage perfection; Use workbooks each day; Stress the "classics" of literature; Avoid wasting instructional time encouraging students to use linguistic and cognitive strategies as they read;* and *Always ask a lot of comprehension questions after children read.* On contexts and practices that "would facilitate learning to read," likewise, nearly all the experts agreed on the following items: *Make reading fun and authentic; Encourage learning about strategies; Encourage learning to paraphrase and summarize; Allow learners to use techniques that help them become consciously aware of what they do as readers: through metacognitive probing, help learners think about how they arrived at an answer, or how what they read influenced their personal understanding;* and *Provide feedback that includes clues about meaning, as well as letter sound information.*

Two of the most interesting aspects of doing this study were reading the notations the experts made concerning suggested items, and the follow-up discussions I had with the expert participants throughout the study concerning their remarks, edits, or qualifiers for some of the items they added, eliminated, or rewrote. Brian Cambourne mostly agrees, for instance, that to *use workbooks each day* without explicit reasons given to and understood by children would make learning to read difficult for them. On the other hand, he also wants it noted that using practice materials, such as workbooks, does not have to be considered poor practice if children understand the reasons they are doing this work and if their responses to questions in the practice materials are genuinely valued (personal communication, May 2, 1995). Then again, while mostly agreeing that if teachers *make reading fun and authentic* they would facilitate learning to read, Cambourne also wants it noted that "learning isn't always *fun*" (personal communication, May 2, 1995).

Rand Spiro, while mostly agreeing that if you *always ask a lot of comprehension questions after children read,* it would make learning to read difficult, also indicated that he believes "it's usually a good idea to have kids discuss what they've read in some way—and I don't know how this would not involve 'comprehension' questions (at least indirectly)" (personal communication, September 27, 1995). As one more example of the qualifiers that the experts wanted noted about certain items, Rand Spiro mostly agreed that we should *allow learners to use techniques that help them become consciously aware of what they do as readers: through metacognitive probing, help learners think about how they arrived at an answer, or how what they read influenced their personal understanding.* Spiro wanted this practice qualified, however, because he indicated that "at higher levels of reading expertise, increasing conscious awareness can cause disintegration of reading processes." So, he says, "My response on this one is 'Yes, but decreasingly so as reading expertise increases'" (personal communication, September 27, 1995). (For listings and discussions of the qualifying statements, see Flippo, 1996.)

An example should suffice to give the reader some sense of the dynamics involved in the study. Referring to *Encourage perfection*, Brian Cambourne crossed it out and indicated, "When an individual seeks his/her own perfection, that is fine. But it must be an internal drive as opposed to perfection imposed by the teacher" (personal communication, May 2, 1995). Wayne Otto, also objecting to this item, remarked, "encourage covers *a lot*" (personal communication, November 23, 1993). When questioned again, in a later interview, he stated, "I disagree because it is legitimate to encourage perfection, but I also see that this could lead to abuse" (personal communication, November 17, 1995).

Discussion

Toward the end of the study, I asked each of the experts to share his or her own individual definition or philosophy statement regarding literacy. These are displayed in Figure 5.

From these statements it becomes clear how, in the decade this study spanned, we have all continued to read, reflect, and learn. I see these learnings, growth, and changes as highly desirable for all of us, experts, researchers, and teachers alike. "Constructivism" and related research that influence our present-day thinking about learning, such as the influences of social processes and cognitive learnings, and the effects of students' interests and motivations on their comprehension, have affected the experts as well. Interestingly, some of the participating experts generally thought to have opposing perspectives have come to describe their views using terms like "social constructivist" and "sociocognitive." In fact, considering the definitions or philosophy statements furnished by most of the experts, it is difficult to detect that they are generally considered to represent several entirely different perspectives.

The data generated by this study do show us that as a field we have learned and grown, and as a result, because of all we know, we tend to shy away from absolutes. No matter whether we call ourselves, or others call us, *whole language* persons, *traditionalists*, or *interactivists*, or we fall into any other camp, we have learned enough to know that certain practices, environments, and conditions usually tend to nurture the development of reading; on the other hand, we have learned enough to know that other practices, environments, and conditions usually tend to make learning to read difficult. (It is important to note that a key word in this discussion is *usually*. The experts' agreements regarding these practices ought always to be considered in the context of actual situations with specific students.)

We see, too, that the experts agreed to many more practices and contexts that would make learning to read difficult for children (especially in the area I have categorized as "Reading Instruction") than they did for those that would facilitate learning to read. This is important because, as we have seen already (Levine, 1996), many of these very practices that the experts believe hinder

Figure 5
Expert Participants: Personal Definitions/Philosophy Statements
Regarding Education and Literacy Development

Richard Anderson
(November 15, 1995)

My current perspective is sociocognitive. The language of student-student and teacher-student interactions provides a social context within which meanings of written texts are constructed. This context, in turn, influences the nature of individual students' attending, thinking, talking, writing, and learning. Discussions of written texts create socially constructed "extended texts." Access to this extended text is governed by students' participation in the lesson. As teachers and students interact to construct the academic content of the lesson, students simultaneously receive information about norms for participation.

Brian Cambourne
(May 2, 1995)

"Effective reading" to me means having sufficient control over language and the processes and skills, and understandings and knowledge of written language to be able to interact with written texts, comprehend what the author(s) of the text intended, and be able to interrogate these texts and "unpack" the agendas of those who wrote them. The major purpose of reading is to provide a mechanism for internalizing the linguistic patterns of various forms of discourse so that learners have a cultural resource that will enable them to get access to power in their culture and bring about social change. It ("effective reading") should be available to as wide a spectrum of the community as possible—therefore it should be taught using a pedagogy which makes it accessible to all, not one which privileges a powerful elite.

Edward Fry
(December 5, 1994)

All any teacher can do is move a student ahead a notch or two. He or she should try to move all children from brightest to dullest ahead. Teachers should have great latitude in selecting methods and no major method should be totally forbidden. Personally I would use a variety of methods such as (a) match student ability to book difficulty (readability), (b) give lots of reading practice in both narrative and expository text, (c) teach vocabulary—high frequency words and roots, (d) teach phonics, (e) teach comprehension, (f) develop writing ability, and (g) give students success, praise, and love.

Yetta Goodman
(December 15, 1994)

Social constructivist learning theory and sociopsycholinguistic transactional reading theory.

Jane Hansen
(November 26, 1993)

I believe the larger the picture provided by and of a reader, the better. We know who a reader is when we know her viewpoint on herself over the years at home and school, her sense of herself in relation to others in school and at home, and the others' sense of her.

(continued)

Figure 5 (continued)
Expert Participants: Personal Definitions/Philosophy Statements
Regarding Education and Literacy Development

Jerry Harste (November 30, 1995)	My paradigm is whole literacy—for me, instructionally, that means building curriculum from kids. I define literacy as a much broader concept than just reading and writing. It's the ability to mediate the world through sign systems—including those from music, math, drama, movement, and art. To be literate is to be able to flexibly orchestrate various sign systems to create text that is successful to the context.
Wayne Otto (November 23, 1993)	Social constructivist—but with a skeptic's stance much of the time.
Scott Paris (November 24, 1993)	A developmental approach emphasizing the collaborative construction and assessment of meaning for authentic purposes that are cognitively engaging, intrinsically motivating, and metacognitively stimulating.
P. David Pearson (March 13, 1995)	Children need to work in classroom communities in which they regularly read and write for, to, and with one another.
George Spache (February 2, 1994)	I believe reading instruction should provide a progression of reading experiences that promote vocabulary growth in critical but enjoyable selections of gradually increasing difficulty. The pupil should be taught and encouraged to use word analysis techniques such as common word elements and the context to aid his comprehension. In primary grades, phonics can be an aid to some pupils. But it is not a basic mode of instruction because many pupils cannot make the auditory discriminations it demands and the knowledge of phonics has no relationship to comprehension. Heavy emphasis upon letter sounds produces readers who are slow and too analytical with consequent poor comprehension.
Rand Spiro (September 27, 1995)	I believe in the importance of employing multiple approaches, each coordinated with the others. Each paradigm for teaching reading and each theory of reading has strengths and weaknesses—the trick is to harness the strengths of each to counteract the weaknesses of the others. A byproduct of this kind of "principled eclecticism" is that readers will become more flexible in adapting their own approaches to the needs of different reading situations. (The above beliefs are consistent with the overarching paradigm of "cognitive flexibility theory.")

progress in reading are the ones now being promoted by legislators and others. While, clearly, these diverse experts have generally very different ideas about "how" reading should be taught, they certainly all see many contexts and practices that would not be wise to impose or force on children.

Not only do their ideas diverge on how to teach reading, but different experts espousing different philosophies can also attribute different meanings to words like *reading* and *comprehension.* This happens, of course, because the experts belong to different communities of discourse. A mutually acceptable scaffolding was therefore needed to allow them each to meaningfully compare items generated by the other participants with their own ideas (and vice versa), and this consideration is what accounts for the qualifying words, and in some cases, the extreme wording of the practices and contexts generated. It also explains the occasionally unwieldy or cumbersome character of the language used to describe them. (Yet as extreme as they might appear in the context of this study, we have already begun to see evidence, as the opening quotation indicates, of legislation in many states aimed at installing these very practices.)

We can say with certainty that quick fixes and simplistic solutions are just that. Rather than pursue such solutions, the experts and I instead would prefer to focus on where we as a field can agree and how we use this information to combat inappropriate and potentially damaging policy decisions. However, the participating experts are equally concerned that teachers and readers of these data understand there are no absolutes when one deals with learning and children—even the best of practices can sometimes be overdone, and even what appears on the surface to be a poor practice is sometimes not unreasonable under certain circumstances. Each of the agreed upon practices, then, should be interpreted within specific contexts with specific situations, students, and their needs in mind. As Pearson (1996) has emphasized, teachers must be able to understand literacy and learning well enough to adapt teaching and learning environments, materials, and methods to particular situations and students.

Conclusions

Teachers should consider these points of agreement when they discuss, plan, shape, and deliver their reading instruction, as well as when they meet or communicate with parents and families and with their supervisors or administrators. Once again, these lists are not meant to be "do" and "don't do" lists. Instead they represent the ideas of experts who are representative of a continuum of beliefs and philosophies. These experts did not participate in this study to impose restrictions on teachers. Professional teachers should be allowed to make their own decisions and plan classroom instruction and learning opportunities based on their situations and the needs, interests, motivations, and strategies of the children with whom they work—not based on any particular list, restrictions, or absolutes.

Second, we are not nearly as divided as some would like the public to believe. There are points of agreement, even among people with the most diverse of philosophies. I believe we need very publicly (a) to share the results of this study with the media, policy makers, parents, communities, and the general public, and (b) to emphasize that no one has endorsed any particular method or approach. Rather, experts have simply pointed out a number of contexts and practices for reading instruction on which they agree. These are relevant to most methods and approaches. Decisions about reading instruction are multifaceted, on the other hand, and only the classroom teacher who works with a child every day is in a position to know what is appropriate instruction for that particular child and when. We as a field want policy to reflect beliefs, ideas, and learnings based on the extensive research and practice in our field (exemplified in the very diverse work of these experts), not simplistic solutions that the media and politicians create and then legislate, and with which most of us disagree.

As a postscript, I think it is important that practicing teachers be given an equal voice concerning beliefs, ideas, and learnings based on their classroom research and practice. I have already begun the process of collecting teachers' responses to the experts' lists (see the call for responses in Flippo, 1999).

AUTHOR NOTES

This article is dedicated to the memory of George Spache, a full participant in this study and a dedicated reading educator and researcher. The field will greatly miss him and remember his contributions.

I wish to acknowledge and thank the Massachusetts Reading Association for the Sylvia D. Brown Memorial Research Scholarship (1991) they awarded me to fund some of the research reported in this study.

REFERENCES
Anderson, R.C., Hiebert, E.H., Scott, J.A., & Wilkinson, I.G. (1985). *Becoming a nation of readers.* Champaign, IL: Center for the Study of Reading.
Cambourne, B. (1988). *The whole story.* Auckland, New Zealand: Ashton Scholastic.
Cambourne, B. (1995). Toward an educationally relevant theory of literacy learning. *The Reading Teacher, 49,* 182–190.
Flippo, R.F. (1996, December). *"Seeds of Consensus": The beginnings of professional unity.* Paper presented at the annual meeting of the National Reading Conference, Charleston, South Carolina.
Flippo, R.F. (1997). Sensationalism, politics, and literacy: What's going on? *Phi Delta Kappan, 79*(4), 301–304.
Flippo, R.F. (1999). *What do the experts say? Helping children learn to read.* Portsmouth, NH: Heinemann.
Fry, E.B. (1977). Fry's readability graph: Clarifications, validity, and extensions to level 17. *Journal of Reading, 21,* 242–252.
Goodman, Y.M. (1996). Revaluing readers while readers revalue themselves: Retrospective Miscue Analysis. *The Reading Teacher, 49,* 600–609.
Goodman, Y.M., Watson, D.J., & Burke, C.L. (1987). *Reading miscue inventory: Alternative procedures.* Katonah, NY: Richard C. Owen.
Graves, D., & Hansen, J. (1983). The author's chair. *Language Arts, 60,* 176–183.

Hansen, J. (1996). Evaluation: The center of writing instruction. *The Reading Teacher, 50*, 188–195.

Levine, A. (1996, October). Parents report on America's reading crisis: Why the whole-language approach to teaching has failed millions of children. *Parents Magazine, 71*(10), 63–68.

Linstone, H.A., & Turoff, M. (Eds.). (1975). *The Delphi method: Techniques and applications.* Reading, MA: Addison-Wesley.

Monson, R.J., & Monson, M.P. (1994). Literacy as inquiry: An interview with Jerome C. Harste. *The Reading Teacher, 47*, 518–521.

Otto, W. (1977). The Wisconsin design: A reading program for individually guided education. In H.J. Klausmeier, R.A. Rossmiller, & M. Saily (Eds.), *Individually guided elementary education: Concepts and practices* (pp. 137–149). New York: Academic Press.

Paris, S.G., & Ayres, L.J. (1994). *Becoming reflective students and teachers with portfolios and authentic assessment.* Washington, DC: American Psychological Association.

Pearson, P.D. (1996). Six ideas in search of a champion: What policymakers should know about the teaching and learning of literacy in our schools. *Journal of Literacy Research, 28*(2), 302–309.

Pearson, P.D., Barr, R., Kamil, M.L., & Mosenthal, P. (Eds.). (1984). *Handbook of reading research.* New York: Longman.

Short, K.G., & Harste, J.C. (with Burke, C.). (1996). *Creating classrooms for authors and inquirers* (2nd ed.). Portsmouth, NH: Heinemann.

Smith, F. (1973). Twelve easy ways to make learning to read difficult. In F. Smith (Ed.), *Psycholinguistics and reading* (pp. 183–196). New York: Holt, Rinehart, and Winston.

Spache, G.D. (1981). *Diagnostic Reading Scales: Revised edition.* Monterey, CA: CTB/McGraw-Hill.

Spiro, R.J. (1980). Constructive processes in prose comprehension and recall. In R.J. Spiro, B.C. Bruce, & W.F. Brewer (Eds.), *Theoretical issues in reading comprehension: Perspectives from cognitive psychology, linguistics, artificial intelligence, and education* (pp. 245–278). Hillsdale, NJ: Erlbaum.

Spiro, R.J., Coulson, R.L., Feltovich, P.J., & Anderson, D.K. (1994). Cognitive flexibility theory: Advanced knowledge acquisition in ill-structured domains. In R.B. Ruddell, M.R. Ruddell, & H. Singer (Eds.), *Theoretical models and processes of reading* (4th ed.), (pp. 602–615). Newark, DE: International Reading Association.

Turner, J.C., & Paris, S.G. (1995). How literacy tasks influence children's motivation for literacy. *The Reading Teacher, 48*, 662–673.

CHAPTER 2

Point of View: Richard C. Anderson

Linda G. Fielding

Not long after I arrived at University of Illinois at Urbana-Champaign as a new doctoral student, I enrolled in a course taught by Richard (Dick) Anderson. By that time in 1982, the Center for the Study of Reading, funded by the Office of Educational Research and Improvement and directed by Dick, had been in operation for about 6 years. Much research had been conducted there about human learning and cognition, basic processes in reading and comprehension, the state of U.S. textbooks and reading instruction, acquisition of vocabulary, and many other areas. The Center was turning its attention more and more to research that might have very direct implications for classroom instruction. It was toward that goal that Dick hired me, with my 10 years' experience as a middle school reading and language arts teacher, as his research assistant that fall. I write this commentary from my vantage point as a participant in some of his research and many discussions with him about reading research, a beneficiary of his counsel as codirector of my dissertation, and an avid reader of the research he continues to conduct.

A Brief Intellectual Biography

A 1960 graduate of Harvard, Dick had taught at Rutgers; had coauthored an influential educational psychology textbook (Anderson & Faust, 1973) and published research about programmed learning, human learning, and cognition; and even had written an influential article about achievement tests (Anderson, 1972) by the time he began discussions with colleagues at the University of Illinois that led to their successful bid for the Center for the Study of Reading in 1976. In the early years of the Center, Dick was involved in ground-breaking research about schema theory that led to new understandings about the role of background knowledge in reading comprehension (Anderson, 1984). Research with William Nagy and other colleagues about how people learn word meanings suggested that learning words in context through wide reading must make a substantial contribution over what is possible through direct instruction in word meanings alone (Nagy, Anderson, & Herman, 1987). This vocabulary research as well as his studies of the role of interest in learning (Anderson, Shirey, Wilson, & Fielding, 1987) contributed to his decision to study the role of independent reading of trade books in children's reading achievement. From this research he concluded that wide independent reading makes substantial contributions to children's present reading achievement and their growth as readers over time (Anderson, Wilson, & Fielding, 1988). With other colleagues he also began to study the reading group as a staple of U.S. classroom reading instruction, and found that a meaning focus during reading lessons was superior in every way to a focus on accuracy of word reading (Anderson, Wilkinson, & Mason, 1991).

Arguably, his most widely read work is the research synthesis *Becoming a Nation of Readers* (Anderson, Hiebert, Scott, & Wilkinson, 1985), which he cowrote as chair of the National Academy of Education–established Commission on Reading. Its purpose was to "summarize the knowledge acquired from research and to draw implications for reading instruction" (p. 3). Five descriptors that answer the question "What is reading?" framed the conclusions—namely, that skilled reading is a constructive, fluent, strategic, and motivated process, and a lifelong pursuit. Critics argued that among other things, the report did not include enough research from nonexperimental paradigms, go far enough in its recommendations, recommend practices consistent with its description of what reading is, address special issues in the education of minorities, or adequately address reading's social dimensions (Davidson, 1988). However, Dick's current investigations of collaborative reasoning during text reading (Anderson, Chinn, Waggoner, & Nguyen, 1998) underscore the social and collaborative dimensions of reading and undoubtedly are fundamental to his current characterization of his theoretical orientation as "sociocognitive" (Flippo, 1998; refer to Chapter 1, p. 17, in this book).

So far I have focused on a chronology of Dick's research and research syntheses. To adequately explain his agreement with the contexts and practices that would facilitate learning to read or make it difficult, I also must comment on other aspects of his intellectual history.

First, his own belief in the social construction of meaning is evident in the talk that has always surrounded my research experiences with Dick. The oral history of the Center has it that noisy, vigorous, and usually good-natured arguments about reading processes laid the foundation for the proposal that originally brought the Center to Illinois. (Incidentally, an anonymous source good-humoredly reported that these discussions easily seeped through office walls, sometimes interfering with the thinking of those not involved.) Friday afternoon research presentations accompanied by ample time for discussion, almost always with Dick in attendance, were a regular occurrence before, during, and after my years at the Center. And regular meetings of Dick's various research teams depended on garnering opinions and suggestions from everyone involved.

Dick also has participated actively in developing and confirming his understandings in other ways. For instance, he always has been committed to learning from experienced teachers about ways to make his classroom-based research more authentic and his suggestions for classroom practice more grounded in reality. The Center-produced videotape series *Teaching Reading: Strategies From Successful Classrooms* (1990) is one example of this commitment; his hiring of me and a number of other former teachers as research assistants is another. Dick's direct involvement with Reading Recovery (Clay, 1993) is yet another example of his own alternative ways of learning. When Reading Recovery began gaining recognition and respect in the United States, Dick was instrumental in bringing it to Illinois. Noteworthy is the fact that he participated in one of the first training groups by tutoring three first-grade youngsters. Dick learned methods of teaching about phonics and word identification in the context of text reading, in connection with what the reader already knows, and as strategies rather than isolated items of knowledge—practices that are more contextualized and reader-specific than the general approaches suggested in *Becoming a Nation of Readers* (Anderson et al., 1985). A final example of Dick's active learning: When Dick became interested in the role of wide reading in learning to read and realized that he had not read any children's literature in some years, he asked me to select several good examples for him. I remember he was particularly impressed with the depth of plot and theme and richness of language in Katherine Paterson's *Bridge to Terabithia* (1977). These examples suggest that although much of Dick's belief system is built on his own research and syntheses of others' research, he also engages in hands-on practices and intellectual exchanges with others who influence his thinking.

Agreement With the Contexts and Practices

Part of my role in writing this contribution is to point out and speculate about the agreed upon contexts and practices from the Expert Study that Dick feels most strongly about. I address these in the order that the contexts and practices are described in the Flippo (1998) article reprinted in the first chapter of this book.

Combining Wide Reading With Other Language Processes

My guess is that Dick is in very strong agreement with all of the practices included in the Expert Study category "combining reading with other language processes." His own most recent research about collaborative story discussions (Anderson et al., 1998) is based on the notion that talking and listening to others' talk are central to meaning construction. In addition, *Becoming a Nation of Readers* suggests writing as an important practice in its own right as well as a vital alternative to a steady diet of workbook pages.

Contexts, Environment, and Purposes for Reading

Both Dick's own research about the role of interest in learning (Anderson et al., 1987) and the characterization of reading as "a lifelong pursuit" in *Becoming a*

Nation of Readers (Anderson et al., 1985, p. 18) support his agreement with the Expert Study statements that reading should focus on functional purposes and students' interests. His own research about children's independent reading (Anderson et al., 1988) was instrumental in providing empirical support for the practice of allotting time and opportunity for reading real books and other materials. On the other hand, it is not surprising that Dick agrees with the suggestion to "use silent reading whenever possible" because it is qualified with, "if appropriate to the purpose" (Flippo, 1998; refer to Chapter 1, p. 14, in this book). *Becoming a Nation of Readers* suggests that "frequent opportunities to read aloud make sense for the beginning reader" (Anderson et al., 1985, p. 51) and that oral reading also makes sense in some contexts beyond the beginning stages. In a more recent re-analysis of data about the value of silent reading, Dick and colleagues also suggested that the value of silent over oral reading may not be as strong as previously thought (Wilkinson, Anderson, & Wardrop, 1988). However, it is important to note that these caveats about silent versus oral reading assume meaning-focused, as opposed to accuracy-focused, oral reading. His own reading group research indicates that meaning-focused prediction questions produce better recall, recall of more important information, and more accurate reading than questions and prompts focused on accuracy of word pronunciation (Anderson et al., 1991).

Materials

My guess is that Dick is in very strong agreement with the suggestions in the Expert Study category "materials." As stated, his own research supports the wide reading of trade books and other authentic reading materials. In addition, research about commercially published reading materials conducted at the Center and summarized in *Becoming a Nation of Readers* directly cautions against many features of materials that would make learning to read difficult, such as using workbooks with every reading lesson, following all suggested teaching procedures to the letter, and assigning more skill sheets to children who do not understand a skill. From his research about the role of interest in learning (Anderson et al., 1987) and the value of trade book reading (Anderson et al., 1988), I am sure he agrees strongly that if the teacher made all reading choices for children or limited their reading to selections in which they had been taught all of the words, learning to read would be difficult. Dick has served as senior advisor for one of the many 1990s basal reader series that also support these ideas.

Reading Instruction

I have already commented on my guess that Dick agrees strongly with the suggestions in the "reading instruction" category of the Expert Study clustered summary agreements, based on his own research about vocabulary learning and independent reading. Another suggestion in this category, to "provide multiple, repeated demonstrations of how reading is done or used" (Flippo, 1998; refer to Chapter 1, p. 14, in this book), is made directly in *Becoming a Nation of Readers* and is based to a great extent on research conducted by colleagues and former graduate students at the Center. Furthermore, it is described as one of the teacher's roles in his recent investigations of collaborative reasoning during story discussions (Anderson et al., 1998), and is illustrated through suggestions to teachers in the basal series for which Dick was senior advisor.

Conclusion

Was I surprised to find Dick in full agreement with the Expert Study lists of contexts and practices that would facilitate learning to read or make it difficult? Not at all. As this chapter illustrates, Dick conducted research in many of these areas himself, and through *Becoming a Nation of Readers* and other reviews he analyzed and synthesized others' research in all of the areas. Furthermore, in the areas in which he has done his own research, there often is a progression from research about basic processes to research about classroom practices. But Dick participates actively in developing his beliefs and understandings in ways other than research and synthesis—through intellectual exchange with other researchers and teachers and various kinds of hands-on practice. Nearly 40 years of active involvement in and critical thinking about the field of reading research would lead almost inevitably to these agreements.

However, I am sure Dick would never want these points of agreement to halt the inquiry process or make us complacent about our consensus. In fact, I expect he would say that we still have much to learn about the finer points of contexts and practices that facilitate learning to read—and that it is in these finer points that the success or failure of a particular practice often lies. In fact, much of his recent research, such as his line of inquiry into small-group reading lessons and collaborative story reasoning, is focused on these finer points. The evolution of Dick's own research over time illustrates his ongoing thinking about what we need to know next to further the improvement of reading instruction. Although he clearly agrees with the listed contexts and practices that evolved from the Expert Study and that are supported by his own and others' research, I am confident that Dick wants us to continue to search for gaps where our knowledge needs to be deepened and extended, and that he will do the same.

REFERENCES

Anderson, R.C. (1972). How to construct achievement tests to assess comprehension. *Review of Educational Research, 42,* 145–170.

Anderson, R.C. (1984). Role of the reader's schema in comprehension, learning, and memory. In R.C. Anderson, J. Osborn, & R.J. Tierney (Eds.), *Learning to read in American schools: Basal readers and content texts* (pp. 243–257). Hillsdale, NJ: Erlbaum.

Anderson, R.C., Chinn, C., Waggoner, M., & Nguyen, K. (1998). Intellectually stimulating story discussions. In J. Osborn & F. Lehr (Eds.), *Literacy for all: Issues in teaching and learning* (pp. 170–196). New York: Guilford Press.

Anderson, R.C., & Faust, G.W. (1973). *Educational psychology: The science of instruction and learning.* New York: Dodd, Mead.

Anderson, R.C., Hiebert, E.H., Scott, J.A., & Wilkinson, I.A.G. (1985). *Becoming a nation of readers.* Washington, DC: National Institute of Education.

Anderson, R.C., Shirey, L., Wilson, P.T., & Fielding, L.G. (1987). Interestingness of children's reading material. In R. Snow & M. Farr (Eds.), *Aptitude, learning and instruction* (pp. 287–299). Hillsdale, NJ: Erlbaum.

Anderson, R.C., Wilkinson, I.A.G., & Mason, J. (1991). A microanalysis of the small-group guided reading lesson: Effects of an emphasis on global story meaning. *Reading Research Quarterly, 26,* 417–441.

Anderson, R.C., Wilson, P.T., & Fielding, L.G. (1988). Growth in reading and how children spend their time outside of school. *Reading Research Quarterly, 23,* 285–303.

Center for the Study of Reading. (1990). *Teaching reading: Strategies from successful classrooms.* Urbana, IL: Author.

Clay, M. (1993). *Reading Recovery.* Portsmouth, NH: Heinemann.

Davidson, J. (Ed.). (1988). *Counterpoint and beyond: A response to* Becoming a Nation of Readers. Urbana, IL: National Council of Teachers of English.

Flippo, R.F. (1998). Points of agreement: A display of professional unity in our field. *The Reading Teacher, 52,* 30–40.

Nagy, W.E., Anderson, R.C., & Herman, P.A. (1987). Learning word meanings from context during normal reading. *American Educational Research Journal, 24,* 237–270.

Paterson, K. (1977). *Bridge to Terabithia.* New York: Avon.

Wilkinson, I.A.G., Anderson, R.C., & Wardrop, J. (1988). Silent reading reconsidered: Reinterpreting reading instruction and its effects. *American Educational Research Journal, 25,* 127–144.

CHAPTER 3

On Being an "Expert" With a Point of View: Ten Years On

Brian Cambourne

More than 10 years ago, Rona Flippo sent me a list of statements about reading that Frank Smith made notorious in the early 1970s (Smith, 1973). In the letter that accompanied this list, she informed me that I was among a small group of "world reading experts" whom she had selected to comment on Frank's list. I was vain enough to succumb to such flattery. For the next 10 years, she regularly asked me to reflect on my comments and those of fellow "experts." So here I am, more than 10 years later, a so-called expert revisiting the opinions I expressed to statements made by myself and statements made by the other experts about ways of facilitating learning to read or making it difficult.

Revisiting My Responses

It is obvious that when I first responded to Smith's list and then those generated by myself and the other experts, I had some strong views about learning and language. It is also obvious that I was predisposed toward what could be described as a "holistic" or "constructivist" perspective with respect to learning and teaching. The origins of these views are not difficult to identify. I am conscious of rejecting the fragmented, mechanistic theories of learning and language with which I had been imbued during my 1950s teacher-preparation course. That is probably why I agreed in the Expert Study that integrating the four modes of language, "so that each feeds off and feeds into the other," would facilitate learning to read; that is probably why I claimed that "multiple repeated demonstrations of how reading and writing is done or used" rather than "deliberately separating reading and writing" or "teaching letters and words one at a time" would facilitate learning to read for children (Flippo, 1998; refer to Chapter 1, pp. 12–14, in this book).

There were other reasons that help explain why I responded the way I did. As a young teacher I continually noticed that there seemed to be a significant number of nonmainstream students in the classes I taught who were capable of the most complex kind of learning outside of the classroom setting, but who failed to learn even the most simple concepts of reading, writing, spelling, math, and so forth that I tried to teach them. I knew from my conversations and interactions with these children that they did not experience the same problems when it came to understanding and mastering the skills, tactics, and knowledge of complex sports like cricket; carrying out complex tasks such as sight-reading complex music and singing it in tune; running a successful after-school lawn-mowing business; reading and understanding the racing guide; calculating odds and probabilities associated with card games; or speaking and translating across two or three languages. These experiences led me to explore models of learning that were different from the mechanistic models to which I had been exposed during my teacher training.

At the same time I was being influenced by the work of others. Frank Smith's work helped me think of the brain as an "organ of learning." This simple analogy led me to explore the hypothesis that the human brain had evolved primarily as a survival mechanism—that is, it had learned to learn in ways that ensured that certain skills and understandings necessary for species survival would be learned successfully and easily. As well, after years of applying Chomsky-an linguistic principles to the reading process, I was introduced to Michael Halliday's functional systemic-linguistic theory (1985). His work helped me understand the functional (i.e., "survival") purposes that language served both in individuals' lives and the cultures in which they lived. It seemed to me that learning to use and understand the language of the culture into which one was born was a universal example of this kind of complex "survival" learning. I therefore decided to try to understand the nature of this kind of learning by systematically observing toddlers in experimenter-free settings (using recording devices and unobtrusively taking field notes) as they used, listened to, and responded to language with caregivers, siblings, relatives, neighbors, friends, and teachers both in home and school settings.

As a consequence of this research and the literature I had reviewed on language acquisition, I concluded that because certain conditions always seemed to be present in the environment in which language was being used and learned, these conditions could be considered "necessary" conditions for such learning to occur.

No wonder I responded the way I did. I was firmly convinced that if I could just work out ways of turning the conditions of learning that underpinned everyday cultural learning into classroom practice, the complexity of learning to read would be significantly reduced. In fact I spent a considerable amount of my research time in those days trying to work out what these conditions were. Eventually I identified these:

- Immersion
- Demonstration
- Engagement

- Expectations
- Responsibility
- Employment
- Approximations
- Response

I firmly believed that if teachers could implement these conditions appropriately, they would begin to make the acquisition of literacy as barrier free and uncomplicated as possible. Given the beliefs I had about such things at the time, it would have been hypocritical of me to respond any other way.

Ten Years On: How Would I Respond?

Although I would not change in any significant way how I would respond to the items included in the lists reprinted in this volume, with the benefit of hindsight I would add this caveat: *Prolonged and persistent observation in classrooms has helped me realize that teaching literacy is a lot more complex than I ever imagined when I first responded to Smith's list.* Part of these observations included the opportunity to ask many teachers variations of these three questions:

1. What is effective literacy?
2. How is it best learned?
3. After it is learned, how should effective literacy be used?

Their responses have helped me understand the following:

- What happens in classrooms in the name of teaching literacy is far more complex than the listing of a set of contexts and practices for facilitating reading, or the careful application of some preferred "teaching method," or indeed the use of a carefully designed set of resources.
- Rather, what one observes in classrooms is embedded in and enclosed by the formal theoretical knowledge and understandings that teachers carry around inside their heads. In the main this comprises knowledge and understandings about learners, the learning process, language, and the role that language plays in learning.
- This formal theoretical knowledge is in turn embedded in and enclosed by another, less formal kind of knowledge and understandings, which comprises a teacher's ideology. By *ideology* I mean beliefs and values about the purpose and nature of literacy, schooling, and society.

Figure 1 is a schematic representation of what I mean.

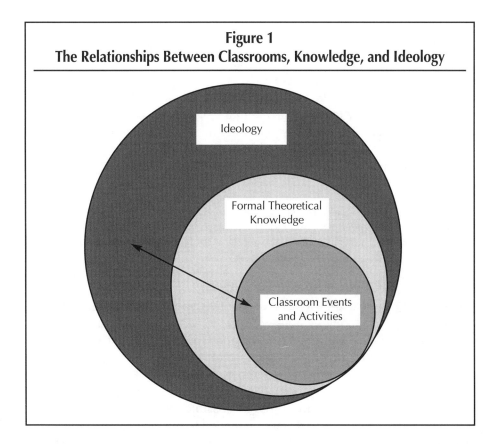

Figure 1
The Relationships Between Classrooms, Knowledge, and Ideology

Ideology

Formal Theoretical
Knowledge

Classroom Events
and Activities

Figure 1 depicts classrooms as a series of "enclosed-enclosing" systems, each of which is related, either through being embedded within or embedding the others. The system comprising the events and activities that occur in classrooms is embedded within a system of formal theoretical knowledge. This in turn grows out of an informal kind of nonconscious system of tacit knowledge (ideology), which comprises the set of beliefs and values about literacy, schooling, education, and the world in general. While the "knowledge" component is relatively easy to get at through interview and debriefing sessions, the "ideological" component is less amenable to conscious awareness, is harder to get at, and is resistant to being made explicit.

"Unpacking" Each System

The Ideological Layer

Although I cannot identify the origins of teachers' values and beliefs, our data indicate that many of our teachers' ideologies were very similar (Cambourne,

1988; Cambourne & Turbill, 1994). They tended to talk about "effective" literacy in terms of "*high degrees of control of language.*" By *control* they meant giving their students access to a wide enough range of linguistic choices that made it possible for them to shape, use, and interpret a wide range of discourses, especially those that were involved in academic learning. The data also indicate that they tended to agree that language and knowing, thinking, understanding, and learning are so closely related that control of one (language) led to control of the others (knowing, thinking, understanding, and learning). As a teacher commented during a debriefing interview,

> I believe that we [teachers] should be helping kids get control of as many forms of language as possible because that's one way of giving our less privileged kids access to power. [Not] power in the sense of dominion over, but power in the sense of being able to negotiate and gain access to the good things of life and to succeed in education.

The Formal Theoretical Knowledge Layer

The formal theoretical knowledge that effective teachers made explicit during the debriefing and sharing sessions we had seemed to be made up from three overlapping domains, namely "Learning and How It Works," "Language and How It Works," and "The Role of Language in Learning."

With respect to the first of these domains, "Learning and How It Works," as a group, teachers held two strong beliefs about learning: (1) learning should be as uncomplicated and barrier free as possible (related to the conviction that unnecessarily complicated learning tended to exclude the less privileged members of our society); and (2) learning should be "durable"—what is learned and mastered should continue to be "known" and used long after formal schooling has finished.

The learning theory that best fitted in with these beliefs was "natural" learning (Cambourne, 1988). Sometimes this was referred to as "child-centered learning," "acquisition learning" (Holdaway, 1974), "whole learning" (Cordeiro, 1992), and "comprehensible input" (Krashen & Terrell, 1983). It is similar to the learning theory that is used to explain how children learn to talk, with an extra dimension—an emphasis on helping learners get "inside" texts and reflect on how they need to be shaped to achieve different communicative and cognitive purposes with different audiences.

With respect to the second of these domains, "Language and How It Works," as a group, teachers drew on the theory of language that was essentially "functional linguistics" as developed by Michael Halliday (1978, 1985). This theory of language describes language in functional terms and among other things supports the notion that control over language is facilitated by a conscious understanding of how linguistic choices can be made to shape text so that specific purposes can be achieved with specific audiences. Halliday-an

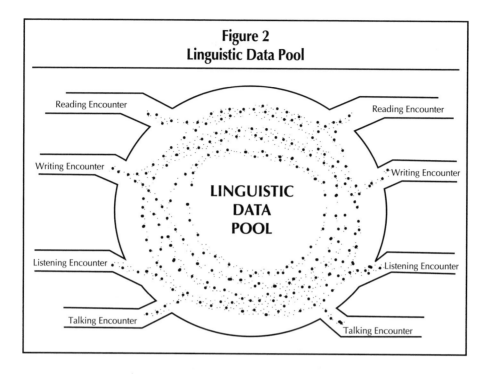

Figure 2
Linguistic Data Pool

Reading Encounter

Reading Encounter

Writing Encounter

Writing Encounter

LINGUISTIC DATA POOL

Listening Encounter

Listening Encounter

Talking Encounter

Talking Encounter

linguists promote this slogan, which was at the core of much of the planning and teaching that occurred in the classrooms in which these teachers taught: "We learn language, we learn through language and we learn about language simultaneously as we use it."

With respect to the third of these domains, "The Role of Language in Learning," these teachers believed that language was the major medium of thinking, learning, knowing, understanding, and problem solving. In this respect they were definitely Whorfian in essence (see Whorf, 1956). They were also cognizant of the "linguistic data pool," a visual metaphor created by Burke (Harste, Burke, & Woodward, 1979; see Figure 2 for my rendition of what a linguistic data pool might look like). All claimed it helped them understand the relationships between reading, writing, listening, talking, linguistic choice, and the construction of texts for different purposes and different audiences.

End Point

So what is the end result of my more than 10 years of involvement with Rona's study? Unfortunately, it sounds like a bland truism: *Effective literacy classrooms are very complex settings.* Given the constraints of this chapter, it is difficult to capture this complexity fully. All I have done is provide some elementary insights into its nature. What is important is that this complexity has to be orchestrated. The more time I spend engaged in research and thinking about literacy, the more I am convinced that those classroom settings we call *effective* are much too complex to be orchestrated and maintained by teachers who are armed only with a set of teaching strategies, activities, or even contexts and practices for facilitating learning to read. At 9:00 a.m. on any school morning when that setting known as Mrs. Brown's first- (or fifth-) grade language session comes to life with its physical properties, its human inhabitants and their ways of operating, no such set of teaching practices alone will be of much use in informing Mrs. Brown about how to organize and orchestrate the complexity of the setting she is about to guide. Rather, the range of contexts, practices, teaching strategies, and options she employs will need to be underpinned by formal theoretical knowledge about learning, about language, and about the role that language plays in learning. Furthermore this formal theoretical knowledge will need to be accompanied by a conscious awareness of her values and beliefs (i.e., her ideology) pertaining to the nature of literacy and the purposes and functions it should serve in our culture. Once these things are in place in the ways described here, she will be creative enough to design her own contextually relevant instruction and be flexible enough to cope with the unpredictability that occurs in the sessions she designs and initiates. Then, and only then, she will be able to truly facilitate learning to read.

REFERENCES

Cambourne, B.L. (1988). *The whole story: Natural learning and the acquisition of literacy.* Auckland, New Zealand: Ashton Scholastic.

Cambourne, B.L., & Turbill, J.B. (Eds.). (1994). *Responsive evaluation: Making valid judgements about students' literacy.* Melbourne, Australia: Eleanor Curtain.

Cordeiro, P. (1992). *Whole learning: Whole language and content in the upper elementary grades.* Katonah, NY: Richard C. Owen.

Flippo, R.F. (1998). Points of agreement: A display of professional unity in our field. *The Reading Teacher, 52,* 30–40.

Halliday, M.A.K. (1978). *Language as a social semiotic: The social interpretation of language and meaning.* London: Edward Arnold.

Halliday, M.A.K. (1985). *An introduction to functional grammar.* London: Edward Arnold.

Harste, J.C., Burke, C.L., & Woodward, V.A. (1979). *Children's initial encounters with print.* National Institute of Education grant proposal.

Holdaway, R.D. (1974). *The foundations of literacy.* Auckland, New Zealand: Ashton Scholastic.

Krashen. S.D., & Terrell, T.D. (1983). *The natural approach: Language acquisition in the classroom.* Oxford, England: Pergamon.

Smith, F. (1973). Twelve easy ways to make learning to read difficult. In F. Smith (Ed.), *Psycholinguistics and reading* (pp. 183–196). New York: Holt, Rinehart & Winston.

Whorf, B.L. (1956). *Language, thought, and reality.* Cambridge, MA: MIT Press.

CHAPTER 4

My Point of View

Edward Fry

I have been asked to focus on my beliefs and position regarding reading instruction in this point-of-view piece. Specifically, I have been asked to focus on my background and my most well-known works, publications, and studies so that readers will know where I am coming from. Rona Flippo believes that it is important for readers of this book to realize that the experts who took part in her study represent different backgrounds, philosophies, and points of view. In the sections that follow, I share some of my professional works and views with you.

Testing

I like testing. I know that recently some of my colleagues do not think much of formal testing or informal testing either. However, most of my career I have been in charge of a university-based reading clinic where parents send their children for reading improvement. Since more children applied than there were spaces, some sort of screening was necessary. Either we admitted students on a first-come, first-served basis, or by a table of random numbers, or by some type of screening process. I opted for a screening process.

Before becoming a university instructor, I spent a year as a teacher of mentally retarded elementary children with IQs ranging from 50 to 75. I was well aware that a child with an IQ of 50 could not learn to read at the same level as a child with normal intellectual ability. To even try to get that child up to grade level frustrated the child, the teacher, and his or her parents with false expectations. In the clinics, therefore, we rejected these below-normal students because the remedial reading instruction we offered was not quite the same as the special education they needed, and we did not wish to create false hope on the part of the parent.

Another curious thing happened with reading clinic applicants. Every semester we saw applicants who were quite normal in every respect. For example, a perfectly normal third grader, reading at third-grade level, would be thrust forward by a parent who wanted the normal student to be a super student. We rejected these students because it is the mission of the regular classroom teacher to improve the reading of these students, not the mission of expensive remedial education (Fry, 1959).

So screening tests were a great help in selecting students of normal learning ability (a nonverbal IQ test) who were underachieving in reading skills (an oral and silent reading test). I am well aware that tests are sometimes inaccurate, but I am also aware of the great waste of time, money, and teaching effort on students who do not need expensive remedial education.

Now testing is not just for reading clinics. I am continually amazed by classroom teachers who just start teaching with no notion of their students' present abilities. They select textbooks, supplemental reading materials, and lessons with some sort of vague hitting toward the middle. These same teachers have been exposed to educational psychology courses in which the normal distribution curve is carefully explained, but somehow it does not sink in that a normal fourth grade can have children reading from first-grade to seventh-grade ability. In only one or two hours, the teacher could administer an oral reading paragraph test to every student in her classroom and see that indeed the normal distribution curve amazingly applies to even her class. Some students read well and others poorly. I believe that they can be assessed by formal or informal tests, and that instruction and material selection can be made much more efficiently.

Readability

Testing is a term usually applied to assessing the student. Readability is an assessment applied to the reading material. For example, is this book at the third-grade level or the eighth-grade level?

The purpose of readability is to help the teacher place a student with a book or material at the proper level. This is sometimes referred to as "matching."

There have been over a thousand research articles on the efficacy of using readability formulas. Basically they show that proper matching increases comprehension, increases inclination to continue reading for pleasure, and facilitates written information communication. Proofs include improved scores on comprehension tests, decreases in oral reading errors, increases in amounts of nonassigned reading, and subjective reader self-reports.

I believe that if every teacher would match the proper reading material to the students' ability there would be much less need for remedial reading. A serious problem in most secondary schools is the dropout rate (about 25% nationally and worse in low socioeconomic status areas). Many of the dropout students are continually given reading materials on the wrong readability level by their well-meaning but nonthinking teachers and administrators. Giving students the wrong material continually tells them that they are failures, so they quit. What good schools need to do is to continually give students successful experiences. I believe that readability formulas can help to do this.

As many readers of this expert piece know, I developed a simple readability graph (formula) based on two inputs: (1) semantics as evidenced by word length, and (2) syntactics as evidenced by sentence length. It is amazing that these two simple inputs have stood up so well in research (Klare, 1984). What many readers might not know is that my readability graph was originally developed in Africa while I was on a Fulbright scholarship. It seems to me that African students are just like U.S. students—they need reading materials at the proper level. And African teachers are just like U.S. teachers—they need simple, reliable methods of judging the readability of a text (Fry, 1977).

The important point is that we need to give students lots of reading practice, most of which should be on reading material that each can successfully read. Yes, some material can be "challenging" (a euphemism for difficult material), but most of the material for pleasure or instruction should be at a reasonable level for that student.

Frequency

Another thing I learned well in directing reading clinics is that teaching time is very limited. Therefore it is extremely important that the teacher focus on exactly what the student needs. An important case in point is vocabulary. What words should be taught first? If you like research, the answer is surprisingly simple. I developed a frequency list called Instant Words based on the Carroll, Davies, and Richman study (1971), and this list clearly showed that the 100 most common words make up 50% of all written material, the first 300 words make up 65%, and the first 1,000 words make up over 90%. Yes, you read correctly—just 100 words comprise half of all the words in *The New York Times*, half the words in an encyclopedia, and half of all the words in any children's book, such as *The Wind in the Willows* (Grahame, 1968).

Beginning readers need to recognize these words instantly. If they have to fool around and try to sound out *the* or *of*, they are not apt to have much interest or brain power left to pay attention to comprehension, fluent oral reading, or enjoying what they read. The same is true of writing. It is practically impossible to write a sentence without using one or more of the first 100 Instant Words.

For those who would like just a bit of technical information on how the list of Instant Words was developed, here it is: The Carroll et al. list, also called the American Heritage list, was a count of 5 million running words (some 87,000 different word forms). The problem was that early computers were not too smart and they gave a different count to any change on word form. Hence a different count (based on total appearances) was given for *run, runs, Run,* and *running*. For the Instant Words, the weights for each of the different word forms were added to the base word *run,* and this of course gave *run* a far different rank. So the Instant Words, while based on the Carroll et al. 5-million-word-count data, have a totally different rank order (Fry, 1957, 1994).

The Instant Words have appeared in numerous college reading methods texts, have been handed around on interminable photocopied sheets, have been published on flashcards, and apparently used by thousands of class-room and remedial teachers. I take some particular pleasure in knowing that they have been a help in adult prison literacy programs, as well.

I have also tried to apply the same sort of frequency thinking to phonics, but not quite so successfully. While there was a massive phonics (phoneme-grapheme correspondence) study done at Stanford (Hanna, Hanna, Hodges, & Rudorf, 1966), the data does not lend itself to a simple count as with indi-vidual words. For openers, phonics is usually taught in some kind of group-ing, such as short vowels, Final E Rule, regular consonants, and so on. But then as you get more technical (as the Hanna et al. study did), position or environ-ment of the grapheme in the word can change the phoneme. A simple exam-ple is the vowel *O* in the words *go* and *got* or the consonant *C* in *city* and *cat*. I tried to make a sort of teacher's compromise between the raw research data and the frequency count of Hanna et al. and an earlier study (Moore, 1951), which resulted in a study I did called "A Frequency Approach to Phonics" (Fry, 1964b). This information has resulted in some phonics charts (as a sug-gested curriculum) that have appeared in charts, flashcards, and other materi-als, and in chapters on phonics in some books, such as my little remedial reading handbook *How to Teach Reading* (Fry, 1995).

Failure

Not everything in the reading field is success. If you have not failed to teach some children how to read, you have not taught very many children. Oh, I know that most journal articles, convention speeches, and teachers' room talk is about success with this method or that student, but I would like to state that if we are careful observers, we all have failures.

One of my greatest failures was with something called the Diacritical Marking System (Fry, 1964a). In the late 1960s and early 1970s, U.S. teachers were being bombarded with the supposed success in England of something called the Initial Teaching Alphabet (ITA), in which the traditional alphabet was revised to make it more phonetically regular and traditional spelling was mod-ified to make spelling more phonetically regular. About the same time, the U.S. Office of Education came up with some grant money to fund the First-Grade Studies to try out different reading teaching methods. Some 27 different re-searchers, mostly at different universities, each compared two or three different methods of teaching reading in first grade (a few studies, like mine, were car-ried on into second and third grade). We all used the same reading tests and did the same statistical analysis—a major research first. I elected to try out ITA and my own version of a similar idea called the Diacritical Marking System (DMS). DMS did not have a different alphabet but used the regular alphabet and regular spelling; hence the word form was not changed, but diacritical marks were added to every word in all the first-grade basal readers. For example, long vowels had a bar over the letter and silent letters had a slash mark through them. To make a long story short, there was not much difference between the reading test scores of those pupils taught with DMS, ITA, or regular old basal readers. Differences between the three methods did not show up at the end of Grade 2 or Grade 3, or between boys and girls, or between bright or slower pupils (Fry, 1966). Hence, due to this study and others, you do not hear too much about ITA or DMS anymore, though we better not forget it because as sure as the sun rises somebody is going to have a new alphabet reform to aid beginning readers. Benjamin Franklin had one, and so did the National Education Association in 1910.

My Agreements

Overall, I agree with all of the items on the Expert Study agreement lists (Flippo, 1998) reprinted in Chapter 1 of this book. However, I would emphasize some of the items more than others, and if I were to individually create my own lists again, I would probably add things as well. In other words, yes these are contexts and practices that would make learning to read difficult and others that would facilitate learning to read, but it is also a matter of emphasis. The items are not all equal to me; I believe that some are more important than others. However, Rona Flippo has done a good job of emphasizing this in her 1998 article and in the first chapter of this book. (As experts in this research project we were asked only to provide and then later to approve positive and negative contexts and practices for teaching reading. If we had also been asked to rank them, we probably would have never gotten closure to this study.)

The great controversy in the most recent years has been between the so-called new whole language or literature approach and the so-designated old-fashioned basic skills approach. The First-Grade Studies (Bond & Dykstra, 1967) taught me that there is not any best method of teaching reading. We had something quite similar to the whole language idea back then, only it was called the language experience approach, and we had some pretty drastic phonics methods too. Some reading experts saw a slight difference favoring phonics, but in my view *there was not a great deal of difference between any of the methods.* However, the indisputable fact is that in using any method there was a great deal of difference between the teachers. Would you believe that teaching ability may also follow the normal distribution curve?

There is nothing wrong with trying out new methods of teaching reading, only it might best be done in a limited-controlled comparison research study— not with something like the whole state of California. If I were a principal or a superintendent or a curriculum director, I would like to think that I would allow each teacher to select his or her own methods of teaching reading, because the method is not as important as that vague and wonderful thing called "teaching ability." Despite the method label put on the district curriculum manual or the basal series, most teachers are somewhat eclectic, and this is probably for the best.

Most reading specialists inside the whole language movement consider me as being outside that movement, and I can agree with that too. But what I would like to think of as my position is that there is nothing wrong with most of the methods and ideas included in whole language instruction. It is fine to have children read good literature and write creative stories, however not to the exclusion of teaching some basic skills like vocabulary, phonics, spelling, and comprehension.

Maybe Rona Flippo is right. Maybe it is important to know how different the experts are who agreed to the contexts and practices listed in this book. Maybe those agreements can be the beginning of some common ground.

REFERENCES

Bond, G.L., & Dykstra, R. (1967). The cooperative research program in first-grade reading instruction. *Reading Research Quarterly, 2,* 135–142.

Carroll, J.B., Davies, P., & Richman, B. (1971). *The American Heritage word frequency book.* Boston: Houghton Mifflin.

Flippo, R.F. (1998). Points of agreement: A display of professional unity in our field. *The Reading Teacher, 52,* 30–40.

Fry, E.B. (1957). Developing a word list for remedial reading. *Elementary English, 34,* 456–458.

Fry, E.B. (1959). A reading clinic reports its methods and results. *Journal of Educational Research, 52,* 311–313.

Fry, E.B. (1964a). A diacritical marking system to aid beginning reading instruction. *Elementary English, 41,* 526–529, 537.

Fry, E.B. (1964b). A frequency approach to phonics. *Elementary English, 41,* 759–765, 816.

Fry, E.B. (1966). First grade reading instruction using the diacritical marking system, the initial teaching alphabet, and a basal reading system. *The Reading Teacher, 19,* 666–669.

Fry, E.B. (1977). Fry's readability graph: Clarifications, validity, and extensions to level 17. *Journal of Reading, 21,* 242–252.

Fry, E.B. (1994). *1000 instant words.* Laguna Beach, CA: Laguna Beach Educational Books.

Fry, E.B. (1995). *How to teach reading: For teachers, parents, and tutors.* Laguna Beach, CA: Laguna Beach Educational Books.

Grahame, K. (1968). *The wind in the willows.* New York: Golden Press.

Hanna, P.R., Hanna, J.S., Hodges, R.E., & Rudorf, E.H., Jr. (1966). *Phoneme-grapheme correspondences as cues to spelling improvement.* Washington, DC: U.S. Department of Health, Education and Welfare.

Klare, G.R. (1984). Readability. In P.D. Pearson, R. Barr, M.L. Kamil, & P. Mosenthal (Eds.), *Handbook of Reading Research* (pp. 681–744). New York: Longman.

Moore, J.T. (1951). *Phonetic elements appearing in a 3000 word spelling vocabulary.* Unpublished doctoral dissertation, Stanford University, Palo Alto, California.

CHAPTER 5

Always a Teacher: From Teacher to Teacher Educator to Researcher

Yetta M. Goodman

There is a Jewish folktale about a teacher in a small stetl (village) in Eastern Europe talking to one of the prominent citizens. The teacher says, "If I were Rothschild [the epitome of a wealthy man to poor Jews], I'd be richer than Rothschild."

"How is that possible?" responds the citizen.

"Because," responds the teacher, "of course, I'd do a little teaching on the side."

This vignette establishes the significance of the role of the teacher in my culture: Teaching is so enriching that no matter in what other work they engage, teachers are enriched as a result of their teaching. Once a teacher, *always a teacher*. I present the knowledge and beliefs about the learning and teaching of reading that I have developed within my professional history of almost a half century with this story in mind. I make clear through my history the support I have for the clustered summary agreements presented in Rona Flippo's Expert Study (1998; refer to Chapter 1 in this book). What I know and believe about reading instruction and learning to read is not solely the result of my role as a reading researcher but has been significantly influenced by my teaching in elementary and middle school classrooms. The understandings I have about the contexts and practices that facilitate learning to read were well in place before I became a reading researcher. My history as a teacher informed my work as a teacher educator and stimulated the questions I continue to explore as a researcher. In these capacities—classroom teacher, teacher educator, and researcher—I always identify myself as a teacher, which includes the notion of lifelong learner. In Yiddish, my native tongue, the words for *to teach* and *to learn* (*leren*) are homonyms.

I am a regents professor at the University of Arizona, in the College of Education, Department of Language Reading and Culture. The regents professor rank is bestowed by the university regents on a selected number of researchers nominated by their colleagues. I am the only professor in the College of Education and one of six women at the University of Arizona with this rank.

My professional journey to becoming a regents professor began as a teacher in a self-contained classroom in an intermediate school in southern California.

Classroom Teacher

From the beginning of my teaching in 1952, I was comfortable calling myself a progressive educator based on my learning about John Dewey's philosophy. I believed, based on my understandings of the work of Jean Piaget, that children constructed their own knowledge. These foundational beliefs were part of my teacher education program and included the writings of Hilda Taba and Helen Heffernan, prominent California educators, who helped me understand the importance of the integration of language arts with social studies; the need for careful planning for a curriculum in which students were involved as active learners; and the important role of the teacher who supports students' intellectual development. I used a range of methods and materials in order to facilitate and to encourage my students to discover their own capabilities. I helped them explore significant concepts by connecting what they were learning to what they already knew and to expand on that learning through their own questions.

In my years of teaching sixth- to eighth-grade students in public school classrooms, we studied their communities and found many ways to present what we were learning to parents, peers, and other school personnel. One of my principals led a schoolwide study of sex education (yes, in the 1950s) in which we studied ourselves, our bodies, and our relationships. We took field trips to help us understand the environment and the world of work. We mapped our families' immigration patterns to California. Students kept samples of their written work and lists of their readings for evaluation purposes. They read from a range of genres, including pamphlets, magazines, and firsthand documents of varying difficulty levels. Although most of my students read and wrote independently, I took dictation from a few who needed support to get their ideas onto paper. Students wrote letters, articles, stories, and reports for authentic purposes. They kept personal dictionaries and gave each other spelling tests based on the words they selected from their work. We read basal stories selectively, and I set aside time for students to read by themselves or quietly with peers.

I set this stage with my own teaching to make clear that although my specific research questions came later, my questions were stimulated by my teaching. I taught struggling readers and writers. I noted how hard these students worked at reading carefully by attending to each word, reading slowly, and sounding out, and how meticulously they tried to write because they wanted to be neat and were afraid to spell. I knew I was successful with such students as I invited them into a rich literate environment in which they were important members making their own contributions to a learning community. They developed their literacy abilities as I provided them with opportunities to use reading and writing to expand on what was important to them.

Teacher Educator

Although my roles as teacher educator and researcher emerged about the same time, I was comfortable in my role as teacher educator long before I comfortably defined myself as a researcher. The research questions I began to explore as a teacher were highlighted throughout my work as teacher educator. For years, I participated in on-site experiences for preservice teachers as they apprenticed themselves to the teaching profession. I visited the classes of graduate students in my university classes and of inservice teachers I met in long-range professional development settings in school districts. Observing teachers at the chalk face provided many opportunities for me to consider the kinds of literacy contexts and practices that do and do not facilitate learning to read.

I observed students in ability reading groups; doing worksheets; copying words, sentences, and morning messages exactly from the board; and playing games with flashcards. I saw teachers correcting the exact same miscues differentially for children in lower and higher reading groups. I observed teachers within seconds of any hesitation by the reader giving the student "the word," telling him or her to "sound it out" or "look more closely." I saw readers look up at their teacher after every word they read to verify that they were right and I saw them change their correct answers because their teacher questioned them. I spent time in classrooms and clinics in which activities were changed every 12 minutes to sustain students' attention. I sat in classrooms in which children were not given material to read until they could speak the "right" dialect or language, in which children were unable to write texts until their handwriting was neat and spellings were accurate. I came to the realization that the *practices* of transmission model teaching control both learning and teaching; the *contexts* of such practices make learning to read and write difficult.

On the other hand, I also observed many teachers who organize classrooms in which students discover themselves as learners, define themselves as readers and writers as they use literacy practices to learn about their world. My understandings about progressive education, of establishing a democratic society in classrooms and organizing learning opportunities for students to construct their own meanings, continue to be confirmed by teachers who support what they are doing with knowledge and understanding. Such teachers, many who identify themselves as whole language teachers, organize their reading instruction in ways that reflect the belief that learning to read is integral to reading to learn. They view reading and writing as tools to learn about the significant aspects of their world.

In the development of my curricula as a teacher educator at the university and in school settings with preservice and inservice teachers, I incorporated my views of constructivism and progressive educational philosophy. With likeminded colleagues, we developed ways to apply whole language principles to help teachers discover their own abilities as teachers and to find ways to answer their own questions (Whitmore & Goodman, 1996). I continue to plan experiences to engage teachers in becoming introspective about their own reading and writing practices in order to have realistic expectations about their students' literacies. Teachers develop a research stance as they participate in miscue analysis of their own students, analyze their students' written compositions, and reflect about their own interactions with students in discussions focused on literacy learning and experiences. They document students' language knowledge and language use. The responses of teachers to their own thoughtful analyses of their students led me to popularize the term *kidwatching* (Goodman, 1978; Goodman & Wilde, 1996).

Kidwatching teachers develop ways to observe their students using a variety of evaluative tools to diagnose strengths and to understand weaknesses. They take careful field notes about their students' literacy events as they watch a group of kids during a science experiment, as they record a reader's miscues during an individual conference, or as they list the resources used by a group at the writing center. They use the knowledge and insights about their students to influence their instructional practices and to make curricular decisions. Although I have popularized the term *kidwatching*, its importance has been highlighted and informed by knowledgeable teachers who use insightful and analytic observations of their students to organize dynamic contexts in which the practices that facilitate learning to read are successful.

Theory and research cannot be directly applied to classroom settings through mandated and scripted lessons for teachers. Theoretical constructs and research insights are sifted through teachers' understandings, adapted into their knowledge base, and as a result become transformed into classroom practice. Such transformations are greatest when teachers view their inquiries from the stance of a researcher. In such cases, there is no separation between educational theory, research, and practice. Within teacher education programs respectful of the concept of *always the teacher*, courses and experiences are organized to involve teachers in discovering their roles as researchers and decision makers in their own classrooms. As teachers define themselves as researchers and become comfortable with that role, they find new ways in which to empower themselves.

Researcher

My research has been informed by my teaching with children and adolescents and my work in teacher education and professional development. Since 1965, I worked with Kenneth Goodman and colleagues in the development of miscue analysis (its procedures and research design). In miscue analysis, readers read orally from a whole story or article. The reader is not given assistance during the reading and is asked to retell after the reading. Miscues are analyzed to determine the degree to which they enhance or disrupt the reader's construction of meaning. From the analysis, we gather insights about the knowledge readers have about the language cueing systems and the ways in which they use a range of reading strategies. The retelling is used to corroborate what we understand from the miscue analysis of the written text. I have miscued over a thousand readers of all ages, with different reading abilities and of different language and dialect communities. I have analyzed tens of thousands of miscues. I have worked with hundreds of teachers as they gain knowledge about individual readers through miscue analysis and use their knowledge to organize instruction to benefit their students.

During collaborations with members of the miscue research team, we realized the power of what we were learning about the reading process and the impact of this knowledge on reading instruction. Since we had all been classroom teachers, we often discussed what we would have done differently if we knew as teachers what we were now learning as reading researchers. We were eager to share what we were learning with other teachers. We planned presentations at professional conferences, organized workshops for school districts, developed syllabi for university courses, and wrote articles and books to inform teachers and researchers about our research findings and our suggestions for classroom applications (Allen & Watson, 1976). We developed materials to guide teachers in using miscue analysis, to help researchers follow miscue analysis research design, and to provide strategy lessons for research purposes and to support developing readers (Goodman & Burke, 1972; Goodman, Burke & Sherman, 1980; Goodman, Watson, & Burke, 1987; Goodman, Watson, & Burke, 1996). The strategy lessons in these works are similar to many of the practices that facilitate learning to read and provide suggestions for facilitating contexts.

Through discussions with teachers about the ways in which they use miscue analysis in classroom and clinical settings, I extended my research focus and began to explore retrospective miscue analysis (RMA). In RMA, readers listen to their own taped readings and with the support of a teacher or a researcher evaluate the influence of miscues on their comprehension. They become consciously aware and begin to articulate their knowledge of language, the reading process, and their use of reading strategies. Through RMA we create environments in which students develop positive views about themselves as literate beings and views about the ways in which being literate impacts their lives. This work highlights the importance of students' expectations about themselves as readers and writers. My research documents that these procedures result in readers developing greater confidence in themselves as readers and at the same time developing greater capabilities as readers. This part of my history is documented in *Retrospective Miscue Analysis: Revaluing Readers and Reading* (Goodman & Marek, 1996).

My understanding of how children learn to read and write continues to be informed by my early literacy research. Early in miscue analysis research, I began to wonder how children come to understand the functions that reading and writing serve in their lives and how they come to understand literacy as an object that they talk about. I documented that children from a range of backgrounds and literacy experiences know a great deal about literacy before they come to school.

My inquiry and understandings about early literacy development led to my roots of literacy metaphor, suggesting that for reading instruction to be effective, teachers need to know about the history of the literacy experiences and knowledge that children have before they come to school (Goodman, 1986). Some of my conclusions are included in a volume with an international group of literacy researchers from Italy, Mexico, Brazil, and Israel, *How Children Construct Literacy: Piagetian Perspectives*, translated into Spanish and Portuguese from English (Goodman, 1990; Goodman, 1991). Literacy is a major cultural phenomenon that needs to be understood within the context of society and not treated as simple reading and writing skills that are taught only in school.

Another volume coauthored with Sandra Wilde, *Literacy Events in a Community of Young Writers*, reports a research study of the writing development in classrooms of Tohono O'odham Indian third and fourth graders (Goodman & Wilde, 1992). As we sat next to each young writer, carefully documenting their writing experiences, it became evident that reading served many purposes for them. They used stories, nonfiction texts, dictionaries, and signs in their environment as resources to use in their writing. We documented that children would remember a word or phrase from a particular book, search for it in the classroom library, and share their finds with their classmates. We became aware of the importance of talk, illustration, and other print media—in the community, on the walls in the school, and in classrooms—on the writing development of the students. We documented students' interests in each other's writing and documented the importance of the classroom social community on writing development. The impact of the social aspects of teaching and learning indicate the paramount importance of the contexts for facilitating learning to read and the role of the teacher in organizing such contexts.

Through my reading and writing research, I have concluded that children invent knowledge about literacy within the constraints of literacy conventions in society. Readers and writers are dynamically involved in their own learning about the reading process and the strategies they use. Kids learn a great deal about the various subsystems of language and how they work in reading as a result of being readers and writers, not as a result of didactic teaching of discrete skills. The latter kind of teaching may result in learning for some students that negatively affects literacy development. These conclusions (Whitmore & Goodman, 1995) highlight the important differences between contexts and practices that make learning to read difficult and those that facilitate learning to read. Research has provided me with a range of rich settings and interactions with children and teachers to help me deepen my theoretical understandings about the teaching and learning of reading, but at the same time, it has helped me wonder about literacy processes and conceive new questions.

In Retrospect

As I come to the end of the history of my professional journey at this time, students from my middle school classrooms in the 1950s come to mind. As my early years as a teacher resulted in my research questions, my theoretical and research knowledge provides insights into my students in a way I did not understand at that time. I understand that Arthur was frustrated every time I asked him to read because he did not believe that he was a reader or a writer. I understand that when William wrote about making himself "dzam" and "pina buder samwhiches," he was reflecting his knowledge of the graphophonic cueing system. When Tanya read only horse stories, she was building concepts and language that stayed with her throughout her life. I have greater insight into why each of them succeeded in learning to read and write. Arthur was the first student in his family to graduate from high school; William became valedictorian of his graduating class; Tanya became a biologist. My work has always focused on ways to document that ethnically, racially, linguistically, and culturally diverse youngsters who are not part of the mainstream are capable learners. I believe that they benefit most from contexts and practices that facilitate learning to read. With such concerns I not only tie my history to the children I taught but to my own childhood experiences as a supposedly unsuccessful learner, often chided for my inadequate performance because of my "Yiddish-speaking home and working-class parents." My understanding about what facilitates or makes learning to read difficult is informed by my personal history as well as my professional one.

It has taken me years to state confidently that my teaching informs my research questions and the selection of my informants, and that reciprocally my research informs my teaching. I believed, as many still do, that university research is where significant ideas have their origin and that research results can be directly applied to classrooms. I now understand the complexity of teaching in the classroom. The Expert Study agreements on what would facilitate learning to read or make it difficult will have minimal impact on schools without professional elementary and secondary teachers who understand what they do in classrooms and why. As teachers research their own questions and use their knowledge and understandings in their classrooms with a passion for teaching and a commitment to learners, dynamic transformations take place.

As a beginning teacher, I applied to my classroom curriculum the research and theory that best fit what I believed. What happens in classrooms is not affected by what researchers do in any direct way. We provide one component of a highly complex, integrative system. As "experts," as we are identified in this book, we need to appreciate the limitations of our roles and work respectfully with others in this enterprise of literacy teaching and learning in schools. Legislation is having significant impact on what happens in classrooms, and as researchers and teacher educators, we cannot ignore these political influences. What happens in classrooms is also influenced by what communities believe about schooling, and the power relationships in the political and business communities. If we work together with greater understanding about the roles we each play, we come to the realization that long-lasting change can only take place in the classroom through support and high regard for the work of the teacher. In this way my concept of *always a teacher* comes to a full circle.

REFERENCES

Allen, P.D., & Watson, D. (Eds.). (1976). *Findings of research in miscue analysis: Classroom implications.* Urbana, IL: ERIC and National Council of Teachers of English.

Flippo, R.F. (1998). Points of agreement: A display of professional unity in our field. *The Reading Teacher, 52,* 30–40.

Goodman, Y. (1978). Kidwatching: An alternative to testing. *National Elementary School Principal, 57,* 41–45.

Goodman, Y. (1986). Children coming to know literacy. In W. Teale & E. Sulzby (Eds.), *Emergent literacy: Writing and reading* (11th ed., pp. 1–14). Norwood, NJ: Ablex.

Goodman, Y. (Ed.). (1991). *Los ninos construyen su lectoescritura: Un enfoque piagetiano.* Mendez de Andes, South America: Aique Grupo.

Goodman, Y., & Burke, C.L. (1972). *Reading miscue inventory: Procedure for diagnosis and evaluation.* Katonah, NY: Richard C. Owen.

Goodman, Y.M. (Ed.). (1990). *How children construct literacy: Piagetian perspectives.* Newark, DE: International Reading Association.

Goodman, Y.M., Burke, C.L., & Sherman, B. (1980). *Reading strategies: Focus on comprehension.* New York: Holt, Rinehart and Winston.

Goodman, Y.M., & Marek, A.M. (Eds.). (1996). *Retrospective miscue analysis: Revaluing readers and reading.* Katonah, NY: Richard C. Owen.

Goodman, Y.M., Watson, D.J., & Burke, C.L. (1987). *Reading miscue inventory: Alternative procedures.* Katonah, NY: Richard C. Owen.

Goodman, Y.M., Watson, D.J., & Burke, C.L. (1996). *Reading strategies: Focus on comprehension* (2nd ed.). Katonah, NY: Richard C. Owen.

Goodman, Y.M., & Wilde, S. (1992). *Literacy events in a community of young writers.* New York: Teachers College Press.

Goodman, Y.M., & Wilde, S. (1996). *Notes from a kidwatcher: Selected writings of Yetta M. Goodman.* Portsmouth, NH: Heinemann.

Whitmore, K., & Goodman, Y. (1995). Reading potentials: Appropriate curriculum and assessment for young children. In S. Bredekamp (Ed.), *Personal and social literacy history of young children* (Vol. II, pp. 146–166). Washington, DC: National Association for the Education of Young Children.

Whitmore, K.F., & Goodman, Y.M. (1996). *Whole language voices in teacher education.* York, ME: Stenhouse.

CHAPTER 6

Evaluation, Writing, and Reading

Jane Hansen

As I think about what I believe and what has prompted the evolution of my beliefs, four experiences from my teacher education days frequently replay themselves. Two involve my professors and two involve the classroom teachers under whom I did my student teaching.

At Drake University in the mid-1960s, we students taught for half days for an entire year in two classrooms, one each semester. My two teachers were as different as night and day. I do not remember the name of the young teacher I served under for my first semester, but I do remember the stack of worksheets she placed on each first-grade child's desk before school each morning. She and I conversed over the ditto machine as she ran off copies of the eight identical, beautiful dittos each child would complete that day. Her sister designed these original creations, and I could not have a copy of any of them. This woman, who lived with her two sisters and mother—all of whom were elementary teachers—was passionate about her profession. She lived it.

My second-semester placement was with silver-haired Mrs. Wilson, who never used one single worksheet in her second-grade classroom. The children made things from colored paper, paints, crayons, scissors, and paste. They did not always sit at their desks, and they did not always work in the classroom—sometimes a few of them worked on the floor in the coat closet. Her husband was the director of curriculum for the Des Moines, Iowa, USA, school district. Without a doubt, I preferred her classroom over my first-semester experience. I remember nothing from my theory classes to support my inclination, but I felt more comfortable there. Maybe it was not exactly because of the paints and paste. Maybe it was Mrs. Wilson's quiet way of letting all of her students know that she loved them as creators, and their sometimes messy creations.

Professor Marvins, a gray-haired, bespectacled, well-suited man, invited us to experiment in his children's literature class. We actually walked to a real classroom as part of that course, saw him shed his suitcoat, sit on a small chair, and come to life as he lived the books he read to the children. Then, each of us took a turn. I clearly remember my very first teaching experience, as I read *Caps for Sale* (Slobodkina, 1985) to second graders. Later, as an elementary teacher, I always read to my students, and as a professor, I continue.

Last week I read *Owls* (1993) by Jean Craighead George, and the students and I talked about these creatures and the great skill of the author. This information book easily held the attention of my audience. I learned years ago from Professor Marvins not to rely on lectures to give information about reading to university students; I create classroom scenes in which the preservice and inservice teachers in my classes experience books. I learned a similar lesson from my other memorable professor, but I doubt she would appreciate my version.

Dr. Weaver, articulate, bone-thin, face lined with experience, and hair dyed to match her black dresses, repeated over and over, in several sessions of our reading methods class, "Don't ever use the phrase *ability groups.* You must not presume to know what a child's ability is; you see every child as a person with ability. However, unfortunately, some of your children will not achieve as much as others. Because of this difference, we form achievement groups."

As an elementary teacher I lived her words. I took care to see each child as someone with ability, and looked closely at the children I placed in groups. As a professor I found I could not live her words; I could not divide my students into achievement groups. Well, I could have, but my soul would not let me. I stopped advocating groups the day I realized I could not treat adults that way; I just could not bring myself to divide the preservice and inservice teachers in my classes into achievement groups. To find another way to teach was not easy, but I had to figure this out. I was learning about writing instruction, and it informed various aspects of my teaching, including my use of groups.

As a relatively new professor at the University of New Hampshire, I accepted an invitation from Donald Graves to conduct research on reading-writing instruction. He had just completed a huge study on the teaching of writing (Graves, 1983), I was a professor of reading, and he wondered if we could combine fields. We researched in Ellen Blackburn Karelitz's first-grade classroom in Somersworth, a blue-collar community. I spent two mornings a week, for 2 years, in Ellen's classroom. She formed no reading groups as her children learned to read from children's literature. They also drew and wrote on blank paper; they seldom saw worksheets. She leaned in closely, spoke softly, heard each child's voice, and listened. They told her what they thought and she did likewise.

I loved this classroom full of the strong voices of busy writers and readers. I was struck by how much sense reading made to them. In contrast to my students when I was a reading resource teacher, Ellen's children expected print to make sense. When they did not know words, they did not substitute them with others that did not make sense and continue as if nothing were amiss. They knew, because they created print, that writers do not put random words on paper. These children wrote their own compositions—their news—every day. They had things to tell, assumed all writers did, and came to the pages of books to find out what those authors had to say.

In order to keep these young children's strong voices vibrant, Ellen thought carefully about various aspects of reading and writing instruction. For example, she could not place some children in low achievement groups, because this might make them feel less worthy than others. If they started to question their status, their voices might become hesitant. This could affect them as writers, as learners, as readers. So, what kind of an organization would she use?

Ellen, Don, and I talked about this. Ellen decided to place the children in a context in which they would want to learn to read, and observe their actions. What would they do when they needed help? Given that only two of them, on the first day of school, could read books from the classroom library, the majority would need lots of help. As for writing, all of them, on that first day, said they could write and they all did—many of them drew pictures, which they called writing. They could write in the form of drawing, but they could not produce print. Eight of them could not write their names. They would need lots of help.

On successive days, when they sat around tables to write, they read and talked about their writing from the previous days. Then they added to it or wrote something new. They wrote and talked among themselves as if writing and talking were one seamless process. Those who could not write their names did not sit off at one table by themselves. The children sat in mixed fashion and got information of all kinds from each other. They asked each other everything from "How do you spell *bicycle*?" to "What time do you have to go to bed?" This procedure continued all year.

On the second day of school, one boy (Mark) had read a book to the class. Ellen had published it the previous evening from the news he wrote on the first day, when he had written three thoughts about a fire in their town. Ellen placed one sentence per page when she typed his book in a large font; Mark created an illustration for each page and practiced reading his book. His own printing had been sparse, because he knew phonics, but not spelling. Mark had put only the sounds he could hear on the page. When Ellen typed it in conventional spelling, many of the words looked unfamiliar to this young writer, but, within minutes, he could read his own language. Mark proudly read his book to the class, seated on the little chair Ellen sat on when she read to the class. Everyone clustered on the carpet, eyes on Mark, as he amazed them with his book. Then they all talked about the fire.

Later that day, Ellen read to the class, as she did more than once a day. She read a book about fire engines, and the children compared what the author of that book wrote to what Mark had written. Ellen started a network of pieces of writing (Blackburn, 1985), some written by classroom authors and others by professionals. The children knew they were part of an august group.

Also on that day, Mandy read a book from the classroom library to the class. This book was about giants and the class talked about these mythical creatures. Mandy's classmates wanted to know how she could read this book. Talk about reading and writing became common very early in these children's careers as readers, learners, and writers.

Every day for the rest of the year, at least two children sat on what became known as The Author's Chair (Graves & Hansen, 1983; Karelitz, 1993) and read to the class. They read their own writing, each other's, their published books, their nonpublished writing, and the writing of professionals. Ellen also read to them frequently. When they talked about what to do to learn to read various books, they often talked about each other.

They learned to use each other as resources for reading, as they did when they sat around their classroom tables to write. When it was time for reading each day, each child either chose to stay with a book from the previous day or to select a new one. In either case, the children often chose books available at the listening center, easy books Ellen had read to the class several times, books written by classmates who could help other children read them, and library books their classmates could read. The children sought help from those who could read. They wanted to learn and they sought assistance. They did not put themselves in achievement level groups. They scattered—in pairs, small groups, and sometimes alone—throughout the classroom. They read.

Ellen spent her time during reading and writing among the children, trying to ensure they were all busy. She spent her time outside the school day thinking about how to ensure the overall classroom context kept all the children immersed in reading, writing, and learning. She did not spend her time creating worksheets for the children. They did not spend much time working on projects, either. This was a classroom for reading and writing, and the students enjoyed doing both.

In 1985, Donald Graves and I asked additional researchers to join us as we undertook a larger reading-writing project with the teachers at Mast Way School in Lee (Hansen, 1987) and then moved on to evaluation. In Stratham, we studied students as evaluators, the prime role they play in writing conferences, and extended that role into reading. In 1990, we trekked down the highway to Manchester, one of New Hampshire's largest cities, and studied students as evaluators of themselves as readers and writers in the context of portfolios (Hansen, 1998). This study opened my eyes a great deal.

I learned that evaluation is the process of thinking about what I am doing, what I have done, and what I intend to do. It is much more complicated than I thought when I saw it as the culminating act for a unit of study. And it no longer made sense to give the title "Evaluation" to the last chapter of a book about reading instruction. Reading instruction begins with evaluation, and evaluation occurs at all times. Plus, when we teach students to use evaluation processes, they tend to understand their work better than when we serve as the sole evaluators. We learned all of this, however, in a roundabout way.

Some students did not find value in the reading and writing they did in school, but they did do some reading and writing outside of school that they considered significant. They started their portfolios with examples of those printed materials. Unfortunately, other students insisted that they did not read or write anything of importance either at school or at home. So we said, "If you aren't a reader or writer, who are you?" They began to create portfolios to answer that question.

They became ethnographers of their lives and began to place varied, and sometimes valuable, artifacts in their portfolios. We saw naturalization certificates, soccer schedules, and birthday cards from fathers in prison. These students, who had seen themselves as insignificant, began to value themselves. As they shared these items in their classrooms, they began to value one another. In this classroom environment, they began to see themselves as readers and writers.

My journey has led me to various beliefs, some of which are mirrored in the points of agreement among the experts in Rona Flippo's study; a cluster of these is titled "Contexts, Environment, and Purposes for Reading," and one item reads, "Create environments, contexts in which the children become convinced that reading does further the purposes of their lives" (Flippo, 1998; refer to Chapter 1, p. 14, in this book). Talk among the students and teacher helps them all become acquainted, helps them respect and care for one another. This is a hallmark of the classrooms I now strive to create in my teacher education classes. In turn, it is my hope that the teachers in my courses go forth to create similar learning environments.

"Combining Reading With Other Language Processes" is another cluster of agreements that pertains completely to my research and teaching. I can no longer teach a writing or reading course, even though some still bear such titles. Anyone who takes a reading course from me studies writing instruction as well. I now fully expect at least one person to approach me after the first session of a reading class with this question: "I meant to enroll in a reading course, but this seems to involve a lot of information about the teaching of writing as well. Do you think maybe I should change to another course?" I do all I can to encourage the person to stay, and the teachers in my classes come to appreciate the inseparability of reading and writing.

Finally, I give my students "lots of time...to do research on a topic, to pursue an interest" (Flippo, 1998; refer to Chapter 1, p. 14, in this book). The teachers in my reading classes conduct teacher research on an aspect of reading instruction that is of particular interest to them. They learn that the stance of a professional is to constantly search for more effective ways to teach, and that we never get it to work all the time. We know what we think we believe today and that, as we continue to learn, our beliefs about what facilitates learning to read will change.

REFERENCES

Blackburn, E. (1985). Stories never end. In J. Hansen, T. Newkirk, & D. Graves (Eds.), *Breaking ground: Teachers relate reading and writing in the elementary school* (pp. 3–13). Portsmouth, NH: Heinemann.

Flippo, R.F. (1998). Points of agreement: A display of professional unity in our field. *The Reading Teacher, 52,* 30–40.

George, J.C., & Minor, W. (illustrator). (1993). *Owls.* New York: HarperCollins.

Graves, D. (1983). *Writing: Teachers and children at work.* Portsmouth, NH: Heinemann.

Graves, D., & Hansen, J. (1983). The author's chair. *Language Arts, 60,* 176–183.

Hansen, J. (1987). *When writers read.* Portsmouth, NH: Heinemann.

Hansen, J. (1998). *When learners evaluate.* Portsmouth, NH: Heinemann.

Karelitz, E.B. (1993). *The author's chair and beyond.* Portsmouth, NH: Heinemann.

Slobodkina, E. (1985). *Caps for sale: A tale of a peddler, some monkeys and their monkey business.* New York: HarperCollins.

CHAPTER 7

Point of View: Jerome C. Harste

Diane DeFord

Ifirst met Jerry Harste when I went to Indiana University in 1974 to complete a master's degree. The fact that I stayed on to complete a doctoral degree was due, in large measure, to this man. As a reading professional he is dedicated to two goals that are critical to learning: inquiry through invitations, and collaboration. What he works to create for himself as a learner he also strives to create for all learners. All of us who studied at Indiana University experienced the call to come to the seminar room to listen to a new idea, to think, to create, and to revise as part of a thought collective (Fleck, 1935/1979).

What I took away from these experiences was the sense that it was not important whether the idea was "good" or not, but that in thinking together, we learned more. Jerry has put this basic theory into practice across years and across institutions as his students moved on to work at other universities. However, they keep the thread of the collective thought intact across space and time.

I was asked to provide this biographical sketch of Jerry. Although I still feel I am a student of his teaching even after 25 years of working as a reading educator, I present his point of view as evidenced in his scholarly writing, organizing it within the framework of categories from the Expert Study (Flippo, 1998; refer to Chapter 1 in this book): (1) Combining Reading With Other Language Processes; (2) Contexts, Environment, and Purposes for Reading; (3) Developing (or Shaping) Students' Perceptions and Expectations; (4) Materials; and (5) Reading Instruction.

Combining Reading With Other Language Processes

Reading is but one mode of language. In some curriculum models, it is often separated from the other modes (speaking, listening, and writing) when "reading instruction" occurs. From Jerry's perspective, this makes learning to read difficult. Rather, reading should be purposefully embedded within settings that encourage speaking, listening, and writing as well. Within his theory of learning, children construct knowledge of the reading process for themselves. He sees the expression of reading, writing, speaking, and listening as *authorship* and the children as *authors*. As they engage in reading, writing, speaking, or listening, they originate or give existence to their ideas and the meanings they create. This is the way children learn. In fact, this is the way we all learn.

By juxtaposing all of the modes of language within a literacy curriculum, common features become apparent to and supportive of the learner. Jerry argues that "this is so because reading and writing, like all forms of communication, involve authoring. They are processes in which we originate, negotiate, and revise ideas" (Harste & Short, 1988, p. 5). In his view, learners seek to make sense and use a host of information from their current beliefs, hypotheses, interests, needs, and purposes to make meaning or form ideas. The curriculum framework that grows out of this perspective is termed the *authoring cycle* by Jerry and his colleagues. The authoring cycle is actually a metaphor for the learning cycle that occurs when children engage in complex literacy events.

Jerry would combine reading with other language processes to accomplish the goals articulated by the other experts as well. When reading and writing are purposefully embedded within a curriculum model that highlights authoring, learners will make meaning and connections through any communication systems available within the setting (language, drama, art, math, and music). Communication is expanded, as is the learner's potential when the language arts curriculum focuses on the social and psychological strategies of successful learners as they employ the language arts as both tools and toys for learning. This stance facilitates learning to read as well as learning of the other communication systems.

Contexts, Environment, and Purposes for Reading

One thread that is visible across Jerry's scholarly writing is his belief that a "low-risk" environment facilitates learning. This is contrasted with the possible no-risk or high-risk environments. The learning setting must provide unlimited time to engage in rich literacy activities that provide demonstrations of reading and writing as ways of exploring and expanding the learner's personal world. In Jerry's words, this is a "self-maintaining environment" (Harste & Short, 1988, p. 117). Another critical ingredient in his supportive context is social interaction. The goal of a self-maintaining environment for authors is to provide time for functional reading and writing activities as well as opportunities to learn from and see their classmates as authors. These natural language contexts provide ample opportunities for learners to engage in and see others engaged in literacy activities.

This perspective offers a conception of curriculum as made up of literacy events and literacy events made up of demonstrations and engagements. By engaging in literacy events and observing demonstrations by other literacy learners, readers and writers will become strategic, or able to vary the content of their strategies and the contexts of their use as needed (Harste, 1986). Some of the contexts that will provide these opportunities for learners include writing and reading to others, producing newspapers, writing and sharing poetry, reading and sharing literature, and reading and writing for a variety of purposes (i.e., journals, stories, information, and lists). When children learn in settings that acknowledge the social and functional nature of language, they learn what it is important to attend to and why (Harste & Short, 1988, p. 118).

Developing (or Shaping) Students' Perceptions and Expectations

Within the authoring cycle, children are learning through engagement and demonstration. As a group of children discuss and reflect on what worked and what did not work, they "come to value the strategies of successful language use and learning" (Harste & Short, 1988, p. 119). As they come to value language, learning, and the strategies that make them successful in literacy activities, they become conscious rather than intuitive in their actions. Jerry and his colleagues believe that "with this consciousness comes choice, and with choice comes empowerment" (Harste & Short, 1988, p. 119). It is this process that shapes children's perceptions and expectations.

Children who have come to own reading and writing in this powerful way interact with and are actively involved in their world as literate beings. They come to see and appreciate their world in new ways. Jerry recounts a story told by Heidi Mills (see Harste & Short, 1988, p. 121) about a preschooler from her classroom on a field trip to the post office. The young child told Heidi, "I can hardly wait to get back to school to write about this in my journal!" Writing is a way of recounting, remembering, and recasting experience to share with others. It provides a different way for the learner to live through this experience at the time the experience is occurring as well as at a different time. As readers and writers shift perspective from participant to spectator, from monitor to critic, from speaker to listener, and from reader to writer or artist, they come to understand the multiple roles they can take as a member of a literate society. This shapes their perceptions and expectations (of self and others) and expands their communication potential.

Materials

I visited the Center for Inquiry a few years ago, the school that Jerry and his colleagues developed based on this theoretical perspective. As I observed children at work, it was clear that life experiences were the cornerstone upon which the curriculum was negotiated. The materials of instruction were predominately those that supported learning in general and literacy development specifically. Reading, writing, speaking, listening, drama, music, and art were the multimodal experiences in which children were engaged. Consequently, there were a variety of text materials that met the range of life experiences children encountered in the real world—a range of literature (fiction and nonfiction, poetry, magazines, newspapers, lists, labels, descriptions, reports, and journals). The classrooms were rich in art supplies, props for drama and movement, and artifacts from the world.

As Jerry and his colleagues write in *Creating Classrooms for Authors* (1988),

> There is in this sense no "pure" act of reading or writing—writers talk, read, write, listen draw and gesture, all in the name of writing; readers discuss ideas they find problematic, listen, sketch, underline, and do a number of other things, all in the name of reading. (p. 53)

In this same way, the materials of instruction are as varied as the needs of the learners—or as the contexts of work learning—demand. There are no formulas or magic combinations of activities that can be set forth to make teaching easy or consistent. The teacher in this environment actively orchestrates and negotiates a complex set of materials, professional knowledge, knowledge of students, interests, social interactions, and instructional decisions. The materials are less important than how they are used to further learning. The variety of materials were used to facilitate work time, authors' sharing time, authors' chair, Readers Theatre, shared reading, author meets author, literature response activities, journal writing, independent reading, and writing. In other words, the materials were functional and served learners to make meaning of their world.

Reading Instruction

Within a dynamic literacy curriculum, the teacher's goal is to introduce, support, and guide students to incorporate the range of strategies and options available to them to process written language. While this goal is being met throughout the school day as learners engage with and observe literacy activities, one way this also happens is through strategy lessons. "Strategy lessons help make students consciously aware of their strategies; this awareness makes choice possible and allows learners to be strategic" (Harste & Short, 1988, p. 102).

Through the vehicle of strategy lessons, how language operates is highlighted and explored. Children learn about new forms of language, about different genres, new techniques, and new ways to use language within and across written language events. From a natural language setting (the reading of a book rich in description, for example), students might have an opportunity to discuss how description paints a picture that is vivid for the reader. Connections are then made to their own writing and other books they have read. Finally, they have an opportunity to return to their own writing and reading to apply what they have learned about the purpose or function of description in text. They learn how to use description to clarify their own meaning or get closer to the author's meaning. Most important, no strategy lesson has only one aspect of language in operation—rather, many language lessons could be demonstrated and explored, but for the teacher's purposes, one aspect is highlighted. "Strategies are not given as formulas or rules to be applied, but rather as options that can be used to construct meaning" (Harste & Short, 1988, p. 101).

The teacher selects different strategy lessons across the year, focusing in each instance on the strategies used by successful readers. A student may also notice a strategy that has been helpful. The goal is to discuss and demonstrate what happens within the reading and writing processes in psychological as well as sociological terms. Self-correction and monitoring, and talking with peers and brainstorming, are examples of these psychological and sociological strategies. The teacher observes patterns within reading and writing to determine what types of strategy lessons are needed. Some of these might have the following foci:

- What do I do when I come to something I do not know when I am reading?
- How are different genres organized?
- How do I use what I know when reading new materials?
- What did what I just read mean? How might I paraphrase this?
- What do I do when I am stuck and do not know what to write next?

The goal of these complex interactions within the ongoing life of the classroom is that strategies from the instructional setting are taken on and used by the students. Scibior (1986) studied the authoring cycle within the classroom setting and found that even though the teachers saw each of the steps of the authoring cycle as distinct, the children began to use this as a learning cycle or a general process framework that guided their learning.

Within a literacy curriculum, students need opportunities to explore choices in reading and how to read and write for sustained time periods. By observing and listening to reading, they hear what fluent reading sounds like and how to read fluently themselves. As a participant in a community of readers within the classroom, through such events as shared reading, they become part of the social contract of readers in the larger society. They engage in grand conversations to share and explore the meanings they and others create, and greet opportunities to explore as well as expand what they are reading. In this way, they become more flexible, able to read a variety of materials. As readers across the world do, they meet and are introduced to authors and the power of authoring. This is Jerry Harste's view of learning to read.

REFERENCES

Fleck, L. (1979). *Genesis and development of a scientific fact.* Chicago: University of Chicago Press. (Original work published 1935)

Flippo, R.F. (1998). Points of agreement: A display of professional unity in our field. *The Reading Teacher, 52,* 30–40.

Harste, J.C. (1986). *What it means to be strategic: Good readers as informants.* Paper presented at the National Reading Conference, Austin, Texas.

Harste, J.C., & Short, K.G. (with Burke, C.L.). (1988). *Creating classrooms for authors: The reading writing connection.* Portsmouth, NH: Heinemann.

Scibior, O.S. (1986). *Reconsidering spelling development: A socio-psycholinguistic perspective.* Unpublished doctoral dissertation, Indiana University, Bloomington.

CHAPTER 8

Point of View: Wayne R. Otto

Robert T. Rude

T he year was 1970. We were in the midst of the Vietnam War and the accompanying protests by college and university students across the United States. The streets passing through the University of Wisconsin-Madison campus were littered with bricks that students, standing on the roofs of high-rise dormitories, had thrown on the patrolling National Guardsmen below them. Innocent students, myself included, were tear-gassed by police brought on campus to control the unrest and protests. Universities— indeed, the country—were being ripped apart at the seams. It was the age of Robert McNamara, Secretary of Defense, and his systems approach to solve the problems of the world. Quantifying educational outcomes in terms of behavioral objectives was a part of many school curricula. It was in this context that the Wisconsin Prototypic Reading System, later known as the *Wisconsin Design for Reading Skill Development* (1970), was born.

The *Design*, as it became known, was developed at the Wisconsin Research and Development Center for Cognitive Learning, one of a handful of educational research centers around the United States. Under funding from the U.S. Department of Education, the *Design* was spearheaded by principal investigator Wayne Otto and a staff of full-time employees and graduate students at the University of Wisconsin-Madison. The ultimate goal of these research and development centers was to infuse the developed programs into U.S. schools.

Wayne's *Design* was truly a grassroots phenomenon. Over the years, administrators, reading specialists, and teachers in several schools and school districts in the Madison, Wisconsin, USA, area had worked with the Research and Development Center staff in an attempt to develop a consentually agreed upon list of reading skills that students should know before they graduated from elementary school. The list eventually consisted of six elements: Word Attack, Comprehension, Study Skills, Self-Directed Reading, Creative Reading, and Critical Reading. One of the major accomplishments of the *Design* team was to develop and field test a series of criterion-referenced reading tests that teachers could use to measure student skill acquisition. The plan was to design tests for the Word Attack element first, then the Study Skills, followed by the Comprehension element. Finally, the latter three sections of the program—

Self-Directed, Creative, and Critical Reading—would be fine-tuned, although there was never an intent to develop criterion-referenced tests for these facets of reading. They were always considered candidates for the more open-ended objectives of the affective domain.

The first three components were developed in roughly that sequence. They lent themselves to being evaluated more readily with formal paper-and-pencil tests than did the last three areas. The Word Attack element, for example, consisted of 45 skills, 39 of which were measured with paper-and-pencil tests. The last three components did not lend themselves to criterion-referenced measures as readily and were, therefore, left more to teachers' interpretation of how to assess and implement the respective skills. The time, resources, and money needed to conceptualize, pilot test, revise, field test, and finally market each of the *Design* components was considerable.

In the early and mid-1970s, teachers relied heavily on basal readers and workbooks. Few integrated literature with reading as we know it today. A small percentage of teachers dabbled with the individualized reading of trade books, but for the most part, instruction was driven by published basal reading systems. In the context of this regimented instructional milieu, the *Design* was cutting edge. Students in the *Design* were administered the criterion-referenced "mastery tests" in groups, the tests were machine or hand scored, and instructional groups were formed based on skill needs. The *Design* allowed teachers to use virtually any basal reader or trade books and yet keep a systemized accounting of the reading skills that each child knew. An additional component of the program was a McBee keysorting system (this was long before personal computers and database management systems were found in schools) that could be used for determining skill needs. Finally, there was a file folder system—a compendium of teaching ideas and related materials, one folder for each skill—that enabled teachers to quickly determine what type of instruction (or materials) could be used during ad hoc skill group sessions. Thus the *Design* was a management system that could be overlaid onto any reading program or plan, thereby providing teachers with a means of knowing what each student knew at any point in time. Teachers could be accountable.

Wayne's *Design* attempted to provide teachers with what they intuitively knew would work with children—focused reading instruction. This is not unlike the principle that guides today's Reading Recovery teachers when they observe children "Roaming the Known." Reading Recovery teachers, however, work with individuals, not groups, and they attempt to build on students' *strengths*, whereas the *Design* was predicated on finding children's *weaknesses* and then eliminating these skill deficits. The *Design* was based on a deficit (medical) model similar to that used at reading clinics throughout the country: Find out what is wrong with the student (patient) and then remediate the problem (disease).

Critics of the *Design* argued that you should not teach reading skills in isolation. It was never the intent of the program, however, that these skills would be taught in a contextual void. The intent was to provide teachers with a system that would free children—as soon as possible—from the drudgery of decoding and get them into reading meaningful text. Nevertheless, some teachers, perhaps those looking for simple solutions to complex problems, began to instruct students almost exclusively with worksheets and dittos that took reading from its meaningful contextual setting and put it into an isolated skill-and-drill routine. In its worst manifestation, some teachers stopped teaching "reading" altogether and only taught "skills." Children were left on their own to discover the joy of literature. For the most part, however, the *Design* was used as a system to piggyback on top of the existing basal reading programs, thereby ensuring that students did not miss essential skills.

One of the many positive outcomes of the *Design's* commercial publication by National Computer Systems was that teachers and administrators were introduced to a legitimate alternative to basal reader instructional programs. Wayne and the other developers did not see the *Design* as a replacement for these programs but simply as a supplement for those teachers wishing to move beyond the current state of reading instruction at the time. The *Design* was a springboard enabling teachers to be responsible, professional decision makers regarding their students. No longer were they limited solely to the scope-and-sequence charts and plans found in commercial basal readers. In that sense, the *Design* was a breakthrough. Furthermore, teachers in the same school or same district who used the *Design* began to communicate with each other about their students' progress as well as how they went about their day-to-day reading instruction. This collaboration also had a positive effect on teachers throughout the country.

In the early to mid-1970s and in the 1980s, however, alternative views of reading began to develop. The *Reading Miscue Inventory* was developed by Yetta Goodman and Carolyn Burke (1972). Teachers began exploring how reading skills could be viewed from a psycholinguistic perspective. Slowly, the importance of a reader's background knowledge and its role in understanding text began to be understood. Qualitative differences in miscues were studied. The psycholinguistic movement helped teachers view reading from a variety of perspectives, the most important one being that the reader's behavior was influenced by a variety of cue sources. Goodman and Burke's investigations were followed by the work of Richard Anderson and his associates (1985) at the Center for the Study of Reading at the University of Illinois. Anderson and his colleagues focused much of their landmark work on the area of reading comprehension. Also in the early to mid-1970s, Frank Smith's views on reading education began to popularize the need for putting both reading and writing in meaningful contexts (1973). Smith espoused the close interrelationship between reading and writing. The later works of Donald Graves

(1983), Jane Hansen (1987), Lucy Calkins (1986), and Nancie Atwell (1987) have helped us integrate the reading-writing connection.

Today, Pat Cunningham and Richard Allington (1999), as well as others, have taken reading instruction to a new level of practicality by focusing on classroom practices that work. Integrating the language arts on a day-by-day level has been explored. Reading Recovery teaching strategies popularized by Marie Clay (1991) have proven effective for beginning readers. The training of Reading Recovery teachers has taught us much about the positive collaborative effects of working together as professionals and the importance of careful observation of student reading behavior. Thus, in the 30-plus years since Wayne and his colleagues conceptualized the *Design*, the field of reading instruction has continued to evolve and mature. Likewise, we as professionals have refined our views of the reading process. Today we understand much better what it takes to become a mature reader. With that brief historical context, some specific comments regarding the *Design* and what we know about reading instruction today are in order.

Combining Reading With Other Language Processes

It is unfortunate that the *Design* was seen only as a stand-alone skills emphasis program. The skill development aspect was merely a means to an end and not an end in itself. Wayne and his colleagues expected that teachers would integrate the *Design* with the other language arts skills in their instructional program. The *Design* was never touted as a *complete* reading system—only as a means of monitoring a student's skill development. Today, of course, we recognize more fully the interrelatedness of reading, writing, listening, and speaking. Language is language. Yet there are still students who benefit from focused skill instruction. Interestingly, the reading skills identified within the *Design* are still found in virtually every reading program on the market.

Contexts, Environment, and Purposes for Reading

Today, astute teachers accept the fact that we—students and adults alike—learn primarily in two ways: through our experiences, and by having good models. We also understand that background experiences play a heavy role in understanding what we read. There is consensus that good teachers of reading model appropriate reading behavior for their students. A 10-minute read-aloud each day sends a powerful message to students. It helps teachers say, "I value reading. As a model, I'm showing you how good readers read." Eventually, all readers will be asked to read silently, however. Therefore, it is important that students be given ample time for silent reading in their classrooms. The *Design* was intended to see that children had the requisite skills to allow them to pursue this independent, silent reading whether it be expository or narrative text. Again, the *Design* was only a monitoring system for skills—not the entire reading system. More than ever before, it is important that today's teachers understand the skill profiles of their students. With today's emphasis on state and national standards, students must be "skill proficient."

Developing Students' Perceptions and Expectations

If the *Design* was guilty of one shortcoming, it was identifying students' *weaknesses* rather than their *strengths*. In the *Design*, students were tested with criterion-referenced tests and grouped together for instruction if they failed to meet a specified criterion level—usually 80% on one of the criterion-referenced paper-and-pencil tests. (Teachers also had the option of making subjective decisions about a student's skill development.) Even in today's more enlightened environment, good teachers use small ad hoc groups to fine-tune students' reading skills and strategies. Their groups are formed after systematically observing the reading and writing behavior of students. The *means* may be different, but the *goal* is the same—to develop fluent, independent readers. When students feel good about themselves as readers, they are more apt to choose reading as a leisure activity. A student with a solid skill base is more apt to be a competent reader than is someone with a patchwork skill background. Good teachers, even back in the 1970s and 1980s, knew the importance of a solid skill development base.

Materials

During the development of the *Design*, there was a purposeful decision made *not* to include instructional material as part of the complete system. Instead, a *Teacher's Resource File* of teaching ideas and a listing of commercially available instruction materials was keyed to each of the skills in the program. Basal reader workbook pages, skill sheets, games, and kits were all coded to skills included in each of the six elements of the *Design*. Some teachers developed elaborate organizational schemes enabling them to retrieve instructional worksheets, tapes, or games at a moment's notice. Other teachers teamed together and pooled their instructional material in school media centers. These materials were shared by all. The hope was that children, after receiving instruction with these materials, would master the skills and then be turned free to read materials of their choice.

It is interesting to look back at the basal readers of the day. In the 1970s, basals differed only minimally from the old Scott Foresman Dick-and-Jane series. The characters may have changed, but the physical layout of the materials and the stories were basically unchanged from 20 years earlier. Today, there has been a drastic shift in story content and physical appearance. Today's basals are usually abridged stories of award-winning Caldecott and Newbery Award books. Famous authors abound. Teachers use the stories in basals to turn student interest to the original works by these famous authors. It is not at all unusual to see and hear first graders talk about Eric Carle, Bill Martin Jr, or Tomie dePaola. Intermediate-grade children discuss Judy Blume, Katherine Paterson, Jerry Spinelli, and Gary Paulsen as if they were familiar neighbors. Does anyone know who penned the infamous Dick and Jane stories? Finally, book reports have been replaced by Book Blurbs and response journals. How we have changed and grown. Today it is not *just* skills, but quality literature as well.

Reading Instruction

While we have made tremendous progress in materials development, there are days when I visit school classrooms wondering if we have made any progress in reading instruction. Some classroom teachers continue placing every child in the same reader, leaving many readers struggling at their frustration reading level. Some teachers continue to use round-robin oral reading as their primary teaching vehicle. When I ask my undergraduate students what they remember most about their elementary school reading instruction, one topic always surfaces—the dreaded practice of round-robin oral reading. It is invariably hated by all. Yet it still exists. But times are changing. More and more teachers are using silent reading. More and more teachers are systematically observing children engaged in reading and writing activities. More and more teachers are using buddy reading. More and more teachers are using instructional strategies that actually *teach* children to become better readers. More and more teachers are using effective comprehension strategies. Given what we know today about reading comprehension instruction, the *Teacher's Resource File* of the *Design* would no doubt be much different from its 1970s incarnation.

Sophisticated teachers of today also understand the qualitative differences among reading miscues. They understand the interrelatedness of the phonological, semantic, and syntactic cueing systems. Young readers are taught that phonics without meaningful contextual reading does not make sense. Young readers are taught metacognitive strategies to help them monitor their reading. If things do not make sense, they are urged to use "fix-up" strategies. Young readers are taught to be writers. Meaning drives all. Without meaning, there cannot be reading. Furthermore, because we understand that background knowledge is such an important component in reading comprehension, we, as teachers, are more willing to accept alternative responses to our comprehension questions. Again, we have learned and grown.

A Personal Concluding Remark

I became a classroom teacher in 1965. When I walked into my first classroom, I had never seen a basal reader. As an undergraduate, my reading methods course was taught by a junior high school English teacher. We spent the semester studying poetry, not learning about teaching reading. Once I entered my first classroom, I learned to follow the teacher's guide religiously and had my students do round-robin reading and workbook exercises. I knew that it was wrong, but I needed a "life preserver" to keep from drowning in ignorance. Today, more than 35 years later, I teach undergraduate and graduate college students. I am a different person than I was back then. Today, my students know and understand things I never expected myself to know. They use portfolios. We read quality children's literature. We write in our journals. We have book discussions. We have hands-on experiences with culturally diverse students at our field sites. We use technology unheard of in the 1960s. We even dabble in poetry.

Frequently I am reminded of a story an old-time reading sage once shared. He was giving a keynote address to a group of teachers. When he had finished, one of the participants raised her hand to ask a question. When called on, she read an excerpt from a professional publication to the keynoter.

"So, what do you think of that quote?" she asked the speaker.

The speaker responded, "I think that's the most absurd thing I've ever heard."

"Do you know who wrote that?" the teacher asked.

"No," responded the keynoter.

"YOU DID!" she shrieked.

The keynoter gathered his thoughts, looked the woman in the eye, and replied, "Well, madam...I've changed."

We have all changed. I have changed. Wayne Otto has changed. And you, the reader, have changed. Without change, there cannot be growth. May we all change—and continue to do so during our professional life—so our students become the benefactors of our wisdom and change.

REFERENCES

Anderson, R., Hiebert, E.H., Scott, J.A., & Wilkinson, I.A.G. (1985). *Becoming a nation of readers*. Washington, DC: The National Institute of Education.

Atwell, N. (1987). *In the middle: Writing, reading, and learning with adolescents*. Portsmouth, NH: Heinemann.

Calkins, L. (1986). *The art of teaching writing*. Portsmouth, NH: Heinemann.

Clay, M. (1991). *Becoming literate: The construction of inner control*. Portsmouth, NH: Heinemann.

Cunningham, P.M., & Allington, R.L. (1999). *Classrooms that work: They can all read and write* (2nd ed.). New York: Longman.

Goodman, Y., & Burke, C.L. (1972). *Reading miscue inventory: Procedures for diagnosis and evaluation*. New York: Macmillan.

Graves, D. (1983). *Writing: Teachers and children at work*. Portsmouth, NH: Heinemann.

Hansen, J. (1987). *When writers read*. Portsmouth, NH: Heinemann.

Smith, F. (1973). *Psycholinguistics and reading*. New York: Holt, Rinehart and Winston.

Wisconsin Research and Development Center for Cognitive Learning. (1970). *Wisconsin Design for Reading Skill Development*. Minneapolis, MN: National Computer Systems.

CHAPTER 9

Developing Readers

Scott G. Paris

T he ambiguous title is deliberate because I want to call attention to *readers* who develop from novices to experts, as well as *teachers* who provide experiences and tutelage that cultivate growth in reading. For my interests, it is important to examine them together, the readers gaining in skills and confidence with the help of others who support their efforts. I am interested in the development of the reader, the teacher, and the conditions that surround them. This chapter examines the roots of my interests and the research that ensued. Then I discuss some of the practices that we, as experts, agreed would facilitate learning to read or make it difficult. At the end, I offer some comments on the goals of reaching common ground among researchers.

Cohort Influences on Beliefs About Reading

I was never trained professionally as a teacher or reading educator and feel humbled to be grouped with genuine experts in reading education in this volume. My desire to help children was fueled by watching my mother bring home the joys and frustrations of teaching fourth graders. The most interesting topics to me during my graduate training in psychology involved children, cognition, and education. In the 1960s and early 1970s, there was a growing excitement about Piaget, memory, concept development, and language because, although we did not know it, the cognitive revolution in psychology and education had begun. I sought out courses in linguistics, educational psychology, and special education to embellish my knowledge, and I worked with children in special education classes. Through a series of unpredictable twists and turns in jobs after graduate school, my initial research on children's memory development led me to children's comprehension of text. All the fascinating questions about the development of cognitive strategies and metacognition that Ann Brown (1975), John Flavell (1977), and others were asking seemed to me to have direct corollaries in the development of reading, and my research pulled me down that path. By the time I joined the faculty at Michigan in the late 1970s, I was an enthusiastic, yet novice, reading researcher.

My career path and interests at that point may be similar to others who came from research backgrounds rather than classroom teaching, but the huge change for me was my decision to work with teachers to implement instructional treatments in schools. It was my good fortune to work with Marge Lipson, David Cross, Janis Jacobs, Evelyn Oka, Richard Newman, and many other talented graduate students at that time. As we created instructional materials to help teachers coach children about strategic reading, most notably our project on Informed Strategies for Learning (Paris, Cross, & Lipson, 1984), we had opportunities to work with a large variety of students and teachers. That is when I saw teachers handcuffed to basals. That is when I saw the paucity of comprehension instruction that Durkin (1978–1979) had noted. I really learned about reading education from watching children in classrooms and talking with teachers. Trying to understand and change classroom reading instruction in the early 1980s gave us insights into the deeply entrenched beliefs and practices that children and teachers bring to the classroom every day. I worked with teachers who were eager to try new approaches, teachers who were reluctant to give up their current styles and materials, and teachers who graded papers during the staff meetings. They all taught me about teaching reading. And those children who were eager, stubborn, or off-task during reading showed me what makes reading easy or difficult.

Of course my beliefs about what facilitates reading or makes it more difficult for children are woven into the prevalent models and theories of the past 20 years as much as they are grounded in the teachers and children who worked with us. I am the sum as well as victim of my accumulated experiences. Like anyone who really believes in contextually, culturally, historically situated practices, I am concerned that our current attempt to cluster beliefs about reading education may hold only transient truths. It seems safe to predict that the experts in 2020 may view this enterprise quite differently. Nevertheless, my charge is to focus on some of the agreements that we reached in the Expert Study (Flippo, 1998; refer to Chapter 1 in this book) about practices that would facilitate or impede children's efforts to learn to read and then explain why I agree with them.

From Having Fun to Showing Off to Learning Through Text

I believe that reading becomes appealing and fun for children when it is embedded in other activities. For preschoolers, it is the social interactions that accompany joint book reading—physical contact, laughter, language games, picture identification, and comments—that make reading with others a valued activity. Parents and teachers need to create these opportunities daily so that children bring books to adults to share before they read independently. As children learn the acts of reading and the skills of letter and word identification, they will want to show off their new competencies to the same adults who have nurtured their joint enjoyment of books. The purposes of social interaction give way to demonstrations of competence, but the motivation to share book reading is at the heart of children's early engagement with literacy. (But that sentence sounds too analytical and detached. What I am talking about is the smile on my daughter's face when she showed off her beginning reading to me at the kitchen table—it was not clear which of us was more proud or more happy of her success.)

Purpose is equally important among older children, but the purposes shift to using literacy to open new avenues for exploring ideas and relationships, such as writing notes to people or reading new stories. The critical distinction for me is embedded in Soviet theories of learning that long ago pointed out that children learn to use skills best when the skills are the means to desired outcomes rather than when skills are acquired as ends in themselves. Some current views denote this as using literacy as a tool for authentic purposes, whereas others emphasize creating situations that include the practices of reading with others as part of a community of readers. Reading a story or book according to the time, manner, and criterion demanded by a teacher is social compliance and not a child-centered purpose. The experts who participated in Rona Flippo's Expert Study agreed that children learn to read when reading is "functional" or used "to pursue an interest" or "when children become convinced that reading does further the purposes of their lives" (1998; refer to Chapter 1, p. 14, in this book). I still believe that these assertions are true, but I also believe that it is difficult to create these personal and authentic goals in some classrooms where materials, schedules, and standards guide reading instruction.

The importance of contexts and purposes is clear in Julie Turner's research (1995) in which she examined literacy activities in first-grade classrooms. She found that some teachers used a preponderance of instructional activities that were characterized as "closed" because they were relatively brief, on-demand tasks that required objective answers. Worksheets and daily oral language (DOL) assignments are good examples. In contrast, other teachers had classroom environments rich in "open-ended" activities in which children engaged in reading and writing for their own purposes and interests with no explicit requirements for producing "correct" responses. It is no surprise that children were more motivated, strategic, collaborative, and engaged in literacy with open-ended activities. Structuring the opportunities for a variety of open-ended literacy activities requires clever teachers. In my view, that is one of the virtues of the whole-language movement in literacy education; it provided opportunities and models for teachers to create rich, authentic, child-centered, open-ended, enjoyable activities. It also provoked commercial publishers to design more creative books and reading materials. As a consequence of the renewed focus on integrated language arts, whole language, and more engaging materials, teachers in the 1990s were more skillful at designing literacy-rich classroom environments with multiple opportunities for children to use reading and writing for fun, for demonstrations of competence, and as tools for learning. This has been a positive development in U.S. schools.

Competing Agenda in Classrooms

As a corollary, there are purposes and contexts identified in our Expert Study list of agreements that may impede children's learning to read. When children have few choices about what they read, little control of the conditions for reading, few opportunities to construct personal meaning in response to reading, little collaboration with their peers, and when the consequences of the literacy activities do not enhance self-efficacy, then children will avoid reading or engage in it grudgingly (Turner & Paris, 1995). Teachers do not set out deliberately to give students closed activities or mind-numbing worksheets. Usually, classrooms that have a preponderance of boring literacy activities are highly structured by mandated curricula and tests. The implicit goals of the teacher often are to stay on schedule with the delivery of the curriculum, administer all the materials in the prescribed order, and assess children's achievement for every unit, theme, and skill. It may be a remnant of the old teaching-for-mastery orientation or a product of the new teaching-for-accountability movement, but it is rarely child friendly.

In fact, the instructional environments of K–5 classrooms are being increasingly crowded by assessment agenda. The proliferation of literacy assessments is an attempt at early identification of children at risk as well as a means of continuous monitoring of progress, but the consequence has been more and more time spent on assessment with less time in school for enjoyable and authentic literacy. There is also an implicit message conveyed to teachers and students that the test is what counts in learning and teaching. I believe that this is an unintended yet deleterious outcome of increased assessment that threatens to undermine the motivation of both teachers and students. It became apparent to me in the 1980s when teachers remarked how much they liked teaching children about strategic reading, but they really had no time for such things because they were not included on the test—the CAT, ITBS, and so forth. Teachers feel pressed by assessment and accountability to structure children's literacy experiences in line with the tests. These externally imposed goals elicit compliance among teachers and children but seem contrary to intrinsic goals and purposes for reading.

The negative effects of repeated assessment appear to me to be embedded in our expert agreements about various factors that would make learning to read difficult, such as, "make sure kids do it correctly or not at all," "focus on the single best answer," "test children...whenever they complete a new story in their basal and each time you have finished teaching a new skill," and "reading correctly or pronouncing words exactly right should be a prime objective" (Flippo, 1998; refer to Chapter 1, pp. 12–13, in this book). The net result, I think, of a preoccupation with assessments as the driving forces for daily curricula is less time and attention for the stimulating, creative, personal uses of literacy for enjoyable purposes and self-directed learning. A critical issue is whether the curriculum is enriched by the focus on high-stakes testing. Some of us believe the answer is definitely "No" (Hoffman et al., 1999; Murphy, Shannon, Johnston, & Hansen, 1998; Paris, 1998).

I subsequently began two lines of research on assessment. One set of studies focused on the impact of standardized testing on students (Paris, Lawton, Turner, & Roth, 1991), teachers (Urdan & Paris, 1994), and parents (Barber, Paris, Evans, & Gadsden, 1992). The outcomes seem intuitive to teachers. Students, especially low test scorers, become more anxious and negative about tests as they progress from grades 2 to 12; teachers feel oppressed and coerced to teach to the tests; and parents are confused by test results but convinced they make students and teachers work harder. The political uses of assessment that have increased every year for the past 30 years continue unabated, and the unintended but negative consequences for stakeholders likewise continue to increase. What would make learning to read difficult? One answer is clear to me: testing children repeatedly with standardized tests unrelated to the daily practices in the classroom and the characteristics of children, especially when coupled with a curriculum that focuses on preparing children to take the tests through excessive practice on component skills (Paris, in press). Then, learning to read is reduced to practicing skills necessary to pass the tests, and reading success is equated with satisfactory test scores. Surely this must be the lowest common denominator of teaching and learning.

Our second line of inquiry spawned by the assessment movement was the creation of literacy portfolios as alternatives to traditional tests. During the early 1990s, I worked with Christa van Kraayenoord in Brisbane, Australia, as we observed primary school teachers and designed performance-based assessments for children 5 to 10 years of age (see Paris & van Kraayenoord, 1998; van Kraayenoord & Paris, 1992, 1994, 1997). Not only did I learn how Australian teachers create integrated curricula with few commercial materials, I learned how assessment can be intertwined with instruction with engaging activities, performances, and projects. About the same time, I also worked with Linda Ayres to design a portfolio system for literacy in an entire district (Paris & Ayres, 1994). We created a portfolio that included children's evidence of their literacy performances, processes, and self-perceptions. The foundation for the system was children's self-assessment of their own accomplishments and exhibitions of their achievements. Our goal was to support the development of children's motivation and self-regulated learning as they engaged in collecting, assessing, describing, and showcasing evidence of their own progress. The ostensible objective was the design of literacy assessments, but the underlying goal was to enhance children's motivated and strategic approaches to reading and writing.

Searching for Common Ground

After years of watching successful teachers in Australia and America, I am convinced that learning to read is made easier for most children by three conditions:

a variety of literacy activities that require children to regulate their uses of literacy; an attentive adult who provides assistance to children during daily reading; and occasional explicit instruction about strategies, skills, concepts, and mechanics of learning to read. Let me say more about explicit instruction because it is missing from my previous comments and from our lists of experts' agreements. I am convinced that some children do not induce aspects of literacy that other children do from routine experiences. Whatever the reasons, some children do not understand rhyming at age 4, phonemic segmentation and blending at 5, word boundaries and concepts about print at 6, onset-rime patterns at 7, narrative story structure at 8, strategies for making inferences at 9, and selective rereading and summarizing main ideas at 10. The list could be expanded, but my point is that these features of reading must be taught explicitly when children fail to learn and use them from their own experiences.

Most educators would agree with the need to equip children with those skills and concepts, but there is no consensus about when and how to teach them. Is there a common ground here? No, not really. In the Expert Study, we did not reach agreement on a scope and sequence of these skills, although there is a consensus about the need for repeated modeling of successful reading skills and the use of diverse materials to support children's practice. I suppose that "balanced instruction" is the common ground as we begin the new millennium, but that eclectic compromise can be interpreted in many ways. Perhaps the terms "needed" or "developmentally appropriate" might fit better here instead because children should only be given explicit instruction on the skills that they are expected to use independently but do not. I would not want to give the entire class lessons on strategies for making inferences if most of the children were already using them, nor would I suggest that every child endure drills on phonemic awareness if they can segment and blend component sounds appropriately. But how can teachers assess each child to know what is needed for individual instruction when they are confronted with large classes of heterogeneous children, often without time, help, or materials to individualize the curriculum?

Teachers who know the diversity of individual problems in learning to read do not expect researchers or legislators to derive a single-minded approach to teach reading to all children. There is no panacea in the methods or materials. Indeed, teachers are suspicious of any such consensus reached by external agents and made into policies because they have witnessed firsthand the potpourri of solutions with new basals, new professional development seminars, new research, and new experts. What they want is freedom, resources, and support to teach children with practices and materials that are individually tailored to each child's developing abilities. This is the essence of a developmental approach to reading because it is the "fit" among the method, the materials, the teacher, and the child—and the interaction among these features in a larger social context—that is more important than any single feature alone.

The notion of "fit" is fundamental for me as a developmental psychologist because it establishes the contextual and changing nature of how children are taught to read. The best evidence that there is no single best method for teaching reading to children is the incredibly diverse and varied ways that children around the world have learned to read during the past 100 years. Some children memorize and chant languages that they do not use beyond school, some memorize hundreds of text symbols and copy them before reading coherent text, some are exposed to interactive book reading from infancy on, and some learn to read in school through drill and practice. It is simply absurd to think that any recent approach—whether based on whole language, phonics, computers, or balanced eclecticism—is a universal panacea. Maybe that is the common ground we reached and perhaps it is the understanding that we should strive for in the future—that there is no panacea, that no single method of reading education will work for all children. Perhaps we should not seek agreements among experts as much as advocate pluralism in the classroom that is based on fitting the best instructional methods and relevant materials to the needs of each child. That may engender more creative and adaptive responses to each child than general arguments about one approach versus another that only foment the so-called "reading wars."

Conclusions

Some may wonder if it is possible to find common ground among academic researchers who thrive on controversy, build their reputations on "new" ideas, and stake claims to intellectual territory based on their contrasting positions. Finding common ground in reading research is anathema to the academic research community because part of our training and academic mission is to uncover the nonobvious and reveal the neglected pieces of a puzzle. Thus, in reading research, researchers often expend efforts studying and arguing against positions that are currently in vogue in order to achieve a public forum for their ideas and right the imbalances in current practices that they perceive. Seeking uncharted territory and establishing new colonies is what academic researchers do more than seeking common ground.

I worry that the public views reading education as a problem to be solved, like a software glitch rather than an infinitely variable set of children trying to adjust to constantly changing conditions in their worlds. When the problem is oversimplified, then searches for solutions become simplistic and alternatives become polarized. In today's educational climate of accountability, the problems and solutions are often reduced to media sound bites and political slogans. Promises to have all children ready for school at age 5 or reading on grade level by a target date are lofty ambitions but largely political rhetoric and false hopes. Failure to solve "the reading problem," popularized in memorable cliches such as "Why Johnny can't read," frustrates the public, and persistent disagreements seem like academic quibbling. Reading researchers should not be seduced by political agenda to "solve" the reading problem with a short list of sanctioned approaches. Such mandates and time lines are contrary to what the research reveals about the complex interplay among children, teachers, schools, homes, curriculum, and instruction. Such uniform solutions also seem to contradict teachers' knowledge of their craft and the uniqueness of each child.

Perhaps we should not search for a solution to a fixed and singular problem with agreements about general orientations but, instead, consider designing instructional environments that fit the needs of specific children. Training teachers might then focus on identifying the needs and strengths of children and matching them with appropriate methods and materials. It is a suggestion that begins with children rather than methods of instruction, curricula, or materials and uses the considerable scientific research on reading to design experiences that are tailored to the child's emerging abilities and uses of literacy. It also builds upon the research that reveals the complexity of reading development and benefits of different kinds of instruction for various children. Perhaps a child-centered, developmental, contextual, and adaptive view of reading instruction can become a position of agreement among reading experts in the future.

REFERENCES
Barber, B.L., Paris, S.G., Evans, M., & Gadsden, V. (1992). Policies for reporting test results to parents. *Educational Measurement: Issues and Practices, 11*, 15–20.
Brown, A.L. (1975). The development of memory: Knowing, knowing about knowing, and knowing how to know. In H.W. Reese (Ed.), *Advances in child development and behavior* (Vol. 10, pp. 104–152). New York: Academic Press.
Durkin, D. (1978–1979). What classroom observations reveal about reading comprehension instruction. *Reading Research Quarterly, 14*, 481–533.
Flavell, J.H. (1977). *Cognitive development.* Englewood Cliffs, NJ: Prentice Hall.
Flippo, R.F. (1998). Points of agreement: A display of professional unity in our field. *The Reading Teacher, 52*, 30–40.
Hoffman, J.V., Au, K.H., Harrison, C., Paris, S.G., Pearson, P.D., Santa, C.S., Silver, S.H., & Valencia, S.W. (1999). High-stakes assessments in reading: Consequences, concerns, and common sense. In S.J. Barrentine (Ed.), *Reading assessment: Principles and practices for elementary teachers* (pp. 247–260). Newark, DE: International Reading Association.
Murphy, S., Shannon, P., Johnston, P., & Hansen, J. (1998). *Fragile evidence: A critique of reading assessment.* Mahwah, NJ: Erlbaum.
Paris, S.G. (1998). Why learner-centered assessment is better than high-stakes testing. In N. Lambert & B. McCombs (Eds.), *Issues in school reform: A sampler of psychological perspectives on learner-centered schools* (pp.189–209). Washington, DC: American Psychological Association.
Paris, S.G. (in press). Trojan horse in the schoolyard: The hidden threats in high-stakes testing. *Issues in Education.*
Paris, S.G., & Ayres, L.R. (1994). *Becoming reflective students and teachers with portfolios and authentic assessment.* Washington, DC: American Psychological Association.

Paris, S.G., Cross, D.R., & Lipson, M.Y. (1984). Informed strategies for learning: A program to improve children's reading awareness and comprehension. *Journal of Educational Psychology, 76,* 1239–1252.

Paris, S.G., Lawton, T.A., Turner, J.C., & Roth, J.L. (1991). A developmental perspective on standardized achievement testing. *Educational Researcher, 20,* 12–20.

Paris, S.G., & van Kraayenoord, C.E. (1998). Assessing young children's literacy strategies and development. In S.G. Paris & H.M. Wellman (Eds.), *Global prospects for education: Development, culture, and schooling* (pp. 193–227). Washington, DC: American Psychological Association.

Turner, J.C. (1995). The influence of classroom contexts on young children's motivation for literacy. *Reading Research Quarterly, 30,* 410–441.

Turner, J.C., & Paris, S.G. (1995). How literacy tasks influence children's motivation for literacy. *The Reading Teacher, 48,* 662–673.

Urdan, T.C., & Paris, S.G. (1994). Teachers' perceptions of standardized achievement tests. *Educational Policy, 8,* 137–156.

van Kraayenoord, C.E., & Paris, S.G. (1992). Portfolio assessment: Its place in the Australian classroom. *Australian Journal of Language and Literacy, 15,* 93–104.

van Kraayenoord, C.E., & Paris, S.G. (1994). Literacy instruction in Australian primary schools. *The Reading Teacher, 48,* 218–228.

van Kraayenoord, C.E., & Paris, S.G. (1997). Children's self-appraisal of their work samples and academic progress. *The Elementary School Journal, 97,* 523–537.

CHAPTER 10

Life in the Radical Middle: A Personal Apology for a Balanced View of Reading

P. David Pearson

Most days, I think I have adjusted to my role as a member of the radical middle in the debates and discussions of reading theory and practice (Pearson, 1996). I am pretty sure that I am somewhere in the middle because colleagues in neither the whole language nor the new phonics crowd seem to accept my position. In the 1980s, when whole language ideas about literacy instruction were on the rise, I was often constructed by others as a cognitive behaviorist, a skills monger masquerading as a champion of comprehension and schema theory. More recently, with the political ascendancy of what I call the *new phonics*—a term I use to characterize what I see as a combined emphasis on phonemic awareness, explicit synthetic phonics instruction, and decodable text—I have been reconstructed by some as a "whole language advocate," a characterization that will no doubt bring a smirk to the lips of respectable whole language folks and a bewildered expression to the countenance of close colleagues and students. Not that there is anything wrong with either position—but neither really fits. I am also pretty sure that I am *radical* about being there, in the middle. In fact, as the debates go on, ad infinitum, and as the research evidence in favor of centrist positions on curricular and instructional issues piles up, I get more radical every day. Instead, I am someone who has great respect for a middle ground, and I believe that most of my well-known work and most of the roles I have played in the field belie this preference. As the most convincing evidence of this middle ground, I would point to my editorial role. First as a coeditor of *Reading Research Quarterly*, then as first editor of the original *Handbook of Reading Research*, and later as coeditor of Volumes II and III of the *Handbook*, I have tried to promote paradigmatic tolerance and respect—not always with resounding success, but always with conviction. Even in my less savory role as a basal author (just short, in the eyes of some, of being a demon), my goal was to make sure that *reading* research was given as much play as *market* research and that literature and integrated curriculum were as prominent as skills and strategies.

Sometimes, however, I find myself resenting the implication, more often left unsaid than proudly asserted, that those who occupy the middle of intellectual controversies are just too wishy-washy to stand for something of substance. If I am completely honest, I usually realize that I am the one who attributes—to those who live at the extremes—the accusation that middle grounders are without conviction. And that realization causes me to wonder how deep my convictions really are. This was just such a mood of self-doubt that swept over me when I sat down to write this personal essay about my views of reading theory and practice. Not surprisingly then, I chose to construct this piece as an apology, an attempt to provide readers (including myself) with as thorough an account as I could muster of why I live in the radical middle.

Let me begin by explaining what I think it means to say I am a member of the radical middle and then provide the apology. These are the premises, the basic tenets, the fundamental beliefs about reading that prompt me to accept that label.

1. *I subscribe to an interactive model of the reading process.* That model's fundamental principle is the relationships among reader, text, and context are constantly shifting. Sometimes we reach out to the text, grabbing whatever meaning we can before the text has a chance to fully assert its own. Sometimes we sit back and let the text, and its meaning, come to us. We call the first top-down, inside-out, or hypothesis-driven reading because the reader dominates. We call the second bottom-up, outside-in, or text-driven reading because the text dominates. Sometimes particular purposes, such as updating knowledge when we read the newspaper or trying to get an author's argument straight, determine the stance we take. In my interactive view, whatever we are and whatever we do as readers changes day by day, hour by hour, and moment by moment.

2. *I accept the research suggesting that the most skilled readers are those who have both well-honed automatic word identification processes and rich stores of knowledge that they use to construct, monitor, and refine the models of meaning they construct as they read.* This view is consistent with the fact that I believe both the miscue research of Goodman and colleagues (see, for example, Goodman, 1967), which suggests that good readers are more likely to make meaning preserving miscues, and the eye-movement research reviewed by Adams (1990), which suggests that instead of sampling text to confirm hypotheses, good readers attend to each and every part of each and every word. When readers are in an automatic processing mode, they just move along, recoding everything in sight to a phonological code that can be processed in working memory. But when the going gets tough (as it often does when miscues are more frequent), good readers shift to a conscious-control mode and use every conceivable resource, including context and meaning, to make sense of things. Thus good readers are both *more* skillful at using context and *less* reliant on it for basic word identification tasks.

3. *I believe that reading occurs as a fundamentally individual process, with eyes on print, consumed by the goal of creating a satisfactory model of meaning that fits both the facts of the text and the facts that a reader brings to the reading.* But reading is also fundamentally a social process, readily influenced by a wide range of social and cultural factors. In the most obvious social sense, we change our minds about what a text means when we discuss it with others. At a more subtle level, we engage in a conversation with an unknown author when we read his or her text. Even more distant, the same cultural forces, some of them handed down over several generations within a community or a culture, that shape our values and our behavior also shape our reading.

4. *I subscribe to the view that reading is the whole point of reading instruction (and, by the way, that writing is the whole point of writing instruction).* Thus a curriculum that postpones real reading for more than an instant does kids a disservice by raising in their minds the possibility that reading may not be the point of reading instruction.

5. *I believe that skills are essential features of both reading and reading instruction.* It would be nice, wonderful in fact, if all kids acquired the skills and strategies they need to be successful independent readers and writers without explicit instruction or any other form of arduous effort on the part of teachers. However both research (see Pearson, 1996; McIntyre & Pressley, 1996) and the experience of teachers suggest that students benefit from the modeling, scaffolding, and guidance that teachers can provide.

6. *I believe skills and skill instruction should always be regarded as means to an end rather than ends unto themselves.* The point of any skill instruction—be it phonics, vocabulary, or comprehension—is that students can understand, appreciate, and critique what they read; in fact, the ultimate test of the efficacy of any skill instruction is not whether students can perform the skill as it was taught but whether it improves their critical understanding. In a sense, the job of phonics is not completed until a reader finds joy, inspiration, or fault with a text.

7. *I believe that reading and writing are synergistic processes—what we learn in doing the one benefits the other.* And this synergy can be seen in all aspects of the processes, from the level of phoneme-grapheme relations (e.g., invented spelling activities benefiting reading phonics) to genre-like features of text (e.g., reading stories to get ideas for how to structure one's own).

Given these fundamental tenets, my position in the radical middle should be at least a little more transparent; equally transparent should be some of the internal contradictions I live with: top-down and bottom-up, text and reader, individual and social, reading and writing, and equal respect for both authentic activity and explicit skills instruction. But I have told you only what I think it means to occupy the position I do, not why I embrace these beliefs. Here is the why.

Sometimes I think that I have a personal attraction to contradiction and dialectic tension. I sometimes say to myself, "Maybe you just enjoy theoretical inconsistency and internal contradictions; perhaps they are your concession to post-modernism." But reading theory and practice are not the only intellectual arenas in which I find myself attracted to embracing what others see as binary opposites. In educational research more generally, I find the debate about qualitative versus quantitative research about as compelling as the new phonics versus whole language debate. I cannot imagine why any field of inquiry would want to limit itself to a single set of tools and practices. Even though I find both debates interesting and professionally useful, I fear the ultimate outcome of both, if they continue unbridled by saner heads, will be victory for one side or another. That, in my view, would be a disastrous outcome, either for reading pedagogy or educational research. A more flattering way to express this same position is to say that I have always aspired to the Greek ideal of moderation in all things or to the oriental notion that every idea entails its opposite. Neither statement would be untrue, but either would fail to capture the enchantment I experience in embracing contradiction.

A second reason for living in the radical middle is the research base supporting it. I read the research implicating authentic reading and writing and find it compelling. I read the research supporting explicit skill instruction and find it equally as compelling. What occurs to me, then, is that there must be a higher order level of analysis in which both of these lines of inquiry can be reconciled. That would be a level in which authentic activity and ambitious instruction were viewed as complements rather than alternatives to one another. The radical middle, with its (or rather my) fascination with apparent contradiction, allows me to work comfortably at that level. It is, most likely, exactly this disposition that allowed me, as a member of the panel on which the Expert Study (Flippo, 1998; refer to Chapter 1 in this book) was based, to find so much to agree with in the statements that emerged in each iteration of the agreement process.

Third on my list is the wisdom of practice as I have come to understand it by interacting with scores of classroom teachers. As the new phonics–whole language debate has played itself out in the last few years, I have found the reaction of classroom teachers particularly insightful. The debate rages in the public press and in academic venues; by contrast, my impressions from talking to teachers about the debate is that they find it fairly unproductive. They tend toward an enlightened eclecticism when it comes to matters of practice. So they see no contradiction in embracing an authentic writing activity in the same breath as a new approach to teaching conventional grammar. Thus, even though the consensus statements in Chapter 1 represent a display of "eclecticism" from experts who represent very different views of reading contexts and practices, classroom teachers who embrace this eclectic stance probably find many, if not most, of them reasonable and helpful. I would probably side with them.

Those who aspire to theoretical consistency find this sort of eclecticism disturbing because they see it as a disconnection between theory and practice. But I find this negative connotation for eclectic positions surprising given the traditional denotation of the word. The dictionary definition of *eclectic* is "selecting or choosing from among various sources." An eclectic stance implies agency (making a selection) and an implicit set of criteria (to make the selection) on the part of the agent. It is exactly this intentionality that I have observed in teachers' eclecticism. My hunch is student engagement (will this appeal to my students?) and perceived helpfulness (will it help them better do their job as readers?) are the two criteria teachers use in deciding whether to incorporate a new practice into their teaching repertoire. It is only fair to confess that I have always taken a decidedly eclectic stance toward my own teaching, both as an elementary classroom teacher and a college instructor.

Fourth is the modest view of evidence that I hold for the positions we advocate in education. Although I think we have learned a great deal in the past 30 years about the nature and development of the reading process, and even more about instructional practices that promote individual growth in reading (for an account of what I think we have learned, see my review of the Snow, Burns, and Griffin 1998 report sponsored by the National Research Council [Pearson, 1999]), I think we can do better. I think there is still room for more evidence and better methods of inquiry. Whatever the reasons, I cannot rid myself of nagging doubts about the strength and quality of our current evidence. And any time one's confidence is shaky, then dispositions of tolerance (for ideas, practices, and research methods) and inquiry (we should try it out and see what happens) make sense to me.

Fifth, the radical middle provides a nice home for the particular approach to curricular balance that I have been moving toward. The metaphor of the fulcrum of the scales of justice has never particularly appealed to me because it suggests that we are carving out a political balance—balancing off one element from the new phonics with one from whole language, anon, anon. But there is another, more powerful metaphor in the "balance of nature." In this ecological approach (see Pearson & Raphael, 1999), balance is not a matter of evening the score; instead it is a matter of assembling an array of skills, strategies, processes, and practices that are sufficiently rich and synergistic to guarantee a full and rich curriculum for all students (one that, incidentally, would honor tenets 4 through 7 in my list of tenets).

So there you have it—my apology for being a member of the radical middle. As I said, it is sometimes a difficult position to maintain. There are those who wonder whether those of us who occupy this middle ground have any standards at all. And there are many ideological bulldozers lurking nearby, ready to forcibly remove you from your newly gained intellectual ground. But it is a satisfying ground to hold. And it offers, unfortunately, all too clear a view of the constant, regular, and periodic swing of the curricular pendulum.

REFERENCES

Adams, M.J. (1990). *Beginning to read: Thinking and learning about print.* Cambridge, MA: MIT Press.

Flippo, R.F. (1998). Points of agreement: A display of professional unity in our field. *The Reading Teacher, 52,* 30–40.

Goodman, K.S. (1967). Reading: A psycholinguistic guessing game. *Journal of the Reading Specialist, 4,* 126–135.

McIntyre, E., & Pressley, M. (Eds.). (1996). *Balanced instruction: Strategies and skills in whole language.* Norwood, MA: Christopher-Gordon.

Pearson, P.D. (1996). Reclaiming the center. In M.F. Graves, P. van den Broek, & B.M. Taylor (Eds.), *The first R: Every child's right to read* (pp. 259–274). New York: Teachers College Press.

Pearson, P.D. (1999). An historically-based review of *Preventing Reading Difficulties in Young Children. Reading Research Quarterly, 34,* 231–246.

Pearson, P.D., & Raphael, T.E. (1999). Toward an ecologically balanced literacy curriculum. In L.B. Gambrell, L.M. Morrow, S.B. Neuman, & M. Pressley (Eds.), *Best practices in literacy instruction* (pp. 22–33). New York: Guilford Press.

Snow, C.E., Burns, M.S., & Griffin, P. (Eds.). (1998). *Preventing reading difficulties in young children.* Washington, DC: National Academy Press.

CHAPTER 11

Point of View: George Spache

Richard D. Robinson

> Reading is more than going rapidly over the lines of print, and it is more than slowly and laboriously plodding along looking carefully at every symbol and form. Rather, reading is a complex of several skills which must function together to produce an amount of comprehension in keeping with the purposes, needs, and methods of the reader.
>
> —George Spache & Paul Berg, *The Art of Efficient Reading* (1955)

Over the past several decades, a wide variety of theories, programs, and materials have been developed related to the effective teaching of reading. Each new idea has been recommended as being a better way to teach reading in comparison with what is currently being used in classrooms. Many, if not most, of these changes follow a fairly well-developed scenario that sees their introduction, extended use in classrooms, and then the eventual replacement of these ideas by other "new" concepts and programs. A classic example is the extended use of phonics as a basis for reading instruction—a particular reading philosophy that has come and gone a number of times (see Spache, 1963, 1964, 1972). With each renewal, advocates of the new approach believe it is truly revolutionary and yet, in most cases, it is often nothing more than new terminology applied to old ideas and concepts.

An outcome of this continual change in reading instruction has been the development of factional groups of educators who advocate an approach or set of materials that they believe is superior to all others. Thus the historical evolution of cadres of teachers who hold to their way of teaching as being the "gospel truth" without regard to other views or approaches to reading instruction (Spache & Spache, 1969).

Despite these differences in reading education, both in terms of philosophical principles as well as actual teaching practices, it is interesting to note how much overlap there is among experts representing diverse philosophies regarding contexts and practices for teaching reading. This is one of the primary conclusions or outcomes of the Expert Study (Flippo 1998; refer to Chapter 1 in this book).

As Director of the Reading Clinic at the University of Florida, George Spache was interested in determining the degree of effectiveness of a variety of reading programs (Spache, 1961). The results of his work showed that while programs differed in terms of specifics, they had much in common, especially in relationship to fundamental beliefs and practices. A corollary to this work was the conclusion that no single approach to reading was clearly superior to all others.

This chapter presents an interpretation of Spache's reading views, based primarily on his lifetime of professional writing and research on this topic. I take full responsibility for my representation of Spache's ideas and thoughts, acknowledging that there may be differing conclusions and opinions. In line with the Expert Study clustered summary agreements reprinted in Chapter 1, I have organized this analysis into the following sections: Combining Reading With Other Language Processes; Contexts, Environment, and Purposes for Reading; Developing (or Shaping) Students' Perceptions and Expectations; Materials; and Reading Instruction.

Combining Reading With Other Language Processes

Spache's writings demonstrate his long belief that the effective teaching of reading should be in the context of the other language processes (Spache, 1964, 1972). For instance, in describing what he considered to be the characteristics of a good reading program, Spache noted that in effective reading instruction "vocabulary, phonic skills, and mechanics of writing—as well as handwriting and the development of speaking, writing, and listening vocabularies—are promoted in multiple uses of the child-produced material" (1976b, p. 342). The language efforts described clearly indicate the widest possible use of all aspects of both oral and written language. It should be noted that an important part of this use of language is based fundamentally on "child-produced materials."

A related approach to reading instruction that Spache advocated was the use of individualized reading. Spache concurred with and cited Veatch's definition of this method of reading instruction: "An individualized reading program provides each child with an environment which allows him to seek that which stimulates him, choose that which helps him develop most, and work at this own rate regardless of what else is going on" (1963, p. 150). Spache's view was that, to be successful, school reading programs need to be constantly aware of individual students' interests and desires and to make every effort to meet these various goals.

Contexts, Environment, and Purposes for Reading

Reading should not be an isolated school experience but rather needs to be incorporated into the context of the student's environment and purposes for reading (Spache & Berg, 1955). Of particular note was Spache's firm belief in the use of trade books or library materials as a fundamental part of all reading instruction. Spache in fact edited a series of teacher-directed books titled *Good*

Reading For Poor Readers (1962–1974). Each of the nine editions contains an extended discussion on how to select the right book for each student and how to effectively use literature in all classrooms. The series emphasizes the fact that while real reading beyond the classroom is important for all students, it is especially critical for those who are having difficulty learning to read. Spache's view was that reading is not just a classroom subject but rather should be made functional and a foundation for all future learning activities throughout a person's life.

Developing (or Shaping) Students' Perceptions and Expectations

Spache's work reflects his belief in the importance of reading as a major influence on both the social and intellectual lives of readers (see 1963, 1976a). Often young children equate their success or failure in school simply by their perceived abilities in reading (Spache, 1976b). This conclusion says to the effective teacher of reading that, in as much as possible, each child's self-image should be enhanced through successful reading. A technique Spache long advocated in helping students develop this positive view of reading as a lifelong activity was the use of bibliotherapy (Spache, 1963, 1976a).

Bibliotherapy is "the treatment of personal problems through the medium of reading" (Spache, 1963, p. 323). When using bibliotherapy readers are able to identify personal characteristics and difficulties in their own lives, which are similar to those described in various types of reading. Success in bibliotherapy requires the teacher to have "a wide knowledge of books and a deep understanding of the personal needs of her pupils" (Spache, 1963, p. 324). While there have been some questions as to the competence of classroom teachers in the use of bibliotherapy, there is much evidence to support its use in the classroom: "Teachers are by training perhaps better equipped to initiate and to follow up on this process [bibliotherapy] by helping the child implement insights in constructive action than are most adults" (Spache, 1976a, p. 341).

It is the primary goal of reading instruction to develop in all readers a positive self-image as well as to help them value reading as a lifelong activity (Spache, 1955, 1963, 1976a). These goals were fundamental in Spache's research and teaching, and he considered them most important in the effective teaching of reading.

Materials

The Basal Reader

For most of Spache's career, the dominant approach to the teaching of reading was use of the basal reader (see Spache, 1963, 1972). Although the basal reader was used by over 90% of schools during that period, it was not without problems. Spache pointed out the following difficulties, evident from almost the beginning of the extensive use of the basal reader: sterility of content, lack of provision for individual differences, and overemphasis on the basal series. Many of these issues apply to "the manner in which basal readers were used rather than against the basal approach itself" (Spache, 1964, p. 73).

Perhaps the most dominant criticism of the basal reader materials is that they are "stereotyped and lacking in vitality, creativity or interest…sterile, lacking in appeal to boys, and unrealistic, in terms of the common experiences of lower middle class boys and girls" (Spache, 1963, p. 25). While Spache might have seen some basis in these arguments, he found that much of this criticism is based on the false assumption that the only reading material a student would use in learning to read is the basal reader. Spache, along with many contemporaries (see Betts, 1954; Dolch, 1949; Russell, 1944), saw the basal reader as a mere "tool" to introduce students to the much wider world of reading. In his view, if the basal reader is the only reading material being used for instruction, this is not the fault of the materials but rather the fault of the teacher using them in this fashion.

Another serious criticism of the basal reader is that it tends to be written for the average student and ignores the remedial and gifted individuals. This despite the fact that the authors of all basal series have encouraged individualization of instruction when teachers use their materials. Spache pointed out, "It is doubtful in the minds of many reading authorities that any one basal book or series can give training in all of the skills and abilities needed, or give the breadth of reading experiences desired. Nor can it provide for the many stages of reading growth" (1963, p. 26). Here again the problem is with how the basal is used rather than with the materials themselves. Throughout his career, Spache continually emphasized the fact that the basal reading series is only a tool to encourage further reading and that it should be used as an introduction to more extensive reading. His *Good Reading For Poor Readers* series details ways in which the classroom teacher needs to move beyond the basal reader into the real world of wide and purposeful reading activities.

It has been said, with some degree of accuracy, that classroom teachers tend to have an over dependence on the extended use of the basal reader. Spache noted the following practices in the use of the basal reader:

> The series is treated as a group of sacred books in which every child must read every page and overlearn every basic vocabulary word. In addition, we see the basal workbooks used slavishly without regard to the child's actual needs, an attitude of worship extended to the core vocabulary of the basal series, a stultifying use of the oral reading circle, and an almost complete reliance upon a visual or "look-say" method of teaching reading. (1963, pp. 27–28)

Practices such as these clearly reflect a fundamental misunderstanding of the primary role of the basal reader. No basal reading series today claims that the program is the only reading students should do. Basal publishers emphasize that their material is "intended as a tool for teaching children to read, and not as a complete program" (Spache, 1972, p. 35). In fact, publishers have made extra effort to encourage wide reading in a great variety of materials.

In reaction to this misuse of the basal reader, we see an effort to change teacher practice to the opposite extreme—no use of basal material at all (see Spache, 1963, 1972; Spache & Spache, 1964). For instance, advocates of individualized reading (Jacobs, 1953; Jenkins, 1957; Veatch, 1957, 1960) are often most critical of the basal reader. As noted earlier, much of this criticism rests not on the basal materials themselves but rather on the unintelligent ways in which they often are used by classroom teachers.

In 1941 Spache noted a number of factors that can enhance reading achievement through the effective use of basal readers: "A reading series should provide...for integration of the reading materials, either through provision of parallel readers, unit reading materials, or books of between-grade difficulty..." (p. 290). Spache believed this to be a fundamental goal of all basal reading instruction.

Workbooks

Accompanying most basal reading textbooks today are supplemental materials, often categorized under the umbrella term *workbooks*. There is perhaps no more criticized area related to the use of the basal reader than the use of workbooks. Many critics see the workbook as being nothing more than organized "busy work" with little if any value for students. There are certainly many stories about the serious misuse of this material, such as the proud teacher who tells of all the students in her classroom completing every page in the workbook by the end of the year.

Arguments abound on both the positive and negative use of the workbook. For instance, teachers who feel positively about the workbook cite it as a source for helping individual students with specific problems as well as containing relevant material carefully planned and related to what has been recently read in the basic readers. Those who oppose workbooks point out the "tendency to overdependence of the teacher upon these tools, their disregard of individual needs, their lack of creativity or training in expression or fluency, and their monotonous, repetitive nature" (Spache, 1963, pp. 28–29).

According to Spache (1963), the answer to this problem lies in the manner in which workbooks are used by the classroom teacher rather than in the workbooks themselves.

Limited Vocabulary

Early in Spache's career the concept of limited or controlled vocabulary was a dominant theme in most reading materials. This limiting of vocabulary was based on many studies of intensive word counts and other types of vocabulary and concept load. Despite the research support, Spache opposed this philosophy of reading materials:

> The adherents of a limited vocabulary will hasten to point out that, in all probability, the child does not learn this wider vocabulary in comics and other recreational material. The same breadth of vocabulary could not be used in basal reading, these protagonists say, for the child cannot readily learn this number of words in a short space of time. We agree, but must point out that this is no proof that basal vocabularies cannot possibly extend beyond the child's daily learning rate. Even though learners are limited in the number of concepts they can absorb in a given time, this does not demonstrate that a spoon-feeding process is best. If we put less emphasis upon over learning of a minute basal vocabulary, and broadened the material, deepened its content, and injected greater intrinsic appeal, reading progress might well be even more rapid and enjoyable.
>
> To the best of our knowledge, there is no proof that over learning of a small core vocabulary is the only possible foundation for learning to read. This belief is predicated upon the assumption that a beginning reader must memorize each and every word he meets, or else he will not be able to read other future materials. If this were true, no primary child could read any book that was not completely parallel to his basal book in vocabulary usage. Yet primary children read literally hundreds of recreational books with enjoyment and adequate comprehension, even though these books collectively introduce many, many new words. This recreational reading begins, in some programs, as early as the preprimer or primer stage—when the child has learned no more than 50 to 150 words. Does not this ability to read independently refute the claim that over learning of the meager basal vocabulary and memorization of every word encountered are essential? (1963, pp. 30–31)

Inflexibility of Method

The dependence on one form or format for reading instruction has long dominated reading instruction. Whether it was, for example, the "look-say" approach or the extensive use of phonics, teachers tended to follow a particular method to the complete exclusion of all other reading plans.

According to Spache (1963), the effective teacher of reading is the one who is not slavishly tied to one approach or philosophy but rather chooses from a wide array of possibilities based on what is best for students.

Excessive Oral Reading

Oral reading has been a constant source of difficulty for many years in reading education. More than 35 years ago Spache wrote, "Observers in primary classrooms receive the impression that both teachers and pupils apparently believe that there is no real reading activity other than oral reading in a circle" (1963, p. 33). This situation in many classrooms, even today, has not changed a great deal. Students spend significant amounts of time reading orally, apparently so that the teacher can tell whether the readers can say the words correctly. Little effort is given for silent reading as well or for determining students' understanding of what is being read (Spache, 1972; Spache & Spache, 1964). Extensive research, as well as actual classroom practice, clearly demonstrates that silent reading should take precedence over oral reading (Spache, 1963). As one little boy said about oral reading in a circle, "We starts at the same place, but some of us gets there first. How come we has to keep lookin' if we knows how to read it?"

Reading Instruction

Spache's feelings about reading instruction may best be understood through his own statements over the years:

> [A good reading program is based on]...a well rounded selection of reading experiences. It includes both recreational and work-type reading, poetry and prose, factual and fictional matter, informational and entertaining materials that extend the child's ideas and knowledge. (Spache & Spache, 1964, p. 92)

> Reading interest can be fostered or stifled by different classroom practices. Among those with positive values are group discussion of what is read, by panel discussions, debates, reading portions aloud, choral reading, etc. (Spache, 1962–1974)

> There is no better tonic for stimulating interest in a [reading] task than recognized success.... (Spache, 1941, p. 287)

> The relative emphasis on phonics has waxed and waned through the years, but heavy doses of it were no panacea for reading failures. (Spache, 1972, p. 153)

> Only when the teacher sees reading as a dynamic interaction between the personality of the reader and literature will her influence grow beyond a mechanical drilling of skills. (Spache, 1963, p. 323)

> In addition to the basal and subject-matter vocabularies, most pupils learn many more words from their recreational, supplementary, and casual reading. (Spache & Spache, 1964, p. 91)

> [Effective reading instruction]...may also be achieved by abandoning rigid standards of progress in the first three grades. Progress should be a continuum rather than a series of distinct steps. Pupils will be permitted to progress at their own rate and will be given varying amounts of time to complete the primary program. (Spache, 1963, p. 35)

> It also becomes apparent that reading success is not promoted by separating the act from related language activities, as in over-emphasis upon skill development, or reading lessons carefully isolated in time and content from other language media, or any classroom practice which assumes that simply practicing in reading aloud or silently is the best program for development of the reading act. (Spache & Spache, 1964, p. 36)

REFERENCES

Betts, E.A. (1954). Three essentials in basic reading instruction. *Education, 74,* 575–582.

Dolch, E.W. (1949). Self-survey of a school program for the teaching of reading. *The Elementary School Journal, 49,* 230–234.

Flippo, R.F. (1998). Points of agreement: A display of professional unity in our field. *The Reading Teacher, 52,* 30–40.

Jacobs, L.B. (1953). Reading on their own means reading at their growing edges. *The Reading Teacher, 6,* 27–32.

Jenkins, M. (1957). Self-selection in reading. *The Reading Teacher, 11,* 84–90.

Russell, D.H. (1944). Opinions of experts about primary grade basic reading programs. *The Elementary School Journal, 44,* 602–609.

Spache, G.D. (1941). New trends in primary-grade readers. *The Elementary School Journal, 42,* 283–290.

Spache, G.D. (1961). Research in reading at the University of Florida, 1950–1960. In E.P. Bliesmer & A.J. Kingston (Eds.), *Phases of college and other adult reading programs. Tenth yearbook of the National Reading Conference* (pp. 141–149). Charlottesville, VA: Jarman Printing Company.

Spache, G.D. (1962–1974). *Good reading for poor readers.* Champaign, IL: Garrard.

Spache, G.D. (1963). *Toward better reading.* Champaign, IL: Garrard.

Spache, G.D. (1964). *Reading in the elementary school.* Boston: Allyn & Bacon.

Spache, G.D. (1972). *The teaching of reading. Methods and results: An overview.* Bloomington, IN: Phi Delta Kappan.

Spache, G.D. (1976a). *Diagnosing and correcting reading disabilities.* Boston: Allyn & Bacon.

Spache, G.D. (1976b). *Investigating the issues of reading disabilities.* Boston: Allyn & Bacon.

Spache, G.D., & Berg, P.C. (1955). *The art of efficient reading.* New York: Macmillan.

Spache, G.D., & Spache, E.B. (1964). *Reading in the elementary school.* Boston: Allyn & Bacon.

Spache, G.D., & Spache, E.B. (1969). *Reading in the elementary school* (2nd ed.). Boston: Allyn & Bacon.

Veatch, J. (1957). Children's interests and individual reading. *The Reading Teacher, 10,* 160–165.

Veatch, J. (1960). In defense of individualized reading. *Elementary English, 37,* 227–233.

CHAPTER 12

Principled Pluralism for Adaptive Flexibility in Teaching and Learning to Read

Rand J. Spiro

I write from the perspective of Cognitive Flexibility Theory (CFT) (Spiro, Coulson, Feltovich, & Anderson, 1994; Spiro & Jehng, 1990; Spiro, Vispoel, Schmitz, Samarapungavan, & Boerger, 1987). In CFT, a successor of schema theories (Anderson, 1977; Anderson, Spiro, & Anderson, 1978; Spiro, 1980), it has been argued for many years that *all* learning, instruction, mental representation, and knowledge application should be governed by a principled utilization of interlocking multiple representations, multiple methodologies, multiple perspectives, multiple case precedents, and multiple analogies (Spiro et al., 1994; Spiro, Feltovich, Coulson, & Anderson, 1989). CFT was designed for learning in ill-structured domains, where cases of knowledge application are characterized *individually* by complexity and *across cases* by considerable variability and irregularity in the conditions of knowledge use. Given the complexity of such domains, single approaches of any kind will be limiting, successful in some contexts and off the mark in many others. This is so whether the domain is a content area like history or biology, a process like reading, or an arena of practical application of knowledge like medicine or teaching.

CFT is intended to prepare people to flexibly and adaptively apply their knowledge to new cases or situations, situations that are often unlike any they have encountered before. Hence the inappropriateness of old-style schema theory, which depends on the retrieval of a pre-stored schema or template from memory, despite the unlikelihood that one would have a prepackaged schema for everything that might be needed, especially in reading (Spiro & Myers, 1984). CFT argues that, when facing a complex new case or situation, you need to assemble elements of prior knowledge and past experience and tailor those elements to fit the new situation's needs. This situation-sensitive assembly of multiple perspectives from prior knowledge is the part of *pluralism* that the title of this chapter refers to that is *principled*—it is not just throwing together any old set of theories, methodologies, and knowledge elements. Rather, one must assemble just those aspects that will help in the current situation, while discounting those aspects that are less helpful. Further, the assembled elements must be meaningfully related to each other and tailored to the specific content of the case at hand. In a sense, one must build a "schema-of-the-moment" (Spiro et al., 1987, 1994; Spiro & Jehng, 1990). For most domains there are strengths and weaknesses of all of the credible approaches, and patterns of combined strength and weakness (across approaches) are usually determined by features of the teaching or learning situation one is facing. The key question for CFT is which approaches, theories, methods, and content schemas are most appropriate for a new situation, and then how are they to be put together (combined, coordinated, aligned) to fit that new context.

It is hard to imagine a domain where these principles would be more applicable than in learning to read and in the teaching of reading. Therefore, it is heartening to see an increasing tendency toward pluralism in the reading field, toward the advocacy of integration of different theoretical and methodological perspectives (see Flippo, 1999; International Reading Association, 1999; Pearson, 1996). And, of course, it should not be surprising to see the agreements in the Expert Study (Flippo, 1998; refer to Chapter 1 in this book), of which I was a part, which indicate a belief that many things that are said to be true of reading and learning to read *are* true—in many but not all situations—for some children, at some times, for some teaching and learning purposes. Furthermore, it will usually be the case that beliefs and practices in the teaching of reading are best applied in combinations, and these combinations will also shift according to changing contexts. In other words, the only summary statement that applies to all of reading is this: *it all depends.*

The skilled teacher of reading will have a rich repertoire to draw upon, and she or he will examine each teaching situation closely—and, based on that close reading, assemble a situation-sensitive approach that draws on different elements of knowledge and different prior-case experiences. Furthermore, this mix will be fluidly changeable as the reading situation evolves and changes. Similarly, the skilled reader will sometimes rely more on the use of knowledge of phonics, sometimes use whole-word approaches; sometimes rely on prior knowledge and contextual information, sometimes accept a premise of novelty and rely less on prior knowledge; sometimes read for accuracy, sometimes skim for gist—all depending on characteristics of what is being read, why it is being read, and who is doing the reading. And, of course, sometimes these strategies of reading are used in combination rather than in isolation from each other. In these senses, there is a principled pluralism required at the "micro" level (the act of reading) that mirrors that which has been argued for at the "macro" level of the field of reading research and the theory of the teaching of reading.

I believe that these issues of cognitive flexibility and situation-adaptive assembly of multiple perspectives are central to the next generation of educational research, not just in the "reading wars," but across the spectrum of learning and teaching. The development of principled pluralisms of the mind and of pedagogy are crucial for learning and teaching in *all* complex domains of knowledge acquisition and application—and we are coming to find that more and more domains that we had thought to be relatively simple and orderly actually have crucial properties of complexity and ill structure. Unfortunately, those approaches that work for learning in simple domains are exactly the opposite of the ones that are best for dealing with complexity—what helps for one, hurts for the other. Examples include single versus multiple representations, compartmentalized versus interconnected knowledge, knowledge-centeredness versus case-centeredness, and retrieval from memory of prepackaged prescriptions for how to think and act versus case-sensitive knowledge assembly (Spiro et al., 1987, 1994). Fortunately, we also now possess new theories and theory-based educational technologies to help foster these more difficult kinds of complex learning that have so often resisted our best efforts in the past (see Spiro, Feltovich, Jacobson, & Coulson, 1992a, 1992b).

One of the most important of the next-generation research questions concerns the manner of operation of principled pluralisms. How does situation-adaptive assembly of knowledge and experience occur, and how should it be fostered (in teachers and students)? There are at least two key elements in the answer to these questions. The first is a recognition of the centrality of case experience (Spiro et al., 1994). The organizing nexus for assembling multiple perspectives is the *case* (example, occurrence, actual event in the world). In ill-structured domains of real-world practice (e.g., reading, or teaching reading), wide-scope generalizations, abstractions, and schemas do not work. Instead, one must attend to "how the world goes" and learn how to piece together and tailor knowledge to the demands of practice—there is no "formula." So it is the case that becomes the organizing focus for knowledge assembly, that provides the guidance for what needs to be part of the schema-of-the-moment and how that assemblage needs to be put together. This contrasts with well-structured domains, where examples or cases are interchangeable illustrations of generic knowledge that spins out in highly routinized ways. In ill-structured domains, the principled basis for adaptive knowledge assembly referred to in the phrase *principled pluralism* is to be found in the landscape of a domain's cases—alignment and coordination of multiple knowledge sources and methods is governed by their fit to the events to which they are being applied and their usefulness in dealing with those events.

An important implication of this shift in emphasis to the situation-adaptive assembly of schemas-of-the-moment out of multiple perspectives is that the structures of prior knowledge must be conceived differently than they were in schema theory. It is no accident that the situated cognition movement has de-emphasized and, at times, been antagonistic to earlier views that placed abstract cognitive structures in a central place. Such views were notorious for their failures to account for novel transfer, the ability to apply knowledge to new situations that differ from the conditions of initial learning. The situations of the world are too rich to permit wide-scope application of generic cognitive structures. However, the problem is not with knowledge structures per se, but rather with the kind of knowledge structure that has typically been proffered. What is required is a different kind of knowledge structure, one that works with the jagged and messy contours of situations in the world rather than smoothing them out—open structures to think with, rather than closed structures that dictate thought. The goal of CFT is to foster the learning of such open, situation-sensitive structures (Spiro et al., 1987, 1992a, 1992b, 1994).

The second key element of preparing people to assemble knowledge in situation-adaptive ways is the role of new technologies. Certain uses of case-based hypermedia are designed to promote knowledge assembly skills by modeling them across a range of contexts (Spiro et al., 1994; Spiro & Jehng, 1990). The nonlinear traversal capability of hypermedia, along with the newly expanded ease of dealing with digital video cases, allows real-world examples to be overlaid by shifting constellations of perspectives and then compared and contrasted in varying ways to illustrate the vagaries of situation-adaptive knowledge assembly across diverse contexts. With this technology it is possible to demonstrate and teach principled pluralism in operation, in all its forms.

Finally, perhaps the most important frontier for next-generation research is that of changing students' and teachers' habits of mind, their underlying epistemic stance toward the world, in the direction of ones that are more compatible with the changing circumstances of knowing and doing that characterize our increasingly complex and rapidly evolving modern world of life and work (Feltovich, Spiro, & Coulson, 1989; Spiro, Feltovich, & Coulson, 1996). We often speak of cognitive structures; rarely do we speak of the underlying assumptions and structures that determine the shape of the cognitive structures that get built, the background "lenses" that prefigure the shape of knowledge (Feltovich et al., 1989). It is these prefigurative schemas that I refer to as habits of mind. There is considerable evidence that the predominant habits of mind are overly simple in a variety of ways (see Spiro et al., 1996) and are thus antithetical to the needs of successful performance in complex domains (such as reading and the teaching of reading). Habits of mind suited to dealing with complexity must be developed; finding ways to do this will be a major challenge of the coming years. Progress in the use of principled pluralisms for the cognitively flexible, situation-adaptive assembly of prior knowledge and experience will be slow until we are able to develop corresponding changes in the underlying habits of mind of teachers and students who would greatly prefer that things were simpler.

In summary, it should be clear to the reader by now what led me to indicate agreement to all of the items in the final lists of the Expert Study. My research has led me to believe that all credible approaches are useful on some occasions, that none are always useful, and that the relevance of one does not preclude the simultaneous relevance of others with which it might be fruitfully combined. This is an inevitable outcome of advocating for a principled pluralism. In the end, it will all depend on an expert teacher making a judgment about which ensemble of approaches and practices to select for a particular student and context. It is the job of those who prepare teachers of reading to ensure that those future teachers understand the implications of principled pluralism and are able to apply knowledge and methods of various types with adaptive flexibility.

ACKNOWLEDGMENTS

The author wishes to acknowledge the many helpful comments and great patience of Rona Flippo. The writing of this chapter was supported in part by grant No. DE-P342A99059 from the Office of Educational Research and Improvement of the Department of Education.

REFERENCES

Anderson, R.C. (1977). The notion of schemata and the educational enterprise. In R.C. Anderson, R.J. Spiro, & W.E. Montague (Eds.), *Schooling and the acquisition of knowledge* (pp. 415–432). Hillsdale, NJ: Erlbaum.

Anderson, R.C., Spiro, R.J., & Anderson, M.C. (1978). Schemata as scaffolding for the representation of information in discourse. *American Educational Research Journal, 15,* 433–440.

Feltovich, P.J., Spiro, R.J., & Coulson, R.L. (1989). The nature of conceptual understanding in biomedicine: The deep structure of complex ideas and the development of misconceptions. In D. Evans & V. Patel (Eds.), *The cognitive sciences in medicine* (pp. 113–172). Cambridge, MA: MIT Press.

Flippo, R.F. (1998). Points of agreement: A display of professional unity in our field. *The Reading Teacher, 52,* 30–40.

Flippo, R.F. (1999). Redefining the reading wars: The war against reading researchers. *Educational Leadership, 57,* 38–41.

International Reading Association. (1999). *Using multiple methods of beginning reading instruction: A position statement of the International Reading Association* [Brochure]. Newark, DE: Author.

Pearson, P.D. (1996). Six ideas in search of a champion: What policymakers should know about the teaching and learning of literacy in our schools. *Journal of Literacy Research, 28,* 302–309.

Spiro, R.J. (1980). Constructive processes in prose comprehension and recall. In R.J. Spiro, B.C. Bruce, & W.F. Brewer (Eds.), *Theoretical issues in reading comprehension: Perspectives from cognitive psychology, linguistics, artificial intelligence, and education* (pp. 245–278). Hillsdale, NJ: Erlbaum.

Spiro, R.J., Coulson, R.L., Feltovich, P.J., & Anderson, D.K. (1994). Cognitive flexibility theory: Advanced knowledge acquisition in ill-structured domains. In R.B. Ruddell, M.R. Ruddell, & H. Singer (Eds.), *Theoretical models and processes of reading* (4th ed., pp. 602–615). Newark, DE: International Reading Association. (Reprinted from: 10th Annual Conference of the Cognitive Science Society. Hillsdale, NJ: Erlbaum, 1988.)

Spiro, R.J., Feltovich, P.J., & Coulson, R.L. (1996). Two epistemic world views: Prefigurative schemas and learning in complex domains [Special issue on reasoning processes]. *Applied Cognitive Psychology, 10*, 51–61.

Spiro, R.J., Feltovich, P.J., Coulson, R.L., & Anderson, D.K. (1989). Multiple analogies for complex concepts: Antidotes for analogy-induced misconception in advanced knowledge acquisition. In S. Vosniadou & A. Ortony (Eds.), *Similarity and analogical reasoning* (pp. 498–531). Cambridge, MA: Cambridge University Press.

Spiro, R.J., Feltovich, P.J., Jacobson, M.J., & Coulson, R.L. (1992a). Cognitive flexibility, constructivism, and hypertext: Random access instruction for advanced knowledge acquisition in ill-structured domains. In T. Duffy & D. Jonassen (Eds.), *Constructivism and the technology of instruction* (pp. 57–75). Hillsdale, NJ: Erlbaum. (Reprinted from *Educational Technology on Constructivism* [Special issue].)

Spiro, R.J., Feltovich, P.J., Jacobson, M.J., & Coulson, R.L. (1992b). Knowledge representation, content specification, and the development of skill in situation-specific knowledge assembly: Some constructivist issues as they relate to cognitive flexibility theory and hypertext. In T. Duffy & D. Jonassen (Eds.), *Constructivism and the technology of instruction* (pp. 121–128). Hillsdale, NJ: Erlbaum. (Reprinted from *Educational Technology on Constructivism* [Special issue].)

Spiro, R.J., & Jehng, J.C. (1990). Cognitive flexibility and hypertext: Theory and technology for the nonlinear and multidimensional traversal of complex subject matter. In D. Nix & R.J. Spiro (Eds.), *Cognition, education, and multimedia: Explorations in high technology* (pp. 163–205). Hillsdale, NJ: Erlbaum.

Spiro, R.J., & Myers, A. (1984). Individual differences and underlying cognitive processes in reading. In P.D. Pearson, R. Barr, M.L. Kamil, & P. Mosenthal (Eds.), *Handbook of reading research* (pp. 471–501). New York: Longman.

Spiro, R.J., Vispoel, W.L., Schmitz, J., Samarapungavan, A., & Boerger, A. (1987). Knowledge acquisition for application: Cognitive flexibility and transfer in complex content domains. In B.C. Britton & S. Glynn (Eds.), *Executive control processes* (pp. 177–200). Hillsdale, NJ: Erlbaum.

PART II

MAKING SENSE OF LITERACY

The pendulum of change in reading education has historically swung from one extreme to another. While each of these extremes has endorsed approaches or methods that have frequently been assumed to be "the answer" to the teaching of reading, inevitably each dominated reading instruction for a period of time and then often was set aside when the next new or resurrected approach took hold. McCullough (1958) characterized this pendulum of change in reading education in the following manner:

> Much of the knowledge we now have about the teaching of reading has been developed by curious and—in terms of the lives of children—wasteful patterns of extremes. We learned a great deal about oral reading by having too much of it, about silent reading by neglecting oral reading, about extensive reading by neglecting intensive, about sight vocabulary by neglecting phonics, about phonics and speed by neglecting comprehension. One would think that it should have finally dawned on us that all of these practices have value and the sensible, most efficient program encompasses them all. (p. 163)

However, in the face of these radical extremes over the years, experienced teachers have tended to continue to use the positive and workable aspects of these approaches to reading in their classroom instruction, electing to teach and use what was most effective and appropriate to their specific students and situations. Thus, over the years, even as arguments have raged inside and outside the reading field and the pendulum has swung back and forth from one extreme to the other, there has gradually developed, through the insight of the typical classroom reading teacher, a "making sense of literacy."

In this section, reading researchers who have an expertise in multicultural education and literacy, teaching struggling readers, and motivation and reading research likewise strive to make sense of literacy. They each reveal to us what is known about their areas of extensive study and to what degree the agreements of the diverse experts in the Expert Study (Flippo, 1998; refer to Chapter 1 in this book) are supported by this related research.

It is evident that classrooms, both today and into the future, are and will become increasingly multicultural in terms of both the curriculum and the student population. Kathryn Au notes the challenges as well as the inherent positive aspects of a multicultural classroom. Her discussion emphasizes the importance of reading as a critical catalyst in the development of a positive belief system related to multicultural concepts and experiences. Centering her remarks around the experts' agreements on reading practices, she effectively illustrates the role of multiculturalism, and shows how the research on multicultural education and students of diverse backgrounds supports the Expert Study findings.

Victoria Purcell-Gates describes, through a personal narrative, her development as teacher of reading for those students who were having difficulty learning to read. In her growth as a teacher of reading, she carefully notes those teacher characteristics that eventually led to success with readers who struggle. Her work also points out those agreed-upon practices and contexts related to identifying and effectively working with the struggling reader.

Finally, Linda Gambrell helps us make sense of literacy by reviewing in depth the existing knowledge base concerning motivation to learn, with particular emphasis on reading motivation. She does note that while there has been extensive research done in the past on motivation to learn, there is still much research to be done related specifically to reading motivation. Gambrell approaches the fundamental issue of the role of reading motivation from the perspective of its theoretical conceptualization as well as a review of related research. She shows that the results of this work can be tied directly to the agreements of the experts as reported in this volume.

Richard D. Robinson

REFERENCES
Flippo, R.F. (1998). Points of agreement: A display of professional unity in our field. *The Reading Teacher, 52*, 30–40.
McCullough, C. (1958). Individualized reading. *NEA Journal, 47*, 162–163.

CHAPTER 13

What We Know About Multicultural Education and Students of Diverse Backgrounds

Kathryn H. Au

Christine Tanioka is an experienced fourth-grade teacher in a school in a rural community on the island of Hawaii. Her students are a mix of ethnicities, including Hawaiian, Filipino, European, and Japanese. Most come from low-income families and speak Hawaii Creole English as their first language. Chris sets up her classroom so that students gain a sense of belonging to a community of readers (for a full description, see Carroll, Wilson, & Au, 1996). In Chris's classroom, the time to teach reading is called the readers' workshop (Au, Carroll, & Scheu, 1997), and it begins with sustained silent reading. During this time, Chris and her students spend about 15 minutes silently reading books of their own choosing.

Chris believes she can foster her students' motivation to read by demonstrating her own love of books. One day, she brought in a shopping bag full of books that she had taken from her nightstand. As she pulled each book from the bag, she told the class what it was about and why it was important to her. One book was about flower arranging, one of her hobbies. Another was about swimming, her children's favorite sport. Another was a novel a colleague had recommended. Her collection included several children's books, which she said she loved best of all.

Chris often gives her students several minutes to share their reading with classmates. She and a few students may give book talks, she may recommend books, and the students may recommend books to one another. Sometimes, when she encounters a reluctant reader, Chris chooses a book from her personal collection to lend that student. Chris further motivates her students by reading aloud a chapter a day from a favorite novel.

Chris devotes time each day to improving her students' skills as readers. She presents the whole class with a minilesson (Calkins, 1994), lasting about 5 to 10 minutes, focusing on procedures, the author's craft, or basic skills. During the first half of the school year, she meets with students in small groups for reading instruction, seeing each group at least three times a week. Often, these lessons of up to half an hour will center on guided discussion of a novel or short story, to sharpen students' comprehension, including their ability to construct a theme (Au, 1992).

Later in the year, when students have gained in reading proficiency and independence, especially in comprehending literature, Chris organizes the class in literature circles. Literature circles are discussion groups of about six students who are reading the same novel (Au, Carroll, & Scheu, 1997). Each day, students read a chapter or so in the novel and write an individual response to their reading. Their responses include questions and issues for possible discussion by their literature circle. Discussions are lively, because Chris has her students read books, such as *On My Honor* (Bauer, 1986), that give them many issues to debate. This fourth-grade classroom is an example of a multicultural educational setting in which students are successfully learning to read.

Students of Diverse Backgrounds

From the perspective of multicultural education, nine variables are considered important in shaping an individual's cultural identity (Gollnick & Chinn, 1990): ethnicity, social class, primary language, gender, age, religion, geographic region, place of residence (whether urban, suburban, or rural), and exceptionality. Three variables—ethnicity, social class, and primary language—pose a challenge to schools in terms of students' literacy learning. In the United States, for example, schools often do not succeed in bringing to high levels of achievement students who are African American, Latino, or Native American in ethnicity, from low-income families, and speakers of a first language other than standard English. (This language may be a dialect of English, such as African American language or Hawaii Creole English, or it may be another language, such as Spanish.) I will refer to these students, including those in the classroom just described, as students of diverse backgrounds. Students of diverse backgrounds may be contrasted with students of mainstream backgrounds. In the United States, these students are generally European American in ethnicity, from middle-income families, and speakers of standard English.

Considerable evidence points to a gap between the literacy achievement of students of diverse backgrounds and those of mainstream backgrounds. A major source of evidence is the National Assessment of Educational Progress (NAEP), which has monitored the literacy achievement of U.S. students at three grade levels for more than 25 years. Results for the 1994 reading assessment for Grade 4 (9-year-olds) revealed the following percentages of students performing below a basic level of proficiency: Whites, 29%; African Americans, 69%; and Hispanics, 64% (Nettles & Perna, 1997). Similar differences were seen at Grade 8 (13-year-olds) and Grade 12 (17-year-olds). Although the gap appears to be narrowing somewhat, we continue to see large differences between the literacy achievement of students of diverse backgrounds and that of mainstream students.

Multicultural education offers a perspective for understanding the literacy achievement gap and thinking about how it might be narrowed. The goal of multicultural education is to bring about changes in schools that will enable all students to attain educational equality (Banks, 1995). Banks (1994) highlights three major approaches to multicultural education. In the curriculum reform approach, educators change the curriculum to give greater prominence to the experience of different ethnic, cultural, and gender groups. In the intergroup education approach, educators enhance students' understanding of and positive attitudes toward marginalized groups. If the students are members of marginalized groups, the goal is to enhance their appreciation of their own culture and heritage. In the achievement approach, educators work to improve the academic achievement of students of diverse backgrounds, who traditionally have not been well served by schools.

This chapter focuses on the achievement approach to multicultural education. I discuss ways of improving the school literacy learning of students of diverse backgrounds within the framework provided by the Expert Study (Flippo, 1998; refer to Chapter 1 in this book). The experts were asked to reach agreement about contexts and practices that would either make learning to read difficult or facilitate learning to read by most students. I try to show how these agreements are particularly important to the school literacy learning of students of diverse backgrounds. For this purpose, I organized the experts' agreements into six topics, as shown in Figure 1. These groupings are similar (but not identical) to those devised by Flippo.

Interpretation of Experts' Agreements

1. Linking All Language Processes

As mentioned earlier, students of diverse backgrounds in the United States often enter school speaking a first language other than standard English. The agreements in the Expert Study do not refer directly to the needs in learning to read of second language learners. Nevertheless, the literacy learning of second language learners is promoted when teachers use every opportunity to bring reading, writing, talking, and listening together, so that each process supports the other.

During literature discussions in Chris Tanioka's class, students sometimes express their ideas in Hawaii Creole English. Chris accepts students' ideas without stopping to correct their language, because she does not want to embarrass students and inhibit their participation. However, when she responds to students' ideas, Chris speaks in standard English. In this way, she models standard English syntax and vocabulary for students. As the discussion continues, students will often use the standard English forms that Chris has just modeled for them.

Figure 1
Summary Agreements in the Six Topics

1. Linking All Language Processes
Do
- Use every opportunity to bring together reading/writing/talking/listening so that each feeds off and feeds into the other.
- Instead of deliberately separating reading from writing, plan instruction and individual activities so that, most of the time, students engage in purposeful reading and writing.

Don't
- Teach reading as something separate from writing, talking, and listening.

2. Ownership and Purposes for Reading
Do
- Provide multiple, repeated demonstrations of how reading is done or used.
- Focus on using reading as a tool for learning.
- Make reading functional.
- Give your students lots of time and opportunity to read real books (both narrative and expository), as well as time and opportunity to write creatively and for purposeful school assignments (e.g., to research a topic, to pursue an interest).
- Create environments/contexts in which the children become convinced that reading does further the purposes of their lives.

Don't
- Avoid reading for your own enjoyment or personal purposes in front of the students.

3. Independent Reading
Do
- Encourage children to talk about and share the different kinds of reading they do in a variety of ways with many others.

Don't
- Require children to write book reviews of every book they read.
- Make a practice of not reading aloud very often to children.
- Stop reading aloud to children as soon as they get through the primer level.
- Select all the stories that children read.
- Remove the freedom to make decisions about reading from the learner.

4. Rejection of a Behaviorist Model of Teaching
Don't
- Make sure children do it correctly or not at all.
- Focus on the single best answer.
- Make reading correctly or pronouncing words "exactly right" a prime objective of your classroom reading program.
- Detect and correct all inappropriate or incorrect eye movements you observe as you watch children in your classroom during silent reading.

(continued)

Figure 1 (continued)
Summary Agreements in the Six Topics

Don't (continued)
- Refrain from giving children books in which some of the words are unknown (i.e., words that you have not previously taught or exposed them to in some way).
- Insist on providing lots of training on all the reading skills prior to letting children read a story silently, even if there is not much time left for actual reading.
- Teach the children in your classroom letters and words one at time, making sure each new letter or word is learned before moving on to the next letter or word.
- Emphasize only phonics instruction.
- Drill children on isolated letters and sounds using flashcards, chalk or magnetic boards, computers, or worksheets.
- Assign a few more skill sheets to remedy the problem if a child is not "getting it."

5. High Expectations
Do
- Develop positive self-perceptions and expectations.
- Use silent reading whenever possible, if appropriate to the purpose.

Don't
- Group readers according to ability.
- Tell students who are weak in reading that reading is a difficult and complex process and that you do not expect them to be able to do the more difficult reading work.
- Have the children do oral reading exclusively.
- Have children orally read a story in small groups, allowing one sentence or paragraph at a time for each child, and going around the group in either a clockwise or counterclockwise rotation.
- Focus on children's learning the skills rather than on interpretation and comprehension.
- Make sure children understand the seriousness of falling behind.
- Encourage competitive reading.

6. Reading Materials
Do
- Include a variety of printed material and literature in your classroom so that students are exposed to the different functions of numerous types of printed materials (e.g., newspapers, magazines, journals, textbooks, research books, trade books, library books, menus, directions).
- Use a broad spectrum of sources for student reading materials.

Don't
- Have children read short, snappy texts rather than whole stories.
- Follow your basal's teaching procedures as detailed without making any modifications.
- Use workbooks with every reading lesson.
- Test children with paper-and-pencil tests whenever they complete a new story in their basal, and each time you have finished teaching a new skill.

During the writers' workshop in Chris's classroom, students engage in peer conferences, when they frequently exchange ideas in Hawaii Creole English. Using their first language allows students' thoughts to flow freely and helps them clarify the ideas they wish to write about. When students have their ideas clearly in mind, they orally rehearse these ideas in standard English. Then they are ready to begin writing down their ideas.

Moll and Diaz (1987) found that Spanish-speaking students showed excellent comprehension of a story read in English when they were allowed to discuss the story in Spanish. The students had many ideas about the story that they were unable to express in English. These investigators concluded that students' comprehension of English texts was being underestimated, because they did not have the opportunity to express their understandings in Spanish.

As these examples suggest, students' proficiency in their first language provides a foundation that teachers can build on to promote reading and writing. The difficulty in schools is that students are often denied the opportunity to use strengths in the first language as the basis for learning to read and write. Research supports the idea that students are best taught to read and write in their first language (Snow, Burns, & Griffin, 1998). Once students have learned to read and write in the first language, usually by the third or fourth grade, the transition is made to reading and writing in the second language. For example, Spanish-speaking students in the United States might first learn to read and write in Spanish, then make the transition to English reading and writing.

In many cases, however, it may not be practical to provide students with initial literacy instruction in the first language. Often the students come from many different language backgrounds or there is a lack of qualified teachers who speak students' first languages. But even when students are learning to read and write in a second language, teachers can take steps to build upon strengths in the first language. For example, a student might be given the opportunity to participate in a literature discussion using the first language. Another student in the class might then translate the first student's points for the teacher and other students. In short, students of diverse backgrounds benefit from literacy learning situations in which all four language processes—reading, writing, listening, speaking—are linked.

2. Ownership and Purposes for Reading

The term *ownership* does not appear in the experts' agreements, but a number of the agreements recognize the importance of students' ownership of literacy. Ownership involves students' valuing of reading and writing at home as well as at school (Au, 1997). Students with ownership use literacy for purposes they set for themselves and make reading and writing a part of their everyday lives. When Chris Tanioka helps her students find books they will enjoy reading, she is trying to build their ownership of literacy.

In the past, educators focused on proficiency, or skill, as the overarching goal. Of course, students' knowledge of reading strategies and skills remains important. However, we now understand that skill in reading should not be separated from the will to read (Winograd & Paris, 1988). For example, we do not consider the teacher's job to be done if a student becomes a skillful reader but reads only for school assignments and never chooses to read for her own enjoyment or information. Such a student does not yet see reading as personally meaningful or understand how reading can be used to meet the purposes she has set for herself. When we make students' ownership of literacy the overarching goal, we remind ourselves to encourage not just proficiency but purposeful, self-motivated reading.

When educators recognize the importance of ownership, they try to help students make connections between literacy at home and literacy in school. Research shows that students of diverse backgrounds often have a variety of home experiences with literacy. For example, the inner-city, African American families studied by Taylor and Dorsey-Gaines (1988) read to gain information about current events. Newspapers, and often magazines, were present in the apartments of all these families. In this case, teachers might make the connection to literacy at home by conducting classroom activities involving the newspaper. Depending on the age and interests of the students, teachers might have them read and respond to articles about sports and entertainment, or to editorials and advertisements.

The difficulty appears to be that the home literacy experiences of students of diverse backgrounds may not be those expected by teachers. Teachers may assume that children are entering school with a background in family storybook reading, a type of reading event not experienced by children in all cultures (Heath, 1982). Teachers may not realize that, if family storybook reading has not been part of home routines, students will need many positive school experiences with storybook reading and other mainstream literacy activities in order to see the benefit of these activities for their everyday lives. To provide these experiences, teachers can read aloud storybooks that children will find interesting and engaging. They can help children see connections between the events in stories and events in their own lives, so that children come to regard reading as personally meaningful.

The example set by the teacher may be important in promoting ownership of literacy by students of diverse backgrounds. We saw how Chris Tanioka shared with her class the books she was reading for her own enjoyment and learning. Some of the students in Chris's class may not have witnessed such enthusiasm for books among the adults in their own families. Through Chris's sharing, they caught a glimpse of how the reading of books can be both joyful and informative, at home as well as at school.

Meaningful and motivating activities can lead all students to achieve higher levels of literacy. However, teachers in mainstream classrooms can usually count on students to complete literacy assignments even when they do not know the purpose behind these activities. The reason is that mainstream students realize the importance of complying with teachers' requests and getting good grades. They know they need to graduate from high school and go on to college to have good life opportunities, including high-paying jobs. Students of diverse backgrounds may lack this same understanding because the connection between schooling and life opportunities may not have been illustrated in the histories of their own families (Ogbu, 1981).

Teachers in classrooms with students of diverse backgrounds cannot count on students to complete literacy assignments they find meaningless. Students may fail to show compliance because they neither see the value of schooling nor understand its long-term consequences for their lives. With students of diverse backgrounds, teachers should be aware of providing immediate, as opposed to long-term, reasons for staying in school (D'Amato, 1988). An immediate reason is provided when students know that they will be engaging in meaningful and motivating literacy activities on a daily basis. Such activities may include listening to the teacher read aloud the next chapter of an exciting book, debating the interpretation of a novel with peers, and conducting research on a topic of personal interest.

3. Independent Reading

As shown in Figure 1, the experts reached agreement on a number of statements highlighting the importance of wide, independent reading. Research points to the benefits of such reading. Wide, independent reading provides students with opportunities to strengthen comprehension, build vocabulary, and orchestrate word-identification skills (Anderson, Wilson, & Fielding, 1988). In addition, the independent reading of self-selected books gives students opportunities to develop their own tastes and interests as readers. Students of diverse backgrounds, like all students, improve their reading abilities when teachers support independent reading.

One of the experts' agreements concerns the importance of having students share the reading they do. Many teachers, such as Chris Tanioka, provide students with a daily time for sustained silent reading of books of their own choosing. Too often, however, teachers do not include time to share reading in connection with sustained silent reading. We have noted how Chris acted as a role model by telling students about the books she was reading. Students can also act as reading role models for one another, if teachers give them the time to share books in class. The sharing of books to celebrate one's own reading and boost the reading of others differs from the typical practice of having students write book reports. The experts agreed that students should not be required to write a review of every book they read. Understandably, students may be reluctant to read if they know they will have to write a book report. Furthermore, the only audience for a book report is usually the teacher.

The sharing of books may take place in informal ways, such as giving students a couple of minutes to discuss their reading with a partner. Or sharing may take place in formal ways, such as having students prepare book talks or book posters to present to the whole class. Sharing activities are especially important in classrooms with students of diverse backgrounds. As pointed out earlier, although students may witness many literacy activities in the home and community, they may not have many avid readers of books as role models. Through the sharing of books, students receive recognition for the reading they are doing, and they gain ideas about what to read next by hearing classmates' recommendations.

The experts agreed that the teacher's reading aloud to students continues to be an important source of inspiration, even when students are able to read many books on their own. Several years ago, I conducted a study in which I interviewed fifth-grade students, most of them of Hawaiian ancestry, about their reading habits. In one of the questions, students were asked about their favorite author. At one school, many students told me that their favorite author was Roald Dahl. Through further questioning, I discovered that these students had all been in the same third-grade classroom. Their teacher loved Roald Dahl and had read aloud two of his books. Inspired by their teacher, the students had gone to the school library and borrowed other Roald Dahl books to read on their own. Clearly, a teacher's enthusiasm can lead students to books they might not have discovered by themselves.

4. Rejection of a Behaviorist Model of Teaching

The experts agreed on 10 statements, listed in Figure 1, which show their rejection of a behaviorist model of teaching and learning. In a behaviorist model, reading is taught as a series of skills presented in a set sequence. Children learn through a process of direct instruction, in which skills are transmitted by the teacher. Skills earlier in the sequence must be mastered before students proceed to skills later in the sequence. This model assumes that all students can and will learn to read through training in the same set sequence of skills. Lower level skills, such as phonics, are emphasized, and skills tend to be taught in isolation, apart from the reading of literature. The emphasis is on correct responses, such as giving the right answer to the teacher's question or pronouncing words "exactly right." Mistakes are believed to be harmful, because they indicate that children are practicing the wrong behavior. To prevent mistakes, the teacher provides training on reading skills and unknown words in advance of having children read on their own.

Many critiques of a behaviorist model of reading instruction are available (Shannon, 1989; Weaver, 1990). In this section I focus specifically on reasons for avoiding use of a narrow, behaviorist model in classrooms with students of diverse backgrounds. First, isolated skill instruction may detract from students' ownership of literacy. As discussed earlier, students of diverse backgrounds need meaningful and motivating literacy learning experiences in the classroom. Isolated skill instruction is likely to be neither. When skills are taught in isolation, it may be difficult for students to see the point of instruction, and they may be less willing to learn skills. Isolated skill instruction may be based on scripted lessons, in which no connections are made to children's own background experiences. Even if skills are learned, students may not understand how to apply these skills to real reading.

Problems of motivation and application can be avoided if skills are taught not in isolation but in the context of meaningful literacy activities, such as the reading of an exciting book or an informational article on a high-interest topic. For example, when children are reading *The Cat in the Hat* (Seuss, 1957), the teacher has the perfect opportunity to teach the *-at* phonogram. The teacher can explain to children that learning this particular skill will help them read this and other books on their own. Children can find *-at* words in *The Cat in the Hat* as well as in other books, and the teacher can create a chart listing all the *-at* words the children have discovered. This is an example of how children can be introduced to a skill in the context of the reading of literature, and then encouraged to apply the skill when they read other books.

Second, students of diverse backgrounds may be prevented from progressing rapidly in learning to read if they are required to proceed through a set sequence of skill instruction in which each skill must be mastered before the next is taught. Research on emergent literacy provides considerable information about how young children develop as readers and writers, but much more remains to be learned, especially about the literacy development of young students of diverse backgrounds (McGee & Purcell-Gates, 1997). We do know that young children growing up in different cultural contexts may develop different understandings of literacy (Heath, 1982). For this reason, among others, it is not the case that one set sequence of skill instruction will be beneficial to all students (Allington, 1997).

Learning to read is not a process of mastering particular skills in a set order. Instead, learning to read appears to be a process of successive approximation (Holdaway, 1979), in which children develop proficiency by engaging in the full processes of reading and writing. For example, children attempt to read books and to write their own stories. While attempting these activities, young children will show behavior that seems sensible to them but that looks unconventional to adults. For example, young children may "read" a story by referring to the pictures, or they may represent a word by writing just its first letter. Such approximations are part and parcel of the literacy learning process.

Children may learn more quickly and develop deeper understandings of literacy if their teacher encourages them to take risks, so they can discover for themselves how reading and writing work. For example, research suggests that children who have the opportunity to invent their own spellings for words become better spellers in the long run than children who learn spelling primarily by rote memorization (Ehri, 1987). The reason is that children who invent their own spellings come to understand for themselves how the English spelling system works; children who do not engage in the process of invention do not develop the same degree of understanding. If children hesitate to read and write because they fear making mistakes, their literacy learning may be slowed. To narrow the literacy achievement gap, we must speed and strengthen the literacy learning of students of diverse backgrounds, by seeing that they are actively engaged in constructing their own understanding of how reading and writing work.

In encouraging children to learn to read and write through a process of successive approximation, teachers such as Chris Tanioka still provide skill instruction (Carroll, Wilson, & Au, 1996). However, teachers determine which skills to teach not by following a set sequence, but by observing children. In this way, the teacher can see which skills children already understand and which skills they are ready to learn next. If children are "reading" pictures instead of print, the teacher can call their attention to the words on the pages of a big book and show them how to track print. If children are writing words using only the first letter, the teacher can show them how to say a word slowly, listen for other sounds, and write down the letters for these other sounds.

Third, use of a behaviorist model of reading instruction in classrooms with students of diverse backgrounds may cause too much time to be given to lower level skills and too little to higher level thinking. Research suggests that a considerable amount of the reading instruction in classrooms with students of diverse backgrounds centers on oral reading (Fitzgerald, 1995). Because the focus is on accurate word-calling, students may get the impression that the most important part of reading is to pronounce the words correctly. In classrooms with Spanish-speaking students and other second language learners, and in classrooms with students who speak a nonmainstream variety of English, teachers may spend considerable amounts of time correcting students' pronunciation of words read aloud (Fitzgerald, 1995; Piestrup, 1973). Moll and Diaz (1987) found that when teachers judged Spanish-speaking students' reading proficiency mainly on the basis of their correct pronunciation of English words, they tended to underestimate their reading achievement. Erickson (1993) suggested that teachers' constant correction of the pronunciation of African American children may signal a denigration of the children's language and communication style. Over time, such signals may contribute to children's unwillingness to participate actively in reading lessons.

Studies demonstrate that the instruction of students of diverse backgrounds tends to be biased toward lower level skills (Allington, 1991; Darling-Hammond, 1995). Every time the pendulum swings "back to basics," these students are likely to receive an even greater dose of isolated skill instruction. Lack of instruction in higher level thinking in literacy—including summarization, interpretation, and critical evaluation—leaves students of diverse backgrounds at a disadvantage in comparison to their mainstream peers. If the literacy achievement gap is to be narrowed, students of diverse backgrounds must be given every opportunity to develop higher level thinking.

5. High Expectations

The experts reached agreement on a number of statements about the importance of teachers having high expectations for students' learning. Although it is difficult to do, teachers must keep expectations high in classrooms with students of diverse backgrounds. Having high expectations for students' literacy learning, in the form of grade-level benchmarks tied to state and national standards, is one factor that can contribute to the improved literacy achievement of these students (Au & Carroll, 1997). Chris Tanioka found grade-level benchmarks useful in guiding her teaching and in making her expectations clear to students. In schools such as the one in which Chris teaches, teachers must be aware of fighting the tendency to have lower expectations for students.

Students of diverse backgrounds tend to be over-represented in low-track, remedial reading, and special education programs, in which expectations for student learning are not high (Darling-Hammond, 1995). In the elementary classroom, students of diverse backgrounds are often placed in the lowest reading group. Studies show that low (as opposed to middle and high) reading groups present students with qualitatively different instructional experiences (Allington, 1983; Barr & Dreeben, 1991). In low reading groups, teachers emphasize oral reading and accurate word-calling. In high groups, the emphasis is on silent reading and comprehension of the text. When a low-group student reads a word incorrectly, the teacher is likely to jump in quickly with the right word (Allington, 1983). Teachers probably make these rapid corrections with good intentions, to save children from embarrassment. In contrast, when a high-group student misreads a word, the teacher often waits for the child to figure out the word herself. The upshot is that low-group students may have less opportunity than high-group students to learn to correct their own mistakes and to gain confidence in their abilities as readers.

These findings suggest that teachers should be aware of providing students of diverse backgrounds with ample time for silent reading and ample instruction in comprehension and higher level thinking. Of course, instruction in word identification cannot be neglected if students are not yet fluent readers. However, even with beginning readers, teachers should make sure students understand that the purpose of reading is not just to identify words but to gain meaning from text.

Students of mainstream backgrounds often expect to compete with other students and strive to be recognized for their superior performance. Individualism, achievement, and competition are all core mainstream values, but these values are not held by all cultural groups in the United States (Spindler & Spindler, 1990). Some students of diverse backgrounds may respond negatively to competitive reading and may appear unconcerned about "falling behind" as readers. For some students of diverse backgrounds, contributions that benefit family and friends may have higher value than their own individual achievement in school. Rather than competing to be recognized individually, some students may prefer opportunities to work cooperatively with peers, such as in a literature circle. While it is essential to hold all students to the same high standards, instructional strategies responsive to differences in cultural values may be needed to help students of diverse backgrounds meet these standards (Au, 1993).

6. Reading Materials

The experts agree that teachers should make a wide variety of printed materials available to students, and that they should avoid many of the practices associated with traditional basal reading programs. These programs continue to be used in approximately 85% of U.S. classrooms (Goodman, 1994). Chris Tanioka, along with most U.S. teachers, taught for years with basal reading programs. However, the nature of texts and instructional recommendations to teachers do seem to be changing. Increasing numbers of teachers report that they supplement the materials provided by basal reading programs with the use of literature. In addition, literature-based instruction is central to all of the major basal reading programs published in the 1990s. Nearly all the selections in the student anthologies consist of literature, in the form of entire trade books or excerpts. Teachers' manuals appear to be moving away from a single, scripted approach to instruction, toward offering teachers a choice of approaches, including cooperative groups.

For educators interested in improving the literacy achievement of students of diverse backgrounds, these trends are all positive. Certainly, reading literature (rather than contrived texts of the "Dick and Jane" variety) is likely to provide students with challenging, interesting, and motivating reading experiences. Morrow (1992) found that students of diverse backgrounds who participated in a literature-based program outperformed control group students on a variety of literacy and language measures, including those for comprehension, story retelling, and story rewriting.

In particular, students of diverse backgrounds can benefit from the reading of multicultural literature as part of the classroom reading program. Works of multicultural literature, often written by authors of diverse backgrounds, present cultures in an authentic manner (Harris, 1992). The use of literature that accurately depicts the experiences of diverse groups may improve students' literacy achievement by increasing their motivation to read (Spears-Bunton, 1990).

When using multicultural literature, attention should be given to the curricular approach as well as to the selection of books. Using Banks' (1989) hierarchy of approaches in multicultural education, Rasinski and Padak (1990) defined several approaches for using multicultural literature, including the transformation and social action approaches. Teachers who follow these approaches use multicultural literature to guide students in the critical analysis of social issues and seek to empower students to take action on these issues.

Teachers in classrooms with students of diverse backgrounds must be especially aware of using the suggestions in the teacher's manual in a flexible manner. Teachers have extensive knowledge of their students' backgrounds that can be applied to help students make personal connections to the story. Students in a reading group in Joyce Ahuna-Ka'ai'ai's third-grade class were reading a story in which the main characters are Japanese Americans. Joyce knew that one of her students, Chad, was part Japanese, and she asked him if he had a Japanese name. Chad said that he did, and he was able to compare himself to the children in the story, who also had both English and Japanese names. Joyce remarked that she would not have thought to ask such a question if she had been following a prescribed list of questions in a basal teacher's manual (Center for the Study of Reading, 1991).

The experts agree that workbooks should not be used with every reading lesson. Often, workbook pages center on the practice of lower level skills. As discussed earlier, it may be more beneficial for students of diverse backgrounds if assignments focus instead on higher level thinking and comprehension. Researchers have looked at the benefits of having students write in open-ended ways about the literature they are reading (Raphael & McMahon, 1994). Students share their written responses with peers in literature circles. Such purposeful writing for an audience of peers will generally be much more meaningful to students than the completion of workbook pages. With workbook pages, students may be more concerned with getting finished than with improving their reading skills (Scheu, Tanner, & Au, 1986).

Conclusion

The Expert Study points to six topics important in improving the literacy education of students of diverse backgrounds and narrowing the literacy achievement gap. In closing, I put forward some suggestions for educators, based on the agreements on each of these topics:

1. Link reading with writing, listening, and speaking, so that students of diverse backgrounds can use their strengths in all language processes when learning to read.

2. Provide students of diverse backgrounds with motivating, purposeful literacy activities that will promote their ownership of literacy.

3. Give students many opportunities for wide independent reading and help them develop their own tastes and interests as readers.

4. Reject a behaviorist model of reading instruction and move instead toward approaches that emphasize higher level thinking with text, promote students' risk-taking as literacy learners, and encourage students' active involvement in developing their own understandings of reading and writing.

5. Hold high expectations for the literacy achievement of students of diverse backgrounds, while realizing that instruction to help students meet these expectations may need to be responsive to their cultural values.

6. Center reading instruction on literature, drawing from our knowledge of students' backgrounds to help them make personal connections to literature and encouraging them to share their thoughts about literature in writing and in discussions with peers.

In short, when I looked at the Expert Study from the perspective of the achievement approach to multicultural education, I found that the agreements fit quite well with research and with my own sense of what it will take to narrow the literacy achievement gap.

REFERENCES

Allington, R.L. (1983). The reading instruction provided readers of differing abilities. *The Elementary School Journal, 83*, 548–559.

Allington, R.L. (1991). Children who find learning to read difficult: School responses to diversity. In E.H. Hiebert (Ed.), *Literacy for a diverse society: Perspectives, practices, and policies* (pp. 237–252). New York: Teachers College Press.

Allington, R.L. (1997, August/September). Overselling phonics. *Reading Today*, pp. 15–16.

Anderson, R.C., Wilson, P.T., & Fielding, L.G. (1988). Growth in reading and how children spend their time outside of school. *Reading Research Quarterly, 23*, 285–303.

Au, K.H. (1992). Constructing the theme of a story. *Language Arts, 69*, 106–111.

Au, K.H. (1993). *Literacy instruction in multicultural settings.* Fort Worth, TX: Harcourt Brace.

Au, K.H. (1997). Ownership, literacy achievement, and students of diverse cultural backgrounds. In J.T. Guthrie & A. Wigfield (Eds.), *Reading engagement: Motivating readers through integrated instruction* (pp. 168–182). Newark, DE: International Reading Association.

Au, K.H., & Carroll, J.H. (1997). Improving literacy achievement through a constructivist approach: The KEEP demonstration classroom project. *The Elementary School Journal, 97*, 203–221.

Au, K.H., Carroll, J.H., & Scheu, J.A. (1997). *Balanced literacy instruction: A teacher's resource book*. Norwood, MA: Christopher-Gordon.

Banks, J.A. (1989). Multicultural education: Characteristics and goals. In J.A. Banks & C.A.M. Banks (Eds.), *Multicultural education: Issues and perspectives* (pp. 2–26). Boston: Allyn & Bacon.

Banks, J.A. (1994). *An introduction to multicultural education*. Boston: Allyn & Bacon.

Banks, J.A. (1995). Multicultural education: Historical development, dimensions, and practice. In J.A. Banks & C.A.M. Banks (Eds.), *Handbook of research on multicultural education* (pp. 3–24). New York: Macmillan.

Barr, R., & Dreeben, R. (1991). Grouping students for reading instruction. In R. Barr, M.L. Kamil, P.B. Mosenthal, & P.D. Pearson (Eds.), *Handbook of reading research* (Vol. II, pp. 885–910). White Plains, NY: Longman.

Bauer, M.D. (1986). *On my honor*. Boston: Clarion.

Calkins, L.M. (1994). *The art of teaching writing* (2nd ed.). Portsmouth, NH: Heinemann.

Carroll, J.H., Wilson, R.A., & Au, K.H. (1996). Explicit instruction in the context of the readers' and writers' workshops. In E. McIntyre & M. Pressley (Eds.), *Balanced instruction: Skills and strategies in whole language* (pp. 39–63). Norwood, MA: Christopher-Gordon.

Center for the Study of Reading. (1991). *Teaching reading: Strategies from successful classrooms* [Six-part videotape series]. (Available from the International Reading Association, 800 Barksdale Road, PO Box 8139, Newark, DE, 19714-8139.)

D'Amato, J. (1988). "Acting": Hawaiian children's resistance to teachers. *The Elementary School Journal, 88*, 529–544.

Darling-Hammond, L. (1995). Inequality and access to knowledge. In J.A. Banks & C.A.M. Banks (Eds.), *Handbook of research on multicultural education* (pp. 465–483). New York: Macmillan.

Ehri, L.C. (1987). Learning to read and spell words. *Journal of Reading Behavior, 19*, 5–31.

Erickson, F. (1993). Transformation and school success: The politics and culture of educational achievement. In E. Jacob & C. Jordan (Eds.), *Minority education: Anthropological perspectives* (pp. 27–51). Norwood, NJ: Ablex .

Fitzgerald, J. (1995). English-as-a-second-language reading instruction in the United States: A research review. *Journal of Reading Behavior, 27*, 115–152.

Flippo, R.F. (1998). Points of agreement: A display of professional unity in our field. *The Reading Teacher, 52*, 30–40.

Gollnick, D.M., & Chinn, P.C. (1990). *Multicultural education in a pluralistic society* (3rd ed.). Columbus, OH: Merrill.

Goodman, K. (1994). Foreword: Lots of changes, but little gained. In P. Shannon & K. Goodman (Eds.), *Basal readers: A second look* (pp. iii–xxvii). Katonah, NY: Richard C. Owen.

Harris, V.J. (1992). Multiethnic children's literature. In K.D. Wood & A. Moss (Eds.), *Exploring literature in the classroom: Content and methods* (pp. 169–201). Norwood, MA: Christopher-Gordon.

Heath, S.B. (1982). What no bedtime story means: Narrative skills at home and school. *Language in Society, 11*, 49–76.

Holdaway, D. (1979). *The foundations of literacy*. Sydney, Australia: Ashton Scholastic.

McGee, L.M., & Purcell-Gates, V. (1997). "So what's going on in research on emergent literacy?" *Reading Research Quarterly, 32*, 310–318.

Moll, L.C., & Diaz, S. (1987). Change as the goal of educational research. *Anthropology and Education Quarterly, 18*, 300–311.

Morrow, L.M. (1992). The impact of a literature-based program on literacy achievement, use of literature, and attitudes of children from minority backgrounds. *Reading Research Quarterly, 27*, 251–275.

Nettles, M.T., & Perna, L.W. (1997). *The African American data book: Preschool through high school education* (Vol. II). Fairfax, VA: Frederick D. Patterson Research Institute.

Ogbu, J.U. (1981). School ethnography: A multilevel approach. *Anthropology & Education Quarterly, 12*, 3–29.

Piestrup, A.M. (1973). *Black dialect interference and accommodation of reading instruction in first grade* (Vol. IV). Berkeley, CA: University of California.

Raphael, T.E., & McMahon, S.I. (1994). Book Club: An alternative framework for reading instruction. *The Reading Teacher, 48*, 102–116.

Rasinski, T.V., & Padak, N.V. (1990). Multicultural learning through children's literature. *Language Arts, 67*, 576–580.

Scheu, J., Tanner, D., & Au, K.H. (1986). Designing independent practice activities to improve comprehension. *The Reading Teacher, 40*, 18–25.

Seuss, Dr. (1957). *The cat in the hat.* New York: Random House.

Shannon, P. (1989). *Broken promises: Reading instruction in twentieth century America.* New York: Bergin & Garvey.

Snow, C.E., Burns, M.S., & Griffin, P. (1998). *Preventing reading difficulties in young children.* Washington, DC: National Academy Press.

Spears-Bunton, L.A. (1990). Welcome to my house: African American and European American students' responses to Virginia Hamilton's *House of Dies Drear. Journal of Negro Education, 59*, 566–576.

Spindler, G., & Spindler, L. (1990). *The American cultural dialogue and its transmission.* London: Falmer Press.

Taylor, D., & Dorsey-Gaines, C. (1988). *Growing up literate: Learning from inner-city families.* Portsmouth, NH: Heinemann.

Weaver, C. (1990). *Understanding whole language: Principles and practices.* Portsmouth, NH: Heinemann.

Winograd, P., & Paris, S.G. (1988). A cognitive and motivational agenda for reading instruction. *Educational Leadership, 46*, 30–36.

CHAPTER 14

What We Know About Readers Who Struggle

Victoria Purcell-Gates

Iwant to begin this piece with the story of how I, a secondary English teacher by training, came to be deeply involved in the field of reading education. Late in the 1960s, I had recently moved to California, newly married and looking for a teaching position. Unfortunately, the time for new hires had passed as we were well into the month of September by the time I began dropping off my resume at school district personnel offices. As fate would have it, though, the U.S. federal government had just given school districts a significant amount of money for programs for the "educationally handicapped" (EH—a term that has since been dropped for the more widely used "learning disabled"), albeit too late for advanced interviewing and hiring for the many new positions this allocation made possible. Therefore, applicants who appeared basically competent and interested were seized upon with gratitude by local school districts that had to suddenly create and fill classes for EH children.

In such a manner, I was hired by a suburban district in northern California and found myself in a trailer parked on the school grounds of a junior high school, facing eight seventh and eighth graders who had failed to learn to read, write, compute, and learn during their school years and who had been designated through testing as EH. These students spent up to 80% of their school time in this class. My job was primarily to teach them how to read and spell. For assistance, I had a coteacher who had developed curriculum for this group, including structured phonics workbooks; graded paperback reading series composed of short reading selections followed by five or six comprehension questions; optional work in a program that consisted of graded, color-coded, stiff cards containing similar reading sections followed by 8 to 10 comprehension questions, which could be self-checked by the students; and an endless supply of dittoed worksheets for skill practice.

Given my almost total lack of knowledge of reading instruction, particularly instruction for children who were experiencing extraordinary difficulty learning to read, I relied heavily on the advice and the instructional strategies of my coteacher. Reading instruction thus consisted of handing out workbooks, making individual assignments from them to account for the individual needs of the students (mandated by the federal policy regarding handicapped students), assigning reading passages (again individualized to fit the tested levels of individual students), and working one-on-one on basic phonics concepts and flashcards with the nonreaders. With two teachers for eight students (we divided ourselves to account for different content instruction and for group versus one-on-one instruction), I was confident that within months these students would begin to read more fluently and effectively. In the meantime, I was learning a great deal about reading instruction as it was then conceptualized by the large majority of teachers in the field.

By December, though, I was beginning to get suspicious. Not one of the students was making any visible progress in reading. While I was perfecting the management techniques needed to keep these students on-task and focused, there appeared to be little payoff to the effort that they and I were putting into the reading lessons. Short-term progress always raised my hopes. Within one setting individual students would appear to grasp phonic principles taught and practiced, correctly marking vowels "long" or "short," correctly blending phonemes together to arrive at a word, correctly dividing multisyllabic words into their component syllables. NOW we have it. I would conclude—now Stephen (or David, or John) would be able to sound out and read the texts presented in the graded readers, on the color-coded cards, or (for the most advanced in the class) in their social studies books. However, whether we tried applying these newly gained skills to text beyond the word level the very same day or waited to the next day, the results were basically the same: no transfer or such little transfer as to barely affect the level of dysfluency with which these students read. The end-of-the-year achievement tests confirmed this pattern; only one child made any measurable progress over the year, and several had fallen lower on the normal curve used to compare their scores to a national sample. I was only partially comforted by the words of my colleagues that the fault for this lack of progress undoubtedly lay with the students, who after all *were* EH.

When the brochure for the local university's summer session for teachers arrived, I quickly signed up for a course on reading development and instruction, looking forward to perfecting my techniques and gaining basic knowledge about learning to read from a developmental perspective. I walked into the first day of class and met my professors, visiting from the Midwest, Ken and Yetta Goodman. My journey of inquiry had begun into the nature of reading acquisition and development and subsequent implications for instruction.

I spent almost the duration of the summer class arguing with Drs. Goodman about instructional techniques. (The gap between a view of reading development that results from skill work versus one that sees it as language development was huge and new in those days.) Still, I left the class with an alternative curriculum for teaching reading that was the result of a required project based on the challenge, "If I believe this miscue data, how would I design a remedial reading class?" As the new year began, I was on my own without my coteacher and I decided to try the new curriculum. Why not? What we had done the previous year had not worked.

The new curriculum consisted of filling the room with trade books at all levels of difficulty, about topics that I judged were of interest to junior high students (primarily boys); implementing a contract-based free-reading program using these books, magazines, and taped stories; and requiring reading responses involving writing, performing, speaking, and drawing. For those students who were not reading well enough to read these texts (those, I determined, who scored below a grade level of 2.5 on norm-referenced tests), I planned work in structured linguistic-based phonics programs to help them acquire the basic skills they needed.

By the end of the first year with my alternative curriculum, I eagerly looked forward to the results of the achievement tests. I had already seen most of my students actually begin to read books and other extended texts. Their spelling and writing was beginning to look more conventional, and several parents had taken the time to question me as to the source of their children's awakening interests in reading. I wondered if they had actually made progress, or if they had just spent the year free-reading at their already-held level of competence. (The few students who had worked with me on skills had not made any visible progress that I could see.) The test results were surprising. The students who had spent virtually all of their time reading and responding to real texts, self-chosen, gained an average of four grade levels. Those students who, instead, spent their instructional time working with me on isolated, basic skills, again failed to show any progress on these achievement tests, confirmed by my observations that they were basically perseverating, or treading water, at this level of basic skill acquisition. For these kids, the general wisdom was that the move from below third-grade reading level to above was particularly intransigent—the fault lay with the kids, again. (We have since all learned a great deal about the limitations of measuring progress by grade levels, and I would not do it today. Rather, I would use such transformed-score measures as NCEs, percentiles, or stanines. However, I do not have access to these from this group taught 30 years ago, and a gain in grade level does indicate extraordinary movement on the normal distribution of norm-referenced scores.)

These results amazed me as well as the district-level EH coordinators, who had become aware of my alternative curriculum and had responded with special inservices for me throughout the year—inservices on the effective use of drill-and-skill instruction. When the district needed to fill a remedial reading position at this same school, there was no opposition from the EH program when I applied and was appointed. I moved from the trailer to a real classroom. I took along my trade books, magazines, and taped books, and left behind the tachistoscope and graded skill materials, except for some phonics workbooks for those very low readers whom I knew I would continue to find.

To bring this saga to a close, suffice it to say that I continued, and elaborated upon, my alternative curriculum based on self-directed reading and response to real texts. I slowly included my very low readers in this program, gradually dropping the teacher-directed skill work as its lack of effect continued. For these readers, I often started them with taped readings and language experience texts. I continued to document impressive gains with pre- and posttests, and virtually all students who took that course improved their reading levels and became actual readers for the first time in their lives.

Several years later, when I began my graduate work toward a doctorate, my personal goal was to explain this to myself. It seemed like magic that by engaging in reading and writing of self-chosen texts students could become better readers and writers. And norm-referenced achievement and diagnostic tests could document this with totally different types of reading tasks (decontextualized and focused on one right answer) both for comprehension and for isolated skills (like decoding, vocabulary, and rate). I was determined to explain this seeming anomaly (I know this appears incredibly out-of-date almost 30 years later) through study of psychology, information processing, and linguistics. I worked at this for about seven years while earning a master's and a doctorate and acquiring a primary research focus in emergent literacy. I continued to work on this after assuming my first university position since I took on the duties of forming and directing a university-based literacy center where graduate students training to be reading teachers could work with students who were having trouble learning to read and write in school. My second university position also involved directing such a center, and I continued to work at explaining this phenomenon with study of the reading process, reader motivation, information processing, language processing, and instruction. At this moment, I am still thinking and studying on this. The rest of this chapter will be my attempt to try to explain what I have decided so far.

Explaining Success Without Resorting to Magic

Truths About Process

A process is learned in process. This is something we all intuitively understand. *Process* is that which is accomplished by the workings of *x* number of different steps; it is a larger whole composed of the operations of component parts. Swimming is a process; skiing is a process; walking is a process; dancing is a process. These are physical processes, composed of many different component processes that must all work together synergistically to achieve the larger process. While moving one's arms in designated ways (termed *swimming strokes*), kicking one's legs in designated ways, and breathing out of the water in designated ways are all component processes of swimming, not one of them alone can be termed *swimming*. Nor can swimming be learned and mastered by practicing and mastering any one of these parts alone. Nor can swimming be mastered by practicing and mastering all of these parts separately and then putting them together. Swimming must be learned by actually swimming, all the while coordinating the processing of the component processes so that swimming—and not sinking—is achieved.

Why can we not master the component processes first and then just put them together to swim, in an additive fashion? Because with a process, the component processes work together synergistically. That is, the ways in which they operate are codetermined by the other processes that are working to achieve the overall process (in the case of our example, swimming). They do not operate exactly the same in process as they do alone. And for the process to be mastered, one must practice the synergistic operation of the component processes; one must practice the overall process.

Reading and writing are also processes—albeit psychological and linguistic ones. While they are for the most part mental processes (the motor processes of moving one's eyes and hands being the only outward physical ones), they still require the synergistic coordination of component processes to achieve the goal processes of reading and writing (Rumelhart, 1977). So while the component processes (or skills) of reading—like eye movements, letter and word perception and recognition, decoding, comprehension, and so forth—can be isolated and practiced, they must be used in process for the synergistic workings of each to result in *reading*, defined as comprehension of print. Since the workings of each part of a process look and act differently in process, the individual processes involved in reading and writing must be, and are, learned in process.

So these truths about process and the relationships between wholes and parts of processes help me understand the success the struggling readers with whom I work achieve as a result of reading whole texts for meaning. While doing this, they practice the parts of the process in process with all of the other parts and thus learn to use those parts in process. Learning and practicing of the parts in process—through reading whole texts for meaning—result in my ability to capture signs of development on norm-referenced tests both for the whole (comprehension) and for each of the parts (vocabulary, decoding, rate). It is not magic after all; it can be explained through knowledge of information processing and process learning.

The Importance of Focusing on Where You Are Going
One of my favorite metaphors for learning to read and for teaching others to read is that of riding a bike. Remember that when riding a bike, and when learning to ride a bike, it is critical that you do not look at the handlebars or even at the ground right in front of the bike. Rather, you must look ahead toward where you intend to go. Only by focusing on your goal do you stand a

chance of keeping your balance and of keeping the bike moving straight and smoothly over the ground. You can see how this principle holds for other processes like walking, talking, and skiing.

This also holds for reading. Struggling readers make more progress, practicing and mastering the parts of the process in process, when they are reading for real purposes. A real purpose is one for which real people read in the real world: for enjoyment and escape; for information; for learning rules; for following directions; for finding out what movies are playing; for playing games; for defending oneself; for maintaining contact with friends and family; for all of the reasons people read print to do things as they move through life, engaging in work and recreation. The purpose of a reading event is the goal of the act, the intentionality of the process; thus, it is the "focus on where you are going," and it plays the same role as this focus does with all processes. It enables the doer to work all the parts together synergistically, to move forward with balance and fluency.

Learning by the Side of the Pool

So far I have focused on those process principles that help explain the success that my students evidenced when I involved them in reading whole texts for real purposes as compared to working on the pieces of the reading process separately. However, since that time in my teaching experience, as I continued to work with readers who struggle for a variety of reasons, I have come to understand how I, while adhering to these principles, can also address the individual confusions and knowledge gaps that are responsible for the difficulties that these readers have. The need to do this, and to go beyond involving struggling readers in the reading of whole texts for real purposes, became increasingly clear to me as I observed individual students who, while becoming more proficient and fluent in ways that showed on norm-referenced tests, also continued to have difficulty with academic literacy tasks. These difficulties were specific to different types of problems that my students evidenced and demanded individual responses from instruction to remediate them.

For this discussion, we need to shift our focus now to the parts of the process. While it is true that the working of the parts is determined by the working of the whole, it is equally true that the misworking of one or more of the parts will hamper, slow down, or bring to a grinding halt the working of the whole. Back to our analogies of swimming or bicycle riding: It is easy to see that a bad stroke will make swimming harder and less fluid, and the wrong pedaling movements will hinder, or render impossible, the efficient movement of the bicycle. Similarly, poor decoding or inefficient comprehension strategies will make the process of reading difficult, dysfluent, and ineffective—that is the purpose for which one is reading is likely to be beyond reach. The smooth operation of the parts of the reading process needs to be ensured to render the whole successful.

A Process Must Be Assessed, and Diagnosed, in Process. I often use the jumping-rope metaphor to help teachers understand their role in assessing or diagnosing problems that could account for struggling readers. Imagine someone came to you and asked you to help a child who could not learn to jump rope. What would you do? After much discussion and work with jump ropes, everyone always comes to the bottom line—the common principle—of what one would need to do: watch that child try to jump rope. And while watching, pay attention to the parts of the process. First, is the rope of the right weight and length for this particular child? Is she holding the rope correctly? Is she using the correct wrist action? Is she jumping in a rhythm that is coordinated with the rope movement? Is her posture enabling her to pass the rope over her head in an efficient manner? And so on. One can do the same thought experiment with the process of bicycle riding. To help someone who is having problems learning to ride a bike, one would watch him riding a bike. While doing so, observe: Is he holding the handlebars correctly? Is he pedaling in the right direction? With the right kind of pressure? And in the right rhythm? Is his posture such that it enables him to lean a little forward to pedal while controlling the handlebars? Is he looking where he is going? So the first principle of diagnosis of a process is to observe that process in process.

The same holds for the reading process. While we can observe the parts of the process in isolation of the others, to truly know the degree and manner in which they affect the whole, we need to observe the parts as they interact synergistically during the operation of the whole process. As a result, we can begin to construct tentative hypotheses about which part, or parts, are misfunctioning and interrupting the smooth operation of the whole. (See Lipson & Wixson, 1997, for a more complete description of the tentative diagnosis of reading problems procedures.) Once this is done, and the diagnosis is confirmed through several types of diagnostic procedures, we can select which parts of the reading process to focus on for what I call "side-of-the-pool" activities and practice.

Side-of-the-Pool Activities. Side-of-the-pool activities are those that isolate pieces of the reading process for concentrated teaching or learning and practice. They are so named because they are akin to hanging on to the side of a swimming pool in order to practice kicking for a while before going back to actual swimming. In a like manner, a teacher may decide, through various assessments and observation, that a learner does not know the graphophonic correspondences for the short vowels. In fact, when this reader attempts to read text, she guesses which vowel sound is represented in a word, using only the contexts of meaning and syntax. When you pull the words out of context, this lack of knowledge becomes clear. This gap in her knowledge results in the mis-functioning of the whole process and causes the reading to be halting and in-accurate, and ultimately results in a loss of meaning. All of these difficulties also make the process fatiguing and dissatisfying so the learner avoids it and perceives it as unpleasant, rendering the learning of the process impossible. This misfunctioning does not only happen with the piece of reading relating to decoding or word recognition. Inefficient use of active comprehension strategies can also hinder the overall process of reading for meaning, and this also can be recognized through observation and through confirming assess-ment procedures.

After tentatively identifying whatever part of the process is causing diffi-culties, side-of-the-pool activities can be implemented. The key to these be-ing identified as side-of-the-pool and not as isolated, unconnected skill work lies in their relation to the whole process. First, students need to be primarily involved in functional reading events; their intentional goal is one that involves reading for meaning to accomplish an authentic literacy purpose. Within this, the teacher, or tutor, can then plan focused skill lessons that help the reader master those skills that are undeveloped, poorly developed, or misapplied and that are making the whole process difficult and hindering ongoing litera-cy development. After working through these skill-based activities, the reader then reenters the "pool," returns to the functional reading activity, practicing the worked-upon skill and using it in conjunction with all of the other com-ponent processes of reading for meaning until it becomes a smoothly func-tioning part of the larger whole. I, and others, have termed this instructional sequence "Whole-Part-Whole."

Explicit Explanations. During these side-of-the-pool activities, teachers are more effective if they use explicit language and engage in explicit explanation of the skills and knowledge to be learned. A swimming coach would not leave a struggling swimmer to discover where and why his kick was off; she would explicitly point out to her student what she believed he was doing wrong and offer clear suggestions as to how he could fix it and do it better. In the same way, a teacher of a struggling reader needs to pinpoint problem skill areas (component processes) and offer clear and explicit explanation of how the reader can fix them so that they can be plugged back into the whole and the goal of reading can be achieved with greater ease and fluency.

This principle of explicit explanation also includes answering questions from students about the process. One of the characteristics common among struggling, remedial readers is a stance of passivity in the face of reading and writing challenges (Johnston, 1985). Often, one can see readers stopping cold when they encounter a word they cannot read in text or avoiding writing words they do not know how to spell. They rely on either the active intervention of a teacher or peers (giving them the word when reading) or avoid the literacy effort altogether. So when, within the energy generated by reading or writing self-chosen texts for authentic purposes, these students take the active route of asking questions about words, needing feedback so that they can get on with their reading or writing, I believe that the teacher needs to give them that feedback clearly and explicitly.

I recently observed in a class of first through third graders with a high proportion of special needs students. The team teachers involved the children in a number of exciting and promising activities that engaged the students in composing, editing, and reading of self-generated texts. During individual writing time, when each student worked on his or her individual texts, I sat with the teacher, who was available for individual consultation. During this time, I observed several children approach the teacher for help with spelling a word. Each time, the teacher made it clear to the students that they were to do the best they could with spelling and that to ask for the correct spelling was inappropriate. In essence, the teacher refused to help them spell conventionally; they were expected to discover the conventional spelling over time on their own. The disappointment and frustration on their faces was clear. It is my belief, and experience, that these students who had been motivated to compose enough to seek out new words to spell would develop much faster if their questions, uncertainties, and attempts were met with explicit feedback that would allow them to move forward. The teacher then could have noted the words she helped them spell and incorporated them into side-of-the-pool activities to be done at another time.

Engagement, Motivation, and Self-Perception

All of this talk of process, side-of-the-pool instruction, and authentic literacy activities is informed and clarified by the recent work on motivation and engagement by the National Reading Research Center (Baker, Afflerbach, & Reinking,1996; Guthrie & Wigfield, 1997; see also Chapter 15 in this book). The factors of engagement and motivation are particularly crucial when considering readers who struggle. These readers seldom perceive themselves as readers; nor do they perceive themselves as capable of learning to read and write. Their difficulties, which for most of them began during their first years of schooling, have convinced them that reading is a difficult, unsatisfying, and unpleasant activity. Thus they avoid reading, thereby depriving themselves of opportunities to practice and solidify the skills they *have* acquired, practice that normally developing readers achieve through self-initiated reading, enabling them to develop further. Without this practice, most struggling readers fail to develop the automaticity needed for fluent, effective reading (Stanovich, 1986).

This scenario is redrawn, however, when struggling readers are involved in choosing their own texts and their own purposes for reading. By focusing on the functionality of reading—the personal, intentional functionality of reading—struggling readers raise their levels of engagement in the reading process to the point that the energy that accompanies this engagement allows for the effort needed to apply newly learned reading strategies to the task at hand. With their eyes on the goal of their reading, students become willing and able to learn the specific skills and strategies needed to reach that goal. Functional, authentic reading activities enable skill and strategy learning.

Further, as struggling readers see and feel themselves actually reading and getting pleasure and satisfaction from it (achieving an authentic literacy goal), they begin to reshape their perceptions of themselves as readers and as learners. They begin to consider the possibility that this is something that they *can* do. They begin to try, take risks, and push themselves, all necessary components of further development. One of the first types of feedback I always get from parents of the children who attend the literacy centers I have directed reflects this change in self-perception as related to motivation and engagement: "My child is trying to read more things." "He is picking up books and magazines on his own and trying to read them." "He is reading road signs and advertisements out loud." This change in self-perception and the related risk taking always precede any real (at least observable) change in ability or skill level for the students. So I do not believe it is primarily related to increased ability to read. Rather, I think it is more related to the newly experienced functionality of reading, brought about by supported involvement in authentic, purposeful literacy activities.

Agreed-Upon Principles Reflected in Success for Readers Who Struggle

This description of readers who struggle and the success they can experience has been an up-close and personal description of my insights, understandings, and beliefs about this topic. These come from my many years of experience teaching and learning from readers of all ages who found learning to read more difficult than the typical learner. My years of working with such readers—and of studying in the areas of psychology, linguistics, anthropology, and teaching and learning—took place in the historical era during which our understandings of the reading process, of cognition, and of language development evolved and came together so that the common understanding of reading was that of a language process and of reading development as a particular instance of language development. Thus, it is not surprising that my insights into the phenomenon of remedial reading reflect many of the points of agreement (see Flippo, 1998; refer to Chapter 1 in this book) made by the experts in this book.

Clearly, the following clustered summary agreements are reflected in my presentation of factors that facilitate success for struggling readers:

- combining reading with other language processes,
- providing functional, authentic contexts and purposes for reading,
- developing students' positive perceptions and expectations,
- using a variety of printed texts to reflect the different genres and functions of reading, and
- placing the focus on the purposes for reading by encouraging and allowing silent reading rather than shining the instructional spotlight on the performance of reading by insisting on oral reading for shows of proficiency and for evaluation.

These positive contexts and practices for reading instruction, as shown throughout this book, are facilitative of literacy development for many kinds of readers and for many kinds of learners. They are not only specific to readers who struggle. As the National Research Council's report on the prevention of difficulties in young children asserts in the introduction to their findings, "Excellent instruction is the best intervention for children who demonstrate problems learning to read" (Snow, Burns, & Griffin, 1998, p. 3).

REFERENCES

Baker, L., Afflerbach, P., & Reinking, D. (Eds.). (1996). *Developing engaged readers in school and home communities.* Hillsdale, NJ: Erlbaum.

Flippo, R.F. (1998). Points of agreement: A display of professional unity in our field. *The Reading Teacher, 52*, 30–40.

Guthrie, J.T., & Wigfield, A. (Eds.). (1997). *Reading engagement: Motivating readers through integrated instruction.* Newark, DE: International Reading Association.

Johnston, P.H. (1985). Understanding reading disability: A case study approach. *Harvard Educational Review, 55*, 153–177.

Lipson, M.Y., & Wixson, K.K. (1997). *Assessment & instruction of reading and writing disability* (2nd ed.). New York: Addison-Wesley.

Rumelhart, D.E. (1977). Toward an interactive model of reading. In S. Dornic (Ed.), *Attention and performance XI.* Hillsdale, NJ: Erlbaum.

Snow, C.E., Burns, M.S., & Griffin, P. (Eds.). (1998). *Preventing reading difficulties in young children.* Washington, DC: National Academy Press.

Stanovich, K.E. (1986). Matthew effects in reading: Some consequences of individual differences in the acquisition of literacy. *Reading Research Quarterly, 21*, 360–406.

CHAPTER 15

What We Know About Motivation to Read

Linda B. Gambrell

There is an extensive body of theory and research-based knowledge about the broad area of motivation to learn. Only recently, however, er, have researchers begun to explore the nature of reading motivation. Although the research base on reading motivation is limited, recent research has provided insights about the relationship between reading motivation and reading achievement. We know there is great variation in the motivation that young children bring to the task of learning to read, and that a significant number of students expend only minimal effort on learning to read. It is also generally acknowledged that there are many cognitive, social, and affective factors that influence the amount of energy that students expend on reading tasks. Consequently, if we can find ways of increasing motivation and the amount of effort that young children expend on literacy learning, the impact on reading achievement would be significant.

Motivation is of considerable consequence in reading development for a number of reasons. First, motivation often makes the difference between learning that is superficial and shallow and learning that is deep and internalized (Gambrell, 1996). Second, we know that children who are motivated and who spend more time reading are better readers (Anderson, Wilson, & Fielding, 1988; Morrow, 1992; Taylor, Frye, & Maruyama, 1990). Third, supporting and nurturing reading motivation and achievement is crucial to improving the educational prospects of all children, and particularly those who find learning to read difficult (Allington, 1986; Smith-Burke, 1989). Teachers have long recognized that motivation is at the heart of many of the pervasive problems we face in teaching young children to read. Because of the powerful influence that motivation plays in early literacy learning, teachers are more interested than ever before in understanding the relationships that exist between motivation and literacy development, and in learning how to help all students achieve the goal of becoming effective, lifelong readers.

The value that teachers, as well as reading experts, place on motivation is supported by a robust research literature that documents the link between motivation and achievement (Dweck, 1986; Elley, 1992; Flippo, 1998 [refer to Chapter 1 in this book]; Gambrell & Morrow, 1998; Guthrie et al., 1996). Highly motivated readers generate their own reading opportunities. They want to read and choose to read for a wide range of personal reasons, such as curiosity, involvement, social interchange, and emotional satisfaction. According to Guthrie et al. (1996), highly motivated readers generate their own literacy learning opportunities and, in doing so, they begin to determine their own destiny as literacy learners.

Historically, researchers have viewed and studied reading primarily as a cognitive process (see Wigfield & Guthrie, 1997, for a more detailed discussion). However, because reading is an effortful activity that involves choice (e.g., Am I going to read or watch television?), motivation is crucial to understanding reading engagement. Pintrich, Marx, and Boyle (1993) have suggested that "cold cognitive models" cannot explain fully children's participation in activities such as reading or their acquisition of reading skills. A more complete picture of the reading process will be possible only when we more fully understand the interplay among motivational, social, and cognitive processes involved in reading.

Motivation is a construct that is complex; consequently, an ever increasing number of motivational theories have been put forth in an effort to explain the role of motivation in learning. Kuhl (1986) used the term to designate all latent and aroused goal states that drive, orient, and select behavior at any given point in time. Wittrock (1986) defined motivation as the process of initiating, sustaining, and directing activity. Maehr (1976) focused on the concept of continuing motivation, which he defined as the tendency to return to and continue working on tasks away from the instructional context in which they were initially presented. More recently, Oldfather and colleagues (Oldfather & Dahl, 1994; Oldfather & McLaughlin, 1993) have defined motivation as the "continuing impulse to learn." In Oldfather's (1993) view, literacy motivation is an ongoing engagement in literacy activities that is propelled and focused by both thought and feeling emerging from the learner's search for meaning.

Contemporary theories of motivation emphasize the importance of self-perception in learning (Dweck, 1986; McCombs, 1989; Weiner, 1990; Wigfield, 1994). Motivation is viewed as a function of individuals' *learned* beliefs about their worth, abilities, or competencies. A vast body of research (Bandura, 1977, 1989; Covington, 1985; Dweck, 1986; Eccles et al., 1993; Weiner, 1990; Wigfield, 1994) supports the contention that learned self-beliefs, expectations, and goals are critical factors that affect motivation and performance. In the following sections, motivation theories are briefly discussed, relevant research is presented, and theory and research-based recommendation for creating classroom contexts that support motivation to read are described.

Motivation: Theoretical Conceptualizations and Related Research

Fundamentally, motivation refers to what moves people to put forth effort. Motivational theorists, therefore, are concerned primarily with the "whys" of behavior. To understand motivation's influence on literacy behavior, theorists and researchers are interested in the choices students make about the reading they do, the amount of effort they exert on reading tasks, and their degree of persistence in the activity of reading.

There are a vast number of motivational theories that are relevant to the topic of motivation to read. Many of these theories overlap in principles and constructs (Bergin & Lafave, 1998); however, current theories of motivation are in general agreement about the importance of self-concept as a learner and learning goals. While there are numerous theories of motivation that have direct implications for reading instruction, four overarching theoretical orientations have helped to inform us about motivation and learning: expectancy-value theory, goal orientation theory, intrinsic and extrinsic theories of motivation, and motivational systems theory.

Expectancy-Value Theory

A number of current theories suggest that self-perceived competence and task value are major determinants of motivation and task engagement (Eccles et al., 1983; Pintrich & Degroot, 1990; Pintrich, Roeser, & DeGroot, 1994; Wigfield, 1994). Eccles et al. (1983) and Wigfield (1994) have advanced an expectancy-value theory (EVT) of motivation that posits that motivation is strongly influenced by one's expectation of success or failure at a task as well as the value or relative attractiveness the individual places on the task. The expectancy component of EVT is supported by a number of research studies that suggest that students who believe they are capable and competent readers are more likely to outperform those who do not hold such beliefs (Paris & Oka, 1986; Schunk, 1985).

In a survey-interview study designed to explore EVT, Gambrell (1995) interviewed third- and fifth-grade students and analyzed their responses by reading ability level (above grade level, on grade level, and below grade level). The results revealed a statistically significant difference among reading ability groups with respect to self-concept as a reader (expectancy). Responses of students reading below grade level in both third and fifth grade were lower in self-perceived reading competence. In addition, at the third-grade level, there were ability level differences with respect to self-perceived competence relative to peers, decoding ability, oral reading, and responding to questions about reading, with the below-grade-level students reporting lower self-perceived competence as compared to the on-grade-level and above-grade-level groups. On the other hand, there were no statistically significant differences among reading ability groups with respect to the value of reading for either grade level. This finding raises some interesting questions with respect to the EVTs of motivation. Perhaps self-concept or expectancy is a more critical factor in the reading motivation of young children than is the construct of value. In this study, elementary students in both third and fifth grade seem to place a high value on reading regardless of their reading ability; however, significant differences in motivation were apparent across reading ability groups with respect to self-perceived competence or expectancy.

Goal Orientation Theory

In goal orientation theory, learning goals are distinct from performance goals (Dweck & Elliot, 1983). A student with a learning goal in reading might want to learn about the topic of aviation, whereas a student with a performance goal would want to learn about aviation in order to make an "A" on a test. Both types of motivation goals can result in increased effort and attention; however, research suggests that learning goals are more likely to result in high-level learning and increased time devoted to the task. Students who have literacy learning goals engage in reading tasks for pleasure or in order to acquire knowledge. Teachers who foster literacy learning goals emphasize understanding, enjoyment, and the usefulness of reading and writing rather than making good grades or competition (doing better as compared to others). On the other hand, teachers who emphasize performance goals are more likely to reward correct performance and emphasize task completion, rather than understanding, enjoyment, and the value of literacy learning. Research by Ames and Archer (1988) suggests that students in classrooms that emphasize learning goals are more likely to have greater use of learning strategies than those in classrooms that emphasize performance goals. In a study with fifth and sixth graders, Meece, Blumenfeld, and Hoyle (1988) reported that students who held learning goals were more likely to report active cognitive engagement in learning tasks, as compared to students who held performance goals. According to Maehr (1976), a learning goal orientation is more likely to foster intrinsic motivation, enjoyment, and continuing impulse to learn.

Intrinsic and Extrinsic Theories of Motivation

Most motivational theorists identify two types of motivation: extrinsic and intrinsic (Deci & Ryan, 1985; Lepper & Hodell, 1989). Behavior is said to be extrinsically motivated when done to satisfy some external goal, such as doing well on a spelling test in order to earn the privilege of a Saturday outing. Intrinsically motivated behavior, on the other hand, is characterized by a desire to engage in an activity because doing so brings personal satisfaction.

Dichotomous theories of motivation that pit learning as a self-initiated process against learning as a conditioning process provide the context for viewing motivation as either intrinsic or extrinsic. According to Deci (1972, 1992) and Csikszentmihalyi (1990), intrinsically motivated actions are performed out of interest and require no incentive other than the spontaneous experience of enjoyment, interest, and satisfaction that accompanies them. Extrinsically motivated behaviors, on the other hand, are performed for the external incentive or consequence that follows from their performance (Bandura, 1977; Skinner, 1953).

While the distinction between intrinsic and extrinsic motivation is an important one, the simplistic intrinsic-extrinsic dichotomy has often led to confusion and misinterpretation. While early studies tended to support the view that intrinsic and extrinsic motivation are antagonistic (Deci, 1971, 1972; Lepper, Greene, & Nesbit, 1973), more recent studies have suggested that, under certain circumstances extrinsic incentives (tangible and intangible) can enhance intrinsic motivation to learn (McLoyd, 1979; Ryan & Grolnick, 1986; Ryan, Mims, & Koestner 1983).

Teacher praise and feedback are intangible extrinsic incentives that have been shown to positively influence student attitudes and behavior. Lepper and Cordova (1992) found that verbal rewards in the form of teacher praise that provided verbal scaffolding, support, direction, and additional information led to more motivated, confident problem solving. In addition, they reported that elaborated or embellished praise was more motivational than tangible incentives. One of the most important findings in the research on motivation and learning is the facilitating effect of teacher praise and feedback on student achievement (Cameron & Pierce, 1994; Deci, 1971). One notable characteristic of both teacher praise and feedback is that they are, by their very nature, always closely linked to the desired student behavior, while tangible incentives (e.g., gold stars, stickers, toys) are usually unrelated to the desired behavior.

While the research provides clear evidence that intangible rewards such as teacher praise and feedback, under certain conditions, enhance intrinsic motivation, the research is less clear about the effects of tangible incentives on student performance. Some studies report a decrease in intrinsic motivation following the receipt of a tangible reward (Deci, 1971, 1972, 1992; Lepper, Greene, & Nesbit, 1973) while others report an increase in motivation (Brennan & Glover, 1980; Karnoil & Ross, 1977). Very little research on the relationship between motivation and the use of incentives has been conducted in the field of reading. Only one study could be located that clearly addressed the issue of incentives and reading development (McLoyd, 1979). In this study, McLoyd examined the effects of high-value versus low-value rewards on children's intrinsic interest in reading a high-interest versus low-interest book. The results of the study revealed that when the amount of time spent reading and the approximate number of words read were used as indices of intrinsic interest in reading, both high- and low-value rewards decreased children's interest in reading the high-interest book. On the other hand, high-value rewards increased significantly children's interest in reading the low-interest book. It appears that highly valued incentives may enhance subsequent interest and involvement in tasks that children find relatively uninteresting.

Based on the results of a study that examined the effects of rewarding children for reading by providing books as an incentive, Gambrell (1996) put forth the reward proximity hypothesis. The reward proximity hypothesis suggests that intrinsic motivation is enhanced when the incentive is linked to the desired behavior. For example, if one wants to foster intrinsic motivation to read, appropriate incentives that are clearly linked to the desired behavior of reading might include books, bookmarks, or even extra time for reading. The reward proximity hypothesis posits that a person's intrinsic motivation will be enhanced if an incentive not only rewards the desired behavior but also reflects the value of the behavior and encourages future engagement in the desired behavior (Gambrell & Marinak, 1997). Clearly, there is a need to investigate the role of incentives in the reading curriculum, particularly given the finding by Moore and Fawson (1992) that 95% of elementary teachers use some variation of a reading incentive program in their classrooms.

Wigfield and Guthrie (1997) also looked at how students varying in motivation differed in the amount and breadth of their reading. They measured both intrinsic and extrinsic aspects of motivation. They found that students who were highest in intrinsic motivation read nearly three times as many minutes per day as did the students who were lowest in intrinsic motivation, and those students who were highest in intrinsic motivation also read more broadly. By contrast, groups high and low in extrinsic motivation did not differ nearly as much on the different measures of the amount and breadth of reading.

Motivational Systems Theory

Ford's (1992) motivational systems theory (MST) centers on three aspects of motivation: personal beliefs, emotional processes, and personal goals.

Personal beliefs are reflected in capability beliefs and context beliefs. Capability beliefs are self-evaluations about whether one has the capabilities needed to attain a goal, while context beliefs are evaluations of whether the environment or context will facilitate goal attainment. Taken together, capability beliefs and context beliefs provide the individual with information that guides decisions about initiating, maintaining, or avoiding learning activities.

According to Ford's MST, *emotional processes* provide an individual with evaluative information about personal values. Emotional processes result in an "energization" of behavior that is reflected in what "turns someone on" or "turns them off," what one likes or does not like, what one values or does not value. The clarity and saliency of personal values influences what is learned and remembered.

Personal goals represent desired future learning outcomes. The term *personal goal* is emphasized because the goals that direct an individual's activity are always within the person (Weiner, 1990). An individual's goals or reasons for engaging in an activity are often contextual in that people will adopt many of the goals shared by other individuals in their environment as well as those assigned by authority figures or significant others, such as parents or teachers.

Ford's MST suggests that people will always try to attain goals they value within the limitations of what they think they can achieve based on their capability and context beliefs. This notion is consistent with Winne and Marx's (1982) assertion that a positive state of motivation is a necessary condition for learning. Ford's MST is also in keeping with Winne's (1985) theory of motivation that suggests that the idealized reader feels competent as a reader, values reading, chooses to read, and engages in reading activities with intensity.

In the MST, goals, emotions, and personal beliefs are related and influence one another. While personal goals, emotional processes, and personal beliefs are internal processes, the MST emphasizes that motivation rests upon the interaction among persons and context. According to Ford (1992) and Bergin and LaFave (1998), context is an essential consideration in understanding motivation.

Taken together, these motivation theories and related research suggest that motivation is strongly influenced by one's expectation of success or failure at a task as well as the value or relative attractiveness the individual places on the task. Students who believe they are capable and competent readers are more likely to outperform those who do not hold such beliefs (Paris & Oka, 1986; Schunk, 1985). In addition, students who perceive reading as valuable and important and who have personally relevant reasons for reading will engage in reading in a more planned and effortful manner (Ames & Archer, 1988; Dweck & Elliott, 1983; Paris & Oka, 1986).

What Research Reveals About Factors Associated With Reading Motivation

Two lines of research have provided important insights about schooling and reading motivation. One line of research explores the decline in motivation to read as children move up the grades in school. The other, more recent line of research has focused on classroom factors associated with reading motivation.

In studies of school motivation, most researchers have found that children begin school with optimistic beliefs and attitudes related to reading. For many children, these initially positive beliefs and attitudes decline across the elementary years (Eccles et al., 1993; Stipek, 1988, 1996). In a large-scale national study, McKenna, Kear, and Ellsworth (1995) documented that positive attitudes toward reading declined as children progressed through the elementary grades. However, in a recent cross-cultural study of young children's motivation to read, Gambrell, Mazzoni, and Korkeamaki (1996) found that motivation to read increased during first grade on fall-to-spring measures and began to decline during second grade for both Finnish and U.S. students. Because U.S.

students begin first grade at age 6 and Finnish students begin first grade at age 7, this study documents a schooling rather than an age effect on reading motivation. This finding suggests that first grade may be a critical time in the development of motivation to read. Additional research is needed that will explore critical dimensions of motivation to read in first grade.

Research by Turner (1995), Morrow and Gambrell (1998), and Guthrie et al. (1998) suggests that the classroom context plays an important role in reading motivation. Turner's (1995) work in first-grade classrooms suggested the importance of open tasks that support students in choosing books, defining activities, and social interaction. The work of Morrow and Gambrell (1998) suggested the following kinds of classroom activities that have been found to foster motivation to read: materials that are easily assessable; teachers who model, guide, and scaffold reading strategies; providing for choice; activities that are meaningful and functional; social collaboration; and opportunities for success. The research conducted by Guthrie et al. (1998) documents teaching practices that foster positive reading motivation, such as conceptual themes, real-world interactions, self-direction, interesting texts, social collaboration, self-expression, cognitive strategy instruction, time for engaged reading, and coherence.

Reading Motivation: Theory, Research, and Expert Agreement

There are several clear themes that run across current theories of motivation and research studies that have focused on classroom factors associated with reading motivation. In addition, the results of Flippo's Expert Study (1998; refer to Chapter 1 in this book) suggest that there is considerable agreement about the important role of motivation. Many of the points of agreement among the experts in Flippo's study appear to be grounded in the belief that motivated children are more likely to engage in meaningful learning and that motivation is an important outcome of instruction (Bergin & LaFave, 1998). There appears to be congruence across theoretical perspectives, research findings, and reading experts—representing a range of diversity in their views and orientations toward reading education—that the following classroom characteristics foster motivation to read: access to reading materials, opportunities for self-selection, social interactions about books, and positive self-perceptions.

Access to Reading Materials

Having access to abundant materials to read—such as books, magazines, and newspapers—is critical to the development of reading motivation. Access to literacy materials encourages students to engage in reading in a voluntary and sustained manner. A number of studies during the past decade have documented that when children have classroom environments that are book rich, the motivation to read is high (Allington & McGill-Franzen, 1993; Elley, 1992; Gambrell, 1995; Guthrie et al., 1996; Lundberg & Linnakyla, 1993; Morrow, 1992; Neuman & Roskos, 1993; Purcell-Gates et al., 1995). In Flippo's Expert Study, reading experts agreed on the importance of giving students time and opportunity to read real books, both narrative and expository. Access to materials that are challenging and offer opportunities for success have consistently been found to promote motivation to read. The results of the studies cited above suggest that book access and time to read are significant factors in literacy development and that greater attention should be devoted to assuring that high-quality classroom libraries are a priority in our schools.

Opportunities for Self-Selection

Self-selection of reading material is strongly linked to motivation to read. The role of choice in motivation in general and reading motivation in particular is well documented (Gambrell, 1995; McLoyd, 1979; Spaulding, 1992; Turner, 1995). Skinner and Bellmont (1993) found that students' intrinsic motivation increased during the academic year when teachers supported student choice of learning tasks and involvement in decision making about learning activities. In addition, students in classrooms in which teachers supported student choice have demonstrated increased persistence, effort, attention, and intrinsic motivation (Ryan & Grolnick, 1986; Skinner & Bellmont, 1993). The research related to self-selection of reading material supports the notion that the books and stories that students find most interesting are those they have selected for their own reasons and purposes (Gambrell & Morrow, 1996; Palmer, Codling, & Gambrell, 1994). Schiefele's (1991) research revealed that students who were allowed and encouraged to choose their own reading material expended more effort in learning and understanding the material.

Turner's (1995) research describes how classroom literacy experiences can be described in terms of task type. Open tasks were those in which students chose books, defined their activities, interacted with their peers, and co-constructed writing assignments. Closed tasks were those in which the teacher determined the reading materials, tasks, and outcomes and students worked individually. Turner reported that open literacy tasks were more often associated with persistence than closed literacy tasks.

In Flippo's Expert Study there was consensus among reading experts that student choice and self-selection of reading materials is an important characteristic of classroom contexts that support literacy learning. For example, the reading experts rejected the notions that the teacher should "remove the freedom to make decisions about reading from the learner," and "select all the stories children read," suggesting a consensus in recognizing the importance of student choice in learning to read. Clearly, there is congruence and consensus across theory, research, and reading experts that opportunities for choice promote students' intrinsic motivation and independence as readers (see Flippo, 1998 [also refer to Chapter 1 in this book]; Gambrell, 1995; Spaulding, 1992; Turner, 1995).

Social Interactions About Books

Current theories of motivation recognize that learning is facilitated by social interactions with others (Guthrie et al., 1998; McCombs, 1989; Oldfather, 1993). A classroom environment that fosters social interaction is more likely to foster intrinsic motivation than more individualized, solitary learning environments (Ames, 1984; Deci & Ryan, 1991; Guthrie, Schafer, Wang, & Afflerbach, 1995). Guthrie et al. (1998) found that students who had opportunities to interact socially with peers during literacy activities were more intrinsically motivated to read, and they read more widely and more frequently than students who were less socially interactive. Studies by Gambrell (1995), Morrow (1992), and Stevens, Madden, Slavin, and Farnish (1987) have also demonstrated that the opportunities for social interaction enhance reading motivation. A number of recent reading studies have revealed that social interaction promotes intrinsic motivation, achievement, and higher level cognition (Almasi, 1995; Guthrie et al.,1995; Guthrie et al., 1998; Slavin, 1984, 1990). The results of the 1992 National Assessment of Educational Progress (Mullis, Campbell, & Farstrup, 1993) revealed that students who participated in frequent discussions about their reading with friends and family were more motivated and had higher reading achievement scores than did students who did not have such interactions.

There was also agreement in the Expert Study about the importance of the role of social interaction in learning to read. The reading experts supported the notion that children should be encouraged to talk about and share the different kinds of reading they do in a variety of ways with many others. Taken together, these studies suggest that motivated readers place a high priority on social interactions associated with discussions about text, and that intrinsic motivation is enhanced when students perceive the learning context to be socially supportive.

Positive Self-Concept as a Reader

There is wide acceptance of the notion that motivation is strongly influenced by one's expectation of success or failure at a task as well as the value or relative attractiveness the individual places on the task. Learning and motivation are enhanced when students believe they are capable and competent (Schunk, 1985). These notions are in keeping with the views of the experts in the Expert Study who reported that it is important to develop positive self-perceptions and expectations, and that it is also important to create classroom environments and contexts in which children become convinced that reading furthers the purposes of their lives.

Summary

There is general consensus about the importance of motivation and developing intrinsic desire to read across current theories of motivation, research, and expert opinion. We know a great deal about the construct of motivation and how to create classroom contexts that support and nurture reading motivation. However, it is worth noting that although there is an extensive theory and research base with respect to motivation and learning, the theory and research on *reading motivation* is only beginning to be explored. Clearly, there are many issues specifically related to reading motivation that will require our attention in the future in order to understand more fully how children acquire motivation to read.

REFERENCES

Allington, R.L. (1986). Policy constraints and effective compensatory reading instruction: A review. In J.V. Hoffman (Ed.), *Effective teaching of reading: Research and practice* (pp. 261–289). Newark, DE: International Reading Association.

Allington, R.L., & McGill-Franzen, A. (1993, October 13). What are they to read? Not all children, Mr. Riley, have easy access to books. *Education Week, 26.*

Almasi, J.F. (1995). The nature of fourth graders' sociocognitive conflicts in peer-led and teacher-led discussions of literature. *Reading Research Quarterly, 30,* 314–351.

Ames, C. (1984). Achievement attributions and self-instructions under competitive and individualistic goal structures. *Journal of Educational Psychology, 76,* 478–487.

Ames, C., & Archer, J. (1988). Achievement goals in the classroom: Students' learning strategies and motivation processes. *Journal of Educational Psychology, 80,* 260–267.

Anderson, R.C., Wilson, P.T., & Fielding, L.G. (1988). Growth in reading and how children spend their time outside of school. *Reading Research Quarterly, 23,* 285–303.

Bandura, A. (1977). *Principles of behavior modification.* New York: Academic.

Bandura, A. (1989). Human agency in social cognitive theory. *American Psychologist, 44,* 1175–1184.

Bergin, D.A., & LaFave, C. (1998). Continuities between motivation research and whole language philosophy of instruction. *Journal of Literacy Research, 30,* 321–356.

Brennan, T.P., & Glover, J.A. (1980). An examination of the effect of extrinsic reinforcers on intrinsically motivated behavior: Experimental and theoretical. *Social Behavior and Personality, 8,* 27–32.

Cameron, J., & Pierce, W.D. (1994). Reinforcement, reward, and intrinsic motivation: A meta-analysis. *Review of Educational Research, 64,* 363–423.

Covington, M.V. (1985). The motive for self-worth. In C. Ames & R. Ames (Eds.), *Research on motivation in education: The classroom milieu* (pp. 77–113). San Diego, CA: Academic Press.

Csikszentmihalyi, M. (1990). *Flow: The psychology of optimal experience.* New York: HarperCollins.

Deci, E.L. (1971). Effects of externally mediated rewards on intrinsic motivation. *Journal of Personality and Social Psychology, 18,* 105–115.

Deci, E.L. (1972). Intrinsic motivation, extrinsic reinforcement, and inequity. *Journal of Personality and Social Psychology, 22,* 113–120.

Deci, E.L. (1992). The relation of interest to the motivation of behavior: A self-determination theory perspective. In K.A. Renninger, S. Hidi, & A. Krapp (Eds.), *The role of interest in learning and development* (pp. 43–70). Hillsdale, NJ: Erlbaum.

Deci, E.L., & Ryan, R.M. (1985). *Intrinsic motivation and self-determination in human behavior.* San Diego, CA: Academic Press.

Deci, E.L., & Ryan, R.M. (1991). A motivational approach to self: Integration in personality. In R.A. Dienstbier (Ed.), *Perspectives on motivation: Nebraska symposium on motivation* (Vol. 38, pp. 237–288). Lincoln, NE: University of Nebraska Press.

Dweck, C.S. (1986). Motivational processes affecting learning. *American Psychologist, 41,* 1040–1048.

Dweck, C.S., & Elliot, E.S. (1983). Achievement motivation. In E.M. Hetherington (Ed.), *Socialization, personality, and social development* (pp. 643–681). New York: Wiley.

Eccles, J.S., Adler, T.F., Futterman, R.B., Koff, S.B., Kaczala, C.M., & Meece, J.L. (1983). Expectancies, values, and academic behaviors. In J.T. Spence (Ed.), *Achievement and achievement motivation* (pp. 75–146). San Francisco: Freeman.

Eccles, J.S., Wigfield, A., Harold, R., & Blumenfeld, P.C. (1993). Age and gender differences in children's self- and task perceptions during elementary school. *Child Development, 64,* 830–847.

Elley, W.B. (1992). *How in the world do students read?* Hamburg, Germany: International Association for the Evaluation of Educational Achievement.

Flippo, R.F. (1998). Points of agreement: A display of professional unity in our field. *The Reading Teacher, 52,* 30–40.

Ford, M.E. (1992). *Motivating humans.* New York: Sage.

Gambrell, L.B. (1995). Motivation matters. In W.M. Linek & E.G. Sturtevant (Eds.), *Generations of literacy: Seventeenth yearbook of the College Reading Association* (pp. 2–24). Harrisonburg, VA: College Reading Association.

Gambrell, L.B. (1996). Creating classroom cultures that foster reading motivation. *The Reading Teacher, 50,* 14–25.

Gambrell, L.B., & Marinak, B.A. (1997). Incentives and intrinsic motivation to read. In J.T. Guthrie & A. Wigfield (Eds.), *Reading engagement: Motivating readers through integrated instruction* (pp. 205–217). Newark, DE: International Reading Association.

Gambrell, L.B., Mazzoni, S., & Korkeamaki, R.L. (1996, April). *Cross-cultural models of home-school early literacy practices.* Presentation at the annual meeting of the American Educational Research Association, New York.

Gambrell, L.B., & Morrow, L.M. (1996). Creating motivating contexts for literacy learning. In L. Baker, P. Afflerbach, & D. Reinking (Eds.), *Developing engaged readers in school and home communities* (pp. 115–136). Hillsdale, NJ: Erlbaum.

Guthrie, J.T., & Alao, S. (1997). Designing contexts to increase motivations for reading. *Educational Psychologist, 32,* 95–107.

Guthrie, J.T., Cox, K., Anderson, E., Harris, K., Mazzoni, S., & Rach, L. (1998). Principles of integrated instruction for engagement in reading. *Educational Psychology Review, 10,* 177–199.

Guthrie, J.T., Schafer, W., Wang, Y., & Afflerbach, P. (1995). Relationships of instruction to amount of reading: An exploration of a social, cognitive, and instructional connection. *Reading Research Quarterly, 30,* 8–25.

Guthrie, J.T., Van Meter, P., McCann, A.D., Wigfield, A., Bender, L., Poundstone, C.C., Rice, M.E., Faibisch, F.M., Junt, B., & Mitchell, A.M. (1996). Growth of literacy engagement:

Changes in motivations and strategies during concept-oriented reading instruction. *Reading Research Quarterly, 31,* 306–325.

Guthrie, J.T., & Wigfield, A. (1997). Reading engagement: A rationale for theory and teaching. In J.T. Guthrie & A. Wigfield (Eds.), *Reading engagement: Motivating readers through integrated instruction* (pp. 1–12). Newark, DE: International Reading Association.

Karnoil, R., & Ross, M. (1977). The effect of performance relevant and performance irrelevant rewards on children's intrinsic motivation. *Child Development, 48,* 482–487.

Kuhl, J. (1986). Introduction. In J. Kuhl & J.W. Atkinson (Eds.), *Motivation, thought, and action* (pp. 1–16). New York: Praeger.

Lepper, M.R., & Cordova, D.I. (1992). A desire to be taught: Instructional consequence of intrinsic motivation. *Motivation and Emotion, 16,* 187–208.

Lepper, M.R., Greene, D., & Nesbit, R.E. (1973). Undermining children's intrinsic interest with extrinsic reward. *Journal of Personality and Social Psychology, 28,* 124–137.

Lepper, M.R., & Hodell, M. (1989). Intrinsic motivation in the classroom. In C. Ames & R. Ames (Eds.), *Research in motivation in education* (Vol. III, pp. 139–186). New York: Academic Press.

Lundberg, I., & Linnakyla, P. (1993). *Teaching reading around the world.* Hamburg, Germany: International Association for the Evaluation of Educational Achievement.

Maehr, M.L. (1976). Continuing motivation: An analysis of a seldom considered educational outcome. *Review of Educational Research, 46,* 443–462.

McCombs, B.L. (1989). Self-regulated learning and academic achievement: A phenomenological view. In B.J. Zimmerman & D.H. Schunk (Eds.), *Self-regulated learning and achievement: Theory, research, and practice* (pp. 51–82). New York: Springer-Verlag.

McKenna, M.C., Kear, D.J., & Ellsworth, R.A. (1995). Children's attitudes toward reading: A national survey. *Reading Research Quarterly, 30,* 934–956.

McLoyd, V.C. (1979). The effects of extrinsic rewards of differential value on high and low intrinsic interest. *Child Development, 50,* 1010–1019.

Meece, J.L., Blumenfeld, P.C., & Hoyle, R.H. (1988). Students' goal orientations and cognitive engagement in classroom activities. *Journal of Education Psychology, 80,* 514–523.

Moore, S.A., & Fawson, P.C. (1992, December). *Reading incentive programs: Beliefs and practices.* Paper presented at the 42nd Annual Meeting of the National Reading Conference, San Antonio, Texas.

Morrow, L.M. (1992). The impact of a literature-based program on literacy achievement, use of literature, and attitudes of children from minority backgrounds. *Reading Research Quarterly, 27,* 250–275.

Morrow, L.M., & Gambrell, L.B. (1998). How do we motivate children toward independent reading and writing? In S.B. Neuman & K.A. Roskos (Eds.), *Children achieving: Best practices in early literacy* (pp. 144–161). Newark, DE: International Reading Association.

Mullis, I.V.S., Campbell, J.R., & Farstrup, A.E. (1993). *NAEP 1992 reading report card for the nation and the states.* Washington, DC: Office of Educational Research and Improvement.

Neuman, S.B., & Roskos, K.A. (1993). Access to print for children of poverty: Differential effects of adult mediation and literacy-enriched play settings on environmental and function print tasks. *American Educational Research Journal, 32,* 801–828.

Oldfather, P. (1993). What students say about motivating experiences in a whole language classroom. *The Reading Teacher, 46,* 672–681.

Oldfather, P. (1995). Commentary: What's needed to maintain and extend motivation for literacy in the middle grades. *Journal of Reading, 38,* 420–422.

Oldfather, P., & Dahl, K. (1994). Toward a social constructivist reconceptualization of intrinsic motivation for literacy learning. *Journal of Reading Behavior, 26*, 139–158.

Oldfather, P., & McLaughlin, J. (1993). Gaining and losing voice: A longitudinal study of students' continuing impulse to learn across elementary and middle school contexts. *Research in Middle Level Education, 17*, 1–25.

Palmer, B.M., Codling, R.M., & Gambrell, L.B. (1994). In their own words: What elementary children have to say about motivation to read. *The Reading Teacher, 48*, 176–179.

Paris, S.G., & Oka, E.R. (1986). Self-regulated learning among exceptional children. *Exceptional Children, 53*, 103–108.

Pintrich, P.R., & DeGroot, E.V. (1990). Motivational and self-regulated learning components of classroom academic performance. *Journal of Educational Psychology, 82*, 33–40.

Pintrich, P.R., Marx, R.W., & Boyle, R.A. (1993). Beyond cold conceptual change: The role of motivational beliefs and classroom contextual factors in the process of conceptual change. *Review of Educational Research, 63*, 167–199.

Pintrich, P.R., Roeser, R.W., & DeGroot, E.A.M., (1994). Classroom and individual differences in early adolescents' motivation and self-regulated learning. *Journal of Early Adolescence, 14*, 139–161.

Purcell-Gates, V., McIntyre, E., & Freppon, P.A. (1995). Learning written storybook language in school: A comparison of low-SES children in skills-based and whole language classrooms. *American Educational Research Journal, 32*, 659–685.

Ryan, R.M., & Grolnick, W. (1986). Origins and pawns in the classroom: Self-report and projective assessments of individual differences in children's perceptions. *Journal of Personality and Social Psychology, 50*, 550–558.

Ryan, R.M., Mims, V., & Koestner, R. (1983). Relation of reward contingency and interpersonal context to intrinsic motivation: A review and test using cognitive evaluation theory. *Journal of Personality and Social Psychology, 45*, 736–750.

Schiefele, U. (1991). Interest, learning, and motivation. *Educational Psychologist, 26*, 299–323.

Schunk, D. (1985). Self-efficacy and school learning. *Psychology in the Schools, 22*, 208–223.

Skinner, B.F. (1953). *Science and human behavior.* New York: Macmillan.

Skinner, E.A., & Bellmont, M.J. (1993). Motivation in the classroom: Reciprocal effects of teacher behavior and student engagement across the school year. *Journal of Educational Psychology, 85*, 571–581.

Slavin, R.E. (1984). Students motivating students to excel: Cooperative incentives, cooperative tasks, and student achievement. *The Elementary School Journal, 84*, 23–63.

Slavin, R.E. (1990). *Cooperative learning: Theory, research, and practice.* Englewood Cliffs, NJ: Prentice Hall.

Smith-Burke, T.M. (1989). Political and economic dimensions of literacy: Challenges for the 1990's. In S. McCormick & J. Zutell (Eds.), *Cognitive and social perspectives for literacy research and instruction* (pp. 1–18). Chicago: National Reading Conference.

Spaulding, C.L. (1992). The motivation to read and write. In J.W. Irwin & M.A. Doyle (Eds.), *Reading/writing connections: Learning from research* (pp. 177–201). Newark, DE: International Reading Association.

Stevens, J.R., Madden, N.A., Slavin, R.E., & Farnish, A.M. (1987). Cooperative integrated reading and composition: Two field experiments. *Reading Research Quarterly, 22*, 433–454.

Stipek, D.J. (1988). *Motivation to learn: From theory to practice.* Englewood Cliffs, NJ: Prentice Hall.

Stipek, D.J. (1996). Motivation and instruction. In D.C. Berliner & R.C. Calfee (Eds.), *Handbook of educational psychology* (pp. 85–113). New York: Macmillan.

Taylor, B.M., Frye, B.J., & Maruyama, G.M. (1990). Time spent reading and reading growth. *American Educational Research Journal, 27,* 351–362.

Turner, J.C. (1995). The influence of classroom contexts on young children's motivation for literacy. *Reading Research Quarterly, 30,* 410–441.

Weiner, B. (1990). History of motivational research in education. *Journal of Educational Psychology, 92,* 616–622.

Wigfield, A. (1994). *Dimensions of children's motivations for reading: An initial study.* Paper presented at the annual meeting of the American Educational Research Association, New Orleans, Louisiana.

Wigfield, A., & Guthrie, J.T. (1997). Relations of children's motivation for reading to the amount and breadth of their reading. *Journal of Educational Psychology, 9,* 420–433.

Winne, P. (1985). Steps toward promoting cognitive achievements. *The Elementary School Journal, 85,* 673–693.

Winne, P., & Marx, R. (1982). Students' and teachers' views of thinking processes for classroom learning. *The Elementary School Journal, 82,* 493–518.

Wittrock, M.C. (1986). Students' thought processes. In M.C. Wittrock (Ed.), *Handbook of research on teaching* (pp. 297–314). New York: Macmillan.

PART III

TOWARD A COMMON GROUND

R eaching a common ground of understanding in the field of reading education should be one of the primary goals of debate and discussion in this academic arena. In this section, invited assessment and reading education authorities and reading researcher Rona Flippo reach toward this common ground by examining the evidence they see.

In the first chapter of this section, Jay Campbell, first author of the 1994 National Assessment of Educational Progress (NAEP), succinctly reviews the NAEP's results and implications, especially in relation to the findings of the Expert Study (Flippo, 1998; refer to Chapter 1 in this book). Although the achievement of a consensus on all matters dealing with reading education would be a difficult and probably impossible accomplishment, Campbell points out that there is clearly a relatively large number of commonalities in terms of accepted literacy practices and contexts. He also observes that the development and understanding of the NAEP, in the context of a broad national constituency, fits readily with the various agreements of the reading experts in the Expert Study, further validating these agreements.

In his contribution to this volume, Timothy Rasinski, who was for many years coeditor of the International Reading Association (IRA) journal *The Reading Teacher*, discusses the seeming contradiction in the fact that although there is now a general coming together of reading professionals on some of the basic tenets of effective reading instruction, as evidenced by the Expert Study, this commonality of beliefs is not evident in the understanding of reading practices by parents and the general public. He clearly blames the educational community for this basic lack of providing vital information to parents on important literacy developments. The result of this communication failure is simply a general public that seeks the "perfect answer" to reading success, often through solutions that may seem attractive on the surface but in reality are superficial at best (Duffy & Hoffman, 1999). Rasinski urges us, now that we have common ground, to let parents and the general public know about it.

Richard Vacca, past President of IRA, continues the discussion, noting the role of policy-driven literacy practices and its relationship with the media in helping determine the public's feelings and beliefs related to current reading instruction. He makes a strong case for the fact that people in the United States— primarily through a series of reports and books such as *A Nation at Risk*

(National Commission on Excellence in Education, 1983) and *Why Johnny Can't Read* (Flesch, 1955), as well as certain test results from the NAEP and SAT—have been convinced that there is a "reading crisis." He notes work by individuals such as Berliner and Biddle (1995), which provides convincing evidence that what is referred to as the "educational crisis" in general and the current "reading disaster" is a misinterpretation or misunderstanding of what is actually happening in our schools. Vacca builds a strong case that the educational community, especially classroom teachers, must become proactive in their important roles as policy makers in the field of reading instruction, and he also urges us to make the agreements from Flippo's Expert Study known to the media and to policy makers.

Rona F. Flippo's summary chapter pulls together what she sees as "the real common ground" in the field of reading. As she notes, the results of her research study and the contributions to this volume clearly indicate agreements between many experts in the field of reading education. This important conclusion, despite wide divergence at times by the resident reading experts on various and other specific points related to reading instruction, is explained and detailed by Flippo. Although it is important to realize that there is a common ground that exists in reading education, it is even more critical to decide how we can use this knowledge to help inform future policy decisions. This common ground among reading researchers, as revealed and summarized in this volume, is noted by Flippo as an opportunity and an invitation to continue the discussion in hopes of sharing common understandings and having more impact on reading-related policies in schools. In fact, Flippo reminds us of her new, ongoing study to solicit the agreements and views of classroom teachers regarding contexts and practices for reading instruction (1999) and urges teachers to take part and get involved.

Richard D. Robinson

REFERENCES

Berliner, D.C., & Biddle, B.J. (1995). *The manufactured crisis: Myths, fraud, and the attack on America's public schools.* New York: Addison-Wesley.

Duffy, G.G., & Hoffman, J.V. (1999). In pursuit of an illusion: The flawed search for a perfect method. *The Reading Teacher, 53,* 10–16.

Flesch, R. (1955). *Why Johnny can't read—And what you can do about it.* New York: Harper & Brothers.

Flippo, R.F. (1998). Points of agreement: A display of professional unity in our field. *The Reading Teacher, 52,* 30–40.

Flippo, R.F. (1999). *What do the experts say? Helping children learn to read.* Portsmouth, NH: Heinemann.

National Commission on Excellence in Education (1983). *A nation at risk: The imperatives for education reform.* Washington, DC: U.S. Office of Education.

CHAPTER 16

A Focus on NAEP Data: What It Means, What It Does Not Mean, and the Findings From the Expert Study

Jay R. Campbell

The contexts and practices identified in the Expert Study (Flippo, 1998; refer to Chapter 1 in this book) that would facilitate learning to read are probably not surprising to most educators. Most of the statements that represent agreement among the experts have been confirmed by research and classroom practice. Many are also consistent with findings from the National Assessment of Educational Progress (NAEP), a large-scale assessment and survey of fourth, eighth, and twelfth graders across the United States. This chapter provides an examination and discussion of the connections that can be made between NAEP data and several key findings from the Expert Study.

NAEP is a project of the National Center for Education Statistics within the U.S. Department of Education. As a monitor of student achievement in the United States for three decades, NAEP has provided educators and policy makers with an abundance of information regarding the status of student learning and the factors associated with achievement. The NAEP assessments provide information on the performance of groups and subgroups of students in a variety of subject areas; the performance of individual students is not analyzed or reported. The most recently developed NAEP reading assessment was administered in 1992, 1994, and 1998 to national samples of fourth, eighth, and twelfth graders and to samples of fourth and eighth graders within individual states.

Results from the NAEP reading assessment, administered three times during the 1990s, have been used at both the national and state levels to inform educational policy initiatives and school reform. The NAEP results include not only students' scores on the assessment, but also information regarding the background and instructional experiences of students. This information is collected through questionnaires administered to students and their teachers. Given the importance of the NAEP data and the implications of the results, it is instructive to examine closely the nature of the assessment instrument and its framework, the background and instructional data collected by NAEP that are associated with achievement, and the degree of interpretation that is warranted by NAEP's findings.

This examination is made particularly meaningful in light of results from the Expert Study indicating that experts from different theoretical perspectives can agree on many ideas for supporting and advancing the reading achievement of students. In fact, much of what has been reported by NAEP from the reading assessments of the 1990s is consistent with findings from the Expert Study—providing some empirical support for what the experts agree contributes to student achievement in reading.

The NAEP Reading Framework and Assessment Content

As with all frameworks that underlie NAEP assessments, the NAEP reading assessment framework was developed through a national consensus process that was responsive to the voices of a variety of educators, curriculum experts, researchers, and concerned members of the general public. Developed during the early 1990s, the current reading framework describes reading broadly, using the term *reading literacy* to describe knowing when to read, how to read, and how to reflect on reading. More specifically, the *Reading Framework for the National Assessment of Educational Progress: 1992–1998* sets forth six important characteristics of good readers that distinguish them from less proficient readers. According to the National Assessment Governing Board, good readers

1. possess positive habits and attitudes about reading;
2. read with enough fluency so that they can focus on the meaning of what they read;
3. use what they already know to understand what they read;
4. form an understanding of what they read and extend, elaborate, and critically judge its meaning;
5. use a variety of effective strategies to aid their understanding and to plan, manage, and check the progress of their reading;
6. can read a variety of texts and can read for different purposes. (1997, p. 9)

The consistency between these characteristics of good readers set forth in the NAEP framework and points of agreement in the Expert Study is worth noting (refer to Chapter 1, p. 14, in this book): The experts agree that students should "develop positive self-perceptions and expectations," similar to the NAEP framework's description of good readers' positive habits and attitudes about reading; also, the experts agree that students should be exposed to "a broad spectrum of sources for student reading materials" and should be engaged in "purposeful reading," similar to the NAEP framework description of good readers as those who read a variety of texts and read for different purposes.

A shared vision of reading education goals is also evident in the type of assessment called for by the NAEP framework and the experts' common ground. For example, the NAEP reading assessment presents students with texts that are authentic and not written specifically for instruction or assessment; that is, they are drawn from reading materials that are typically available to students in and out of school. The texts are reproduced in test booklets in a manner that replicates as closely as possible the way they appeared in their original source. NAEP's emphasis on assessing reading with authentic reading materials is consistent with the experts' agreement that students should be given opportunities to read real books.

The NAEP reading framework also calls for the assessment of students' ability to read a variety of text types. In recognition that reading is an interactive and constructive process that varies depending on the type of text being read and the purpose for reading, the NAEP reading assessment measures students' ability to read and understand different types of texts. The assessment includes texts written for literary experiences, for providing information, and for describing how to perform a task. Once again, this would appear to be consistent with the experts' agreement that students should be exposed to a broad spectrum of sources for student reading material and the different functions of numerous types of printed materials.

Yet another similarity between the NAEP reading assessment and the experts' common ground may be seen in the emphasis placed on integrating reading and writing activities. Although the NAEP reading assessment is distinct from the writing assessment, over half of the comprehension questions on the reading assessment require written answers. Students are asked to demonstrate the ability to construct and extend their understanding of texts in answering what is referred to as constructed-response questions. With short constructed-response questions, complete answers typically require one or two sentences. With extended constructed-response questions, a paragraph or more is often required to demonstrate extensive understanding of the text. Thus, the ability to construct written interpretations of text is clearly valued and emphasized on the NAEP reading assessment.

It should, perhaps, be of no surprise that a national assessment framework developed through a process of national consensus building on what is valued in reading education should be so well aligned with the shared values of a group of national reading experts. The NAEP assessments are intended to represent commonly held objectives for student achievement. In some sense, they are based not only on what the experts can agree on, but on what most educators and concerned citizens believe should be the goal of education.

NAEP Findings on Factors Associated With Reading Achievement

As described earlier, the NAEP assessments include not only measures of achievement in various subject areas, but also survey questionnaires completed by students and their teachers about a variety of experiences and activities that are thought to be related to achievement. Students' and teachers' responses to these questionnaires provide a context for understanding students' performance on the NAEP assessments. In the area of reading, the three assessments conducted during the 1990s collected information through these survey questionnaires about reading and literacy-related activities in and out of school. Because the students who took the assessment also responded to the survey questions, as did their teachers, it is possible to use NAEP data to examine the relationship between reading achievement and a variety of school and home activities. A brief overview of some of the major findings from these assessments provides support for many of the findings in the Expert Study. In order to facilitate a comparison between findings from the NAEP reading assessments and the Expert Study, the following discussion is framed according to the clustered categories of statements agreed to by the reading experts in the Expert Study.

Combining Reading With Other Language Processes

The experts seem to agree on the importance of integrating the language arts in students' instructional experiences. Writing about reading and talking about reading are two ways to provide for integrated instruction that are mentioned in the experts' agreements. Findings from the NAEP assessments support this conclusion. Results from the 1998 assessment indicated that fourth, eighth, and twelfth graders who were asked on a weekly or monthly basis to write extended answers to questions about what they read scored higher on the NAEP reading assessment than did students who reported being asked to do so only a few times a year or less (Donahue, Voelkl, Campbell, & Mazzeo, 1999). Also, findings from the 1994 assessment indicated that fourth- and eighth-grade students whose teachers used classroom assessment practices that included paragraph-length responses to reading had higher scores, on average, than did students whose teachers never or hardly ever assessed reading this way (Campbell, 1997).

Results from both the 1994 and 1998 assessments revealed a positive relationship between student achievement and integrating reading, talking, and listening through discussing or explaining ideas in reading materials. Students in Grades 8 and 12 who were given opportunities on at least a weekly basis to explain their understanding or to discuss various interpretations of what they read had higher reading scores than students who did so less frequently (Campbell, Donahue, Reese, & Phillips, 1996).

Contexts, Environment, and Purposes for Reading

The experts' agreements in this area emphasize multiple reading experiences, frequent opportunities to read, and purposeful reading. The NAEP results support these conclusions. For example, data collected in 1998 indicated that the amount of reading done each day had a positive relationship with reading achievement. Students in Grades 4, 8, and 12 who indicated reading more than 10 pages each day had higher reading scores, on average, than did students who read fewer pages (Donahue et al., 1999). Also, fourth graders in 1992 who said they read silently in class almost every day had higher scores than students who did not (Mullis, Campbell, & Farstrup, 1993).

Developing Students' Perceptions and Expectations

According to the experts, learning to read is facilitated by developing a sense of one's self as a reader and recognizing that reading is integral to daily life. Several findings from the NAEP reading assessments are consistent with these ideas. For example, students in Grades 4, 8, and 12 who said they frequently read for fun had higher reading scores than students who did so rarely (Campbell et al., 1996). It is likely that students who read for fun daily or weekly have acquired a positive perception of themselves as readers and expect reading to be a rewarding or enjoyable experience. Spending time talking to family and friends about reading may also be an indication that these important affective traits are developing. Students at all three grades who reported frequent discussions about what they read had higher reading scores than students who said that they rarely had such discussions (Donahue et al., 1999).

Materials and Reading Instruction

The experts' agreements related to the types of materials and instructional contexts and practices that facilitate reading development suggest that a broad range of materials and opportunities to read for a variety of purposes is advantageous. In 1992, NAEP asked the teachers of fourth graders how much emphasis they placed on literature-based instruction in their classrooms. Nearly half of the fourth graders were taught by teachers who said that they placed heavy emphasis on this instructional practice. The students of these teachers had higher reading scores than the students whose teachers indicated only moderate emphasis and little or no emphasis on literature-based instruction (Mullis, Campbell, & Farstrup, 1993). If literature-based reading instruction involves the use of varied and multiple reading materials, this NAEP finding supports the experts' agreements in these clusters. A related instructional activity is allowing students to read books of their own choosing in the classroom. At the fourth-grade level, this activity had a positive relationship with reading achievement according to the NAEP findings. More frequent opportunities to read self-selected books as a part of instruction were associated with higher reading scores (Donahue et al., 1999).

Interpreting Data From the NAEP Reading Assessments

The NAEP reading assessment is a measure of the reading comprehension skills and abilities of groups of students across the country and within states that have chosen to participate in NAEP's state-by-state assessments. It provides for the reporting of average scores for the groups of students that are sampled and assessed. For example, results from the assessment indicate the level of achievement attained by all fourth graders in the country or in a state. Results are also reported for subgroups of students within a particular grade. For example, the average reading scores of male students can be compared to that of female students, and the average scores of African American students can be compared to that of white students. Scores for individual students cannot be analyzed and reported.

The fact that the NAEP assessment is a group assessment, rather than an individual assessment, makes it possible for the assessment to be administered across the country and within states without the pressures of typical high-stakes assessments that report individual scores and are often used for accountability monitoring. This makes the assessment less likely to be one that has been the subject of direct teaching and preparation; that is, it is unlikely that teachers are "teaching to the test." Because the framework is intended to represent a national consensus on reading objectives for each grade assessed, it is broadly defined to fit with a variety of curricula and instructional approaches. It is expected that the objectives of the NAEP assessment represent shared goals for schools and districts across the nation.

Although these aspects of the NAEP assessment make it a valuable instrument for assessing students from across the country who are involved in a range of curricular programs, they present some limitations to how the findings can be interpreted. Because the assessment provides information about both achievement and the contextual factors related to achievement, these two components of NAEP findings and the degree or type of interpretation warranted by both are discussed below.

Interpretations of Student Achievement From NAEP Data

The first important aspect of any assessment that must be considered in interpreting its results is a clear understanding of what the assessment was intended to measure. The NAEP reading assessment is an assessment of reading comprehension. The test is constructed of authentic, intact texts. Students are asked to demonstrate their understanding of the texts through responses to both multiple-choice and constructed-response questions. The questions are written to elicit the processes of constructing and extending meaning from texts. The performance of students on each individual question is analyzed, and the results are summarized on a 0 to 500 scale. The average scale score attained by a particular group of students is an indication of how well students are able to comprehend the texts that have been selected as age and grade appropriate. Thus, it would be inappropriate to interpret these results as an indication of any other aspect of student learning and achievement. For example, although written responses represent a majority of the types of answers provided by students taking the assessment, these responses are scored strictly on the basis of evidence of understanding the text, not on criteria related to writing ability. Likewise, it would be inappropriate to infer directly from the NAEP reading results that students who scored low on the assessment were necessarily deficient in phonics or phonemic awareness skills. The assessment is intended to measure comprehension skills, not phonics skills. Although students who demonstrate lower reading comprehension proficiency may also demonstrate lower proficiency in phonics skills, the link between these two skills is not addressed by the NAEP assessment.

This may be a particularly important point for state policy makers who use NAEP data from the state-by-state assessments to gauge the effectiveness of literacy and reading education programs. For example, if the fourth graders assessed in a state performed lower on the NAEP assessment one year than did fourth graders who were assessed in the same state during an earlier year, it is likely to concern policy makers and the citizens of that state. If a subsequent assessment shows further trends toward lower performance among fourth graders, there may be a call for action on the part of educators and policy makers. It is important to keep in mind that the NAEP reading assessment is a single assessment of a specific academic skill—reading comprehension. The factors related to achievement in reading comprehension are multiple and varied, and are not entirely addressed by the NAEP assessment alone. Although the NAEP results may point to possible weakness in the curriculum or school policies, they should be considered along with other sources of information in determining the most appropriate actions to be taken.

Another aspect of the assessment that must be considered in interpreting the achievement results is one mentioned earlier—that the NAEP assessment does not provide for the reporting of individual students' scores, only average scores for groups and subgroups of students. This is an important point, because the average score attained by a certain group or subgroup of students does not show the range of performance within that group or subgroup. Thus when NAEP results indicate that the average scale score of white students is higher than that of African American students, this clearly is not an indication that every white student outperformed every African American student.

The fact that NAEP data represent averages rather than findings for individual students is a relatively obvious and easily understood constraint on the interpretation of results. Other aspects of the assessment and the data collected may present less obvious limitations to interpreting NAEP data. For example, interpretations of NAEP data must also account for the fact that the average scores are estimates of the average performance of students. Although NAEP data indicate the average reading score for fourth, eighth, and twelfth graders, these scores are estimates based on representative samples of students in each grade. Every fourth, eighth, or twelfth grader in the nation or in a particular state did not take the assessment—only a representative sample of these students were assessed. The reports that are published based on NAEP results take into account the degree of uncertainty associated with data based on samples rather than the entire population, and only indicate differences between the average scores of students in various groups, or changes in performance across time, when those differences or changes are statistically significant.

A final consideration in the interpretation of NAEP achievement data relates to the "low-stakes" nature of this assessment. The fact that individual scores are not reported for students may be an advantage, because a longstanding criticism of large-scale standardized tests—that teachers may narrowly fit their teaching to the contents of the test—is likely not a problem with the NAEP assessment. Teachers know that they will not be held directly accountable for the performance of students in their classrooms.

Despite this advantage, the reporting of only group scores for the nation and for states may present a disadvantage that must be considered. If students know that they are not receiving individual scores for their performance on the assessment, there is the possibility that they will not try their hardest. There is some indication that this is a potential problem, particularly among the older students. As a part of the questionnaires administered to students who take the NAEP assessment, students are asked to indicate how important it was to them to do well on the assessment. Students' responses to this question in the 1998 reading assessment indicated that 86% of fourth graders, 58% of eighth graders, and only 31% of twelfth graders felt it was important or very important to them that they did well (Donahue et al., 1999). Thus, although most of the fourth graders sampled indicated that they wanted to do well on the assessment, this was true for less than one third of the twelfth graders.

Interpreting NAEP Results on Factors Associated With Achievement

The responses of students in the NAEP assessment and their teachers to questionnaires provide an important context for interpreting the achievement scores. Because NAEP collects this information for students who are assessed, it is possible to examine the relationship between students' home and school experiences and the reading scores attained by students on the assessment. As described in the previous section of this chapter, many of the NAEP findings on factors associated with achievement are consistent with the experts' agreements on what facilitates learning to read. Nevertheless, it is important to understand the limitations of interpreting NAEP results in this area, and to acknowledge that some findings would appear to be inconsistent with those of the experts.

An example of one NAEP finding that may be inconsistent with findings from the Expert Study can be found in results from the 1994 assessment (Campbell et al., 1996). Based on fourth graders' reports of how frequently they were asked by their teachers to work in a reading workbook or on a worksheet, this instructional activity had a positive relationship with achievement. That is, students who said they did this almost every day had higher scores, on average, than students who said they did this less frequently. This would appear to be inconsistent with the experts' agreement that using "workbooks with every reading lesson" would make learning to read difficult.

The relationship between this activity and reading achievement was different, however, when it was examined using teachers' responses to the same question. Based on the responses of the students' teachers, this activity was negatively associated with achievement. That is, students who were taught by teachers who said they had their students work in workbooks or on worksheets almost every day had lower average scores than students who were taught by teachers who indicated that they engaged students in this activity less frequently.

This discrepancy between results based on students' responses and those based on teachers' responses points to one limitation of NAEP findings on factors associated with achievement. Two possible explanations must be considered. It is possible that fourth graders are not able to accurately describe the frequency of an instructional activity such as working in workbooks or on worksheets. Thus, the analysis of their responses may be less valid than the analysis of responses provided by their teachers. A second explanation, though less appealing, must be considered. It is also possible that teachers responding to questionnaires may estimate the frequency of such activities in a manner that favors the socially desirable response. If this is true, it would not be unique to teachers; it is a well-documented fact of survey-type research. In either case, the conclusiveness of findings based on self-reported information from students or teachers should be interpreted cautiously.

Beyond the limitation of self-reported information about instructional experiences, another serious constraint on interpretations of NAEP results is the fact that the questionnaires are asking students and teachers to describe current classroom practices. Because the NAEP assessment is administered in late winter of the school year, the students assessed have been with their current teachers less than 6 months. Thus, the activities and instructional approaches described by students' and teachers' responses to the questionnaires reflect only the last 5 to 6 months of students' schooling. The questionnaires do not capture the educational experiences of students prior to the current school year. It must be assumed that the school years preceding the current one have had a substantial impact on students' current academic achievement. Therefore, if a particular instructional approach described by teachers in their responses to the questionnaire does not show a relationship to reading scores, it may be due to the fact that it only represents a few months of students' entire school history.

A final limitation to interpreting NAEP results on factors related to achievement concerns the nature of the relationship. It is important to recognize that these relationships should be interpreted as correlations, not causal relationships. Although the NAEP data may indicate a statistically significant relationship between a certain classroom activity and students' reading achievement, the underlying cause for the relationship cannot be determined from NAEP data alone. A number of contextual factors may contribute to any one significant finding. For example, the NAEP finding described earlier—that frequent reading of self-selected books had a positive relationship with achievement—may have several explanations. First, it is possible that this activity does have a direct impact on reading development. There is some evidence from other research that supports this interpretation (Guthrie & Alvermann, 1999). Nevertheless, other interpretations must be considered. One alternate explanation is that teachers who frequently allow students to choose their own books also support students' reading development through related activities that have a greater impact on their achievement. These may include having students talk about their reading in small groups, assigning projects or reports based on their reading, or having students keep reading logs and journals to record their reading experiences. Yet another alternate explanation may be that teachers who have higher performing students are more likely to allow reading of self-selected books than are teachers who have lower performing students. In this case, it would not be the frequency of the activity that causes higher achievement; it would be students' higher achievement that causes the teacher to use this activity frequently. Clearly, the most appropriate way to interpret NAEP findings on factors associated with achievement is in the context of other research and with an understanding of classroom practices.

Implications of NAEP Data and the Expert Study

This examination of the NAEP reading assessment and findings from the Expert Study suggest several implications for those who seek to increase students' reading achievement. First, it is clear that there are many contexts, practices, and objectives for reading instruction that are shared, not only by the experts in the Expert Study, but also by a broad national constituency—like the one that developed the NAEP reading assessment framework. Reaching consensus on a topic as hotly debated as "reading instruction" is not a small accomplishment. Nevertheless, both the findings from the Expert Study and the broad view of reading embodied in the NAEP reading framework indicate that it is possible. Perhaps it can be concluded that discussions about teaching reading do not always have to regress into highly politicized, vitriolic debates that result in the exclusion of voices and a narrow view of reading. Moreover, when efforts are made to include as many voices as possible and to build consensus among an array of perspectives, it results in a valuable resource for educators and policy makers.

The similarities between NAEP's perspective on reading and the experts' agreements reinforce the notion that there is a common ground for agreement among most reading educators, which is not just a collection of platitudes or abstract ideas. This common ground includes very specific contexts and practices, approaches, activities, and uses of materials that have direct implication for classroom practice and policy setting. As described earlier, there are a number of limitations on the degree of interpretations that can be made based on NAEP data. Although the NAEP findings point to several activities and instructional approaches that have a positive relationship with reading achievement, NAEP data alone do not provide conclusive evidence of what works in classrooms. Reviewing the NAEP results, however, in light of the findings of the Expert Study is one way to begin to use the NAEP data to determine best practices and effective approaches. If a diverse group of experts who have extensive experience in classrooms and knowledge of research agree on a number of specific contexts and practices that facilitate learning to read, and if data like that collected by NAEP are consistent with their shared recommendations, it may be that the field of reading has a core knowledge base for informing school policies and practices.

A final implication of this examination of NAEP and the Expert Study is that our abilities to agree on a core set of best practices, and the possibility that what we agree on can be confirmed through research and large-scale collections of data, cannot be considered the final goal we are striving toward. Any one particular context, practice, activity, or objective for teaching reading or supporting students' literacy development can only be considered effective when it has had a direct impact on an individual student's learning. The Expert Study and the NAEP reading assessment reflect and support the true work that takes place in classrooms and homes every day. It is, however, in the efforts of teachers and parents that truly effective practices can be observed and measured. Researchers, experts, and large-scale educational programs like NAEP should seek to provide the most useful and relevant information to guide and reinforce the efforts of those directly responsible for helping children learn to read.

REFERENCES
Campbell, J.R. (1997). *NAEP facts: Reading assessment in the nation's fourth- and eighth-grade classrooms.* Washington, DC: National Center for Education Statistics.
Campbell, J.R., Donahue, P.L., Reese, C.M., & Phillips, G.W. (1996). *NAEP 1994 reading report card for the nation and the states.* Washington, DC: National Center for Education Statistics.
Donahue, P.L., Voelkl, K.E., Campbell, J.R., & Mazzeo, J. (1999). *NAEP 1998 reading report card for the nation and the states.* Washington, DC: National Center for Education Statistics.
Flippo, R.F. (1998). Points of agreement: A display of professional unity in our field. *The Reading Teacher, 52,* 30–40.
Guthrie, J.T., & Alvermann, D.E. (Eds.). (1999). *Engaged reading: Processes, practices, and policy implications.* New York: Teachers College Press.

Mullis, I.V.S., Campbell, J.R., & Farstrup, A.E. (1993). *NAEP 1992 reading report card for the nation and the states.* Washington, DC: National Center for Education Statistics.

National Assessment Governing Board. (1997). *Reading framework for the National Assessment of Educational Progress: 1992–1998.* Washington, DC: Author.

CHAPTER 17

A Focus on Communication With Parents and Families

Timothy V. Rasinski

From my perspective, the major finding from this search-for-common-ground study is that the perceived gulf that exists between orientations to research and practices in literacy education by literacy researchers and scholars is not as large as it may seem. Moreover, at the foundation for all approaches, regardless of theoretical or pragmatic orientation, there is a common value—the desire to improve the efficacy of literacy education so that all learners may be able to attain full and functional levels of literacy. This should be looked on as good news. There is more that we—as a body of literacy scholars, researchers, and practitioners—agree on than we disagree on.

However, I was asked to respond to this study and its results not from the point of view of the profession, but from the point of view of communication with parents and families. And in this regard, I hate to be the bearer of bad news: There is not a gulf that exists between literacy educators and the general public—it is more of an ocean. We literacy educators seem to get so caught up in our own disputes, we fail to address the concerns and questions raised by parents and members of the general community. As Allen Berger states in an article on writing for the public in *The Reading Teacher*, "One of the things that strikes me as wrong with educators is that we talk to ourselves too much. Now there's a lot right with that: it's what in part makes us a profession. But what's wrong is that while we're communicating with each other in educational publications others are talking about us in other publications" (1997, p. 6).

And guess what the U.S. media and the public have to say about us educators? Consider the following statements about education and reading that I have collected from my local newspapers by international pundits as well as by parents with children in local schools:

In a country that has 90 million functional illiterates and ranks 49th among nations of the world in stamping out this malaise, while spending nearly $6,000 annually per student, the real fraud is how reading is taught in [United States] classrooms. (Cameron Humphries, *Cleveland Plain Dealer*, December 23, 1994)

Whole language movement discredited, as it should be. It ignores the rules of grammar and punctuation. (John Rosemond, syndicated columnist on parenting, *Akron Beacon Journal*, November 21, 1995)

The answer [to today's education problems] lies in the deliberate dumbing down of educational standards, half-baked, failed education theories,...and teachers and administrators who, for the most part, represent the very bottom of the intellectual academic barrel. (Walter Williams, columnist, *The Cincinnati Enquirer*, March 24, 1996)

It is important that parents be aware of what...many educators today will not tell them. Parents are not told that many children do not learn to read if in a literature-based or whole-language program. (Kathleen DeJeau, teacher and parent, *Akron Beacon Journal*, October 24, 1994)

And this written by one of the United States' most well-known commentators:

Summertime, and the living is easy. Schools are empty, so the damage has stopped. During this seasonal respite from the educational system's subtraction from national literacy, consider why America may be graduating from its high schools its first generation worse educated than the generation that came before. (George Will, *The Washington Enquirer*, July 2, 1995)

While arguing among ourselves, it appears that we have neglected the public and parents whom we ultimately serve as educators. Parents and the public want to know what we think about teaching reading, what are the best kinds of materials for children to read at different age levels, what they can do as parents to help their children become better readers and writers. And, despite all the debate between educators, we seem to have little to say to parents.

A few years ago, when the *Hooked on Phonics* (1999) craze was going strong, I noticed that many parents of the children who were attending our reading clinic had purchased the program for use with their own kids. I also noticed that our local public library had purchased several copies of the program. It was so popular, parents who wanted to check it out had to add their names to a waiting list.

I wondered what accounted for this unprecedented popularity for a reading program that was more than just a little suspect in its claims. So I began to ask parents who had used *Hooked on Phonics* what drew them to it. Most of the parents had children who were struggling in reading. Most were parents of elementary school children, though a few got the program for use with their middle grade children. They mentioned, of course, the marketing blitz that had flooded the radio airwaves. All the parents I talked with could tell me the phone number to order the program, and they were able to tell me other specific bits of information from the advertisements. But, in every single case, parents also mentioned to me that they were not receiving the types of information from the schools that they could use to help their children.

All parents told me that their children's classroom or special reading teachers or school principal told them about reading aloud regularly to their children. But, that is pretty much where the advice left off. Parents were told to make sure their children read daily, that their children get their homework assignments completed on time, and that parents visit the library with their children. Parents wanted more, but more was not forthcoming. One parent reported to me that the teacher she spoke with said that reading instruction should be left to teachers; parents and outsiders have a tendency to mess things up for children trying to learn to read.

And when they were not able to get more information from their schools, in a well-meaning attempt to help their children overcome their difficulties in reading, they fell prey to the glitzy radio advertising that was promising—no, guaranteeing—instant success.

We might want to blame the teachers for not informing parents, for not bridging the gap between home and school, especially when it comes to reading. Many teachers do not like interacting with parents. But in reality, if there is blame to be given out, it needs to be placed at the feet of literacy educators in higher education. Teachers do not tell parents how to help their children in reading because those of us who work in training teachers at the undergraduate and graduate levels do not tell teachers how they can connect with parents. Informal surveys of new teachers acknowledge the lack of leadership colleges have provided in this area. New teachers report that many feel uncomfortable working with parents and adult members of the community, and most report that they had little or no training in the undergraduate programs in how to work with parents and the community for the benefit of children.

If you teach courses in literacy education at the college level, examine your curricula. Does your undergraduate curriculum have a course for working with parents in reading? Does your graduate curriculum have such a course? My guess is that very few programs have a course dedicated to working and communicating with parents to improve children's literacy learning. There may be a chapter in a methods textbook dedicated to the subject, or there may be a class session in one course dedicated to teacher-parent-community connections. That amount of coverage almost seems to be little more than lip service to this issue.

And this is truly unfortunate. For if you are talking about research-based information, *we have it* in the effects of community-home-school connections and student achievement in reading. Study after study has shown positive effects of parental involvement in the literacy education of their children—from Dolores Durkin's (1966) seminal study of early readers to more recent work that has studied actual instructional activities coordinated with the school that parents can engage in to promote their children's literacy learning (Rasinski, 1995). For example, findings from the 1994 National Assessment of Educational Progress (Campbell, Donahue, Reese, & Phillips, 1996) indicate significant relationships between various home factors and students' reading achievement at all levels tested. In their book *The Reading Crisis* (Chall, Jacobs, & Baldwin, 1990), renowned literacy scholar Jeanne Chall and her colleagues note that children who spend time with parents and other adults have a significant advantage in literacy learning, particularly in vocabulary and language, over children whose time is spent more with persons of their own age. In one of the largest international studies of literacy learning ever conducted (Postlethwaite & Ross, 1992), researchers found that the degree of parent cooperation with the school was the highest ranked of 56 indicators of student reading achievement across the 26 countries that participated in the study. In the United States, the parental cooperation variable ranked second in overall importance in distinguishing between more effective and less effective schools in the teaching of reading. The authors of the report write, "It is clear that parent cooperation is important and that all effort should be made to foster it" (p. 32). It is fairly well accepted among literacy scholars that parent involvement is important and that it leads to increased and improved student reading.

One irony of this situation is that despite the growing knowledge base about the importance of and methods for working with parents in children's reading development, it just does not seem to happen often in classrooms and schools. If it does happen, it is usually because of dedicated and knowledgeable teachers and principals who work to make it happen. Less often can such bridges between school and home be attributed to the work of literacy scholars working outside of the schools in and around higher education.

A second irony is that although the United States and state governments do not find themselves deterred from entering into the highly volatile politicized arena of reading education, they do little to promote the programs, policies, and procedures that we know will work—advocating and promoting connections between parents, teachers, and literacy learning. In my home state of Ohio, for example, legislators found it necessary to dictate school and university curricula, making it a requirement for elementary students and college students who want to become teachers to take a course in direct, intensive, and systematic phonics. Although most literacy educators would agree on the need for phonics instruction, there is still considerable debate about the nature and format for such instruction. Nevertheless, the "phonics bill" passed both houses of the Ohio General Assembly with ease and was made law. Other states have moved, in recent years, in similar directions.

If it was that easy to pass a law mandating school practice in an area for which there is considerable professional disagreement, one might think that there would be little difficulty in passing some sort of requirement for universities and schools to work in concerted fashion to promote a widely agreed upon and research-based literacy agenda—home-school collaboration in children's literacy learning. Wrong. I know of no such recent state-mandated requirement; nor do I know of one on its way. Although we communicate fairly well and can agree among our professional selves about what is right about literacy instruction, we do not seem to do such a good job when communicating with families and the public. As a result, parents and the public look on educators with suspicious eyes and we miss out on a wonderful opportunity to have a monumental effect on children's literacy development.

It seems to me that if we can stop the bickering among ourselves about who is wrong and what is wrong—which Rona Flippo's Expert Study (1998; refer to Chapter 1 in this book) suggests is certainly possible—and look around and listen carefully, we would see that a significant amount of the general population knows very little of what we have to say, often receives what we have to say in distorted ways, and as a result learns to distrust literacy educators, scholars, and researchers. Indeed, because we allow the media to make unsubstantiated and distorted attacks on us without retort or opposition, the general population sees us and our work as irrelevant.

Newsweek columnist Robert Samuelson (1995) in a rare positive endorsement of education titled "Three Cheers for Schools," nevertheless says that his "main gripe with our local school is that it doesn't tell parents what's expected of students, or how, exactly, parents can help" (p. 61). Common ground needs to be found between the literacy education community and parents and the public.

We rarely seem to try for informed understanding beyond our own insulated professional educational groups. Indeed, I note with irony that not one of the items generated by the experts in the Expert Study involved connecting reading and writing with the community or involving parents and families in the educational process of their children. It seems that we may have, as a profession, a type of block or bias against connecting with and finding consensus with the community and parents.

Even when I read about some of the most ill-informed and mean-spirited attacks on teachers, teacher educators, and school researchers, I rarely find that faculty from an elementary, middle, or high school; members of the local council of the International Reading Association (IRA), National Council of Teachers of English (NCTE), Teachers Applying Whole Language (TAWL), or other literacy group; or, for that matter, faculty members for local colleges of education respond vigorously and convincingly to such faulty explanations and distortions of our work. Perhaps we are all so busy with our work, teaching, service, research, that we do not have time to respond or communicate. Unfortunately, those seeds of criticism, if left unanswered and unresponded to, will eventually grow into major obstacles to progress in education. We are reaping some of the effects of our lack of connection to public and parents even now.

So then, what do we do? It seems to me that we need to expand our search for consensus and common ground—or at least our search for a fair presentation of our positions—to parents, the media, and the general public. We need to state our understandings of literacy learning and teaching clearly, passionately, forcefully, and repeatedly to the public; we need to answer attacks on our profession and our work; we need to confront those who would slander us.

More important, for the sake of children, we need to build bridges of understanding and mutual cooperation between literacy educators and homes. Those of us in higher education need to work with teachers in schools and teachers in training to provide them with methods for communicating and collaborating with parents—and with actual instructional content in literacy that they can share with parents—so that parents and teachers can work together to enhance children's literacy learning. Many of the methods already exist and have been developed by teachers who understand the importance of school-home connections. For example, Don Howard (1997), a teacher in Lyon Elementary School in Glenview, Illinois, USA, has developed and implemented several school-home initiatives that have strengthened the connections and developed mutual trust and support between teachers and parents. Howard's initiatives include collaborative goal-setting accomplished during the first parent-teacher conference of the school year; curriculum chats four to five times a year in which Howard explains the curriculum he tries to implement and entertains questions and concerns from parents about the curriculum; extracurricular courses for children taught by parents before and after school and during lunchtime in the school building on topics for which certain parents have expertise; and Friday (parent) volunteers who act as readers, storytellers, and conversationalists for children each Friday afternoon. These are the types of connections that need to form the content of teacher education training in working with parents. According to Howard, "Good things happen when parents and teachers are willing to work together and create a team that blends the strengths of home, school, and community into a common ground for learning." The foundation for this collaboration between teachers and parents needs to be set in our teacher training programs.

At the professional level there is much that we can do. Our professional organizations have great publishing programs for informing members of the profession about research results, new teaching methods, and up-and-coming materials for literacy instruction. We communicate among ourselves, but our organizations do not do such a good job connecting with the public. I am certainly not an expert in communicating with the public, but such experts do exist. Our professional organizations need to enlist the support of those experts so they can advise us on ways to mobilize our profession in making those critical connections.

IRA is a professional organization dedicated to the improvement of literacy education. It has thousands of members. Just think of the potential impact those members could have if they wrote letters to editors of local newspapers about how to teach reading and how parents and communities can help. Imagine the impact on the public if every ill-informed criticism of literacy education was met with a multitude of responses by IRA members offering alternative views, views validated by actual practice and research. IRA might wish to produce more materials aimed at the general public. This could be done through collaborative projects with popular general readership magazines or through joint ventures with commercial publishers.

In addition to correcting misconceptions held by the public about literacy education, the content shared with parents and the larger community needs to include specific information on how parents and guardians in particular, and the community in general, can foster literacy development among children. Some of the common understandings from the Expert Study may form the starting point for such communications. For example, providing demonstrations of how reading is done or used is an activity that parents and other members of the community could easily implement in the context of their normal lives. Similarly, parents and community members, without much difficulty at all, could contribute to environments in which children learn that reading does further their life's purpose. Moreover, parents and other community members such as medical doctors, dentists, store managers, and the like could make significant contributions to the goal of making a variety of printed material available and accessible to developing readers. These and other agreed-upon literacy practices and goals from the Expert Study could make communications with parents and the community informed, substantive, and ultimately helpful for students.

I think that much common ground exists between the literacy profession and parents and the general public. However, that common ground needs to be constantly nurtured, especially by those of us for whom literacy education is our profession. Once firmly established, that ground can be the foundation for magnificent bridges between literacy educators and the public.

Consensus is great—but it is not enough. Within our professional field, consensus can certainly help us feel good about ourselves and the work that we do. However, consensus within can also be a dangerous sedative. We can have consensus within our professional groups until the cows come home, but if those seeds of consensus are not spread and nurtured among parents, the public, and the media, we will find that our small, self-indulgent professional garden of Eden is surrounded by a jungle of ignorance, half-truths, and political agendas that will stifle any attempt we might make to expand the horizons of our field.

REFERENCES

Berger, A. (1997). Writing about reading for the public. *The Reading Teacher, 51*, 6–10.

Campbell, J.R., Donahue, P.L., Reese, C.R., & Phillips, G.W. (1996). *NAEP 1994 reading report card for the nation and the states.* Washington, DC: National Center for Education Statistics.

Chall, J.S., Jacobs, V.A., & Baldwin, L.E. (1990). *The reading crisis: Why poor children fall behind.* Cambridge, MA: Harvard University Press.

DeJeau, K. (1994, October 24). Reading between lines of language program. *Akron Beacon Journal*, p. A22.

Durkin, D. (1966). *Children who read early.* New York: Teachers College Press.

Hooked on phonics. (1999). San Francisco: Gateway Learning Corporation.

Flippo, R.F. (1998). Points of agreement: A display of professional unity in our field. *The Reading Teacher, 52,* 30–40.

Howard, D. (1997, April). One teacher's story: Parent partnerships. *School talk.* (No volume number, unpaged.)

Humphries, C. (1994, December 23). Why Johnny can't read. *The Cleveland Plain Dealer,* p. 11B.

Postlethwaite, T.N., & Ross, K.N. (1992). *Effective schools in reading: An exploratory study.* The Hague: International Association for the Evaluation of Educational Achievement.

Rasinski, T.V. (1995). Fast Start: A parental involvement reading program for primary grade students. In W.M. Linek & E.G. Sturtevant (Eds.), *Generations of literacy: Seventeenth yearbook of the College Reading Association* (pp. 301–312). Harrisonburg, VA: College Reading Association.

Rosemond, J. (1995, November 21). "Whole language" movement discredited, as it should be. *Akron Beacon Journal,* p. D3.

Samuelson, R.J. (1995, December 4). Three cheers for schools. *Newsweek, 126,* 61.

Will, G.F. (1995, July 2). Teach Johnny to write. *The Washington Enquirer,* p. C7.

Williams, W. (1996, March 24). Dumbed-down U.S. values curtail wealth. *The Cincinnati Enquirer,* p. D3.

CHAPTER 18

A Focus on the Media, Policy-Driven Literacy Practices, and the Work of Reading Professionals

Richard T. Vacca

School-based reading professionals have difficulty recognizing their role in the educational policy process. Nor do they tend to view themselves as policy makers. Most classroom teachers and reading specialists, for example, believe that an educational policy maker is someone who is likely to be the school board member, legislator, or education agency official. The traditional view of a policy maker, after all, is someone who represents the "top level" of a visible bureaucratic hierarchy. Reading professionals, on the other hand, define themselves as classroom teachers or reading specialists or instructional leaders who deliver educational services in a variety of school contexts that are at the "bottom level" of a bureaucratic hierarchy—such as the classroom. Yet a compelling case can be made for classroom teachers and reading specialists as educational policy makers in their own right.

Fraatz (1987) argues that "a complete picture of the educational policy process and its outcomes requires systematic attention to the contributions made by those who actually deliver educational services to children in public schools" (p. 2). Historically, to be sure, the role of top-level policy makers on school boards, in legislatures, and in state and federal education agencies has been to establish the legal and fiscal frameworks in which educators operate. Professional educators historically have utilized their knowledge and expertise in subject matter areas to make sense of legislation, regulations, and educational directives as they go about the business of designing and enacting curriculum to meet the learning needs of children and adolescents. In other words, the decisions of policy makers *outside* the school are always mediated by the day-to-day decisions of policy makers *inside* the schools (Fraatz, 1987). Policy matters related to curriculum and instruction historically have been left to the discretion of professional educators.

Not so in the 1990s. The discretionary powers held by reading professionals in making curricular and instructional decisions are ever so gradually being eroded in the name of systemic education reform in the United States. Advocates of systemic reform believe that changing teaching is the most direct way to change students' learning (Valencia & Wixson, 1999). Systemic reformers believe that "top-down" policy mandates will lead to "bottom-up" instructional improvement in classrooms, schools, and districts. As a result, policy mandates about the *kind and amount* of literacy instruction in classrooms and *the levels of reading required for successful promotion* from grade to grade are dominating state and federal legislation (Valencia & Wixson, 1999). Two of the major "tools" used by top-level policy makers—literacy standards and assessment—have attained enormous importance in reading and learning to read and are influencing literacy practice in classrooms, schools, and districts.

In this chapter, I examine the complex and interlocking relationship between policy-driven literacy practices and the role of the media in shaping public perceptions of education in general and literacy learning in particular. The role of the media in shaping public perceptions of literacy in the United States has been a strong catalyst in the systemic reform movement. Here is what I see happening: National reports, such as *A Nation at Risk* (National Commission on Excellence in Education, 1983), have painted a dire picture of the failure of American schools to develop a literate student body capable of competing economically with other technologically advanced countries. The media, which is the main vehicle for dissemination and commentary in relation to national and state reports on education, affects the way the public thinks about literacy achievement and literacy learning. In turn, politicians and policy makers, ever responsive to public opinion and concern, have made reading achievement and learning to read as much a political issue as an educational one by enacting legislation that undergirds modern education reform. According to Valencia and Wixson (1999), "This modern reform movement has been characterized by efforts to create new 'policy instruments' to elicit, encourage, or demand changes in teaching and learning" (p. 1).

Reading Crisis or Challenge? A Personal Perspective

The 28th Annual Phi Delta Kappa/Gallup Poll of the Public's Attitudes Toward Public Schools (Elam, Rose, & Gallup, 1996) reflects the importance that the United States public attaches to its schools. For example, by a margin of 64% to 25%, people believe that it is more important for the federal government to improve public education than to balance the federal budget. Despite the bashing that public schools have taken in the media and in national reports of education, people rate their local teachers highest in commitment to school improvement, but also highly rate school superintendents, school boards, governors, and legislators as committed to school improvement.

The steady rise of public education as an important domestic issue in the United States corresponds to its depiction as being in a state of crisis and failure. Whether there is an education crisis in the United States, as it has been portrayed in the media and in national reports, is a point hotly contested by prominent educational researchers and scholars. Berliner and Biddle (1995), for example, argue convincingly that the opponents of public education have manufactured an educational crisis based on misinterpretations of educational statistical data. Bracy (1997) contends that education reformers and critics suffer from "nostalgia" and "amnesia" in their interpretation of education indicators, such as SAT scores and NAEP scores, which have been used to characterize the academic achievement of students. A historical analysis of educational progress in the 20th century leads Bracy to conclude that *A Nation at Risk*, which became the lightning rod for systemic reform, was a "masterpiece of propaganda." According to Bracy (1997), "A more selective use of data is hard to imagine" (p. 55).

A significant dimension of the purported education crisis has been the interpretive spin put on data from state reading proficiency tests, national assessments of reading (see Chapter 16 in this volume), and international comparisons of reading achievement. These data have been used to perpetuate the notion that there is widespread reading failure among today's U.S. children and adolescents in comparison to past generations or other countries, despite evidence to the contrary. This is not to say that reading professionals should rest on their laurels. Instead, we must strive to engage children and adolescents in literacy programs that produce high levels of achievement. The literacy demands on today's school-aged students are greater and more complex than at any time in U.S. history. What it means to be a proficient reader today has changed dramatically to reflect what a reader must actually do. As Cunningham and Allington (1999) put it, "The 'bar has been raised' and we must raise the level of our daily literacy instruction" (p. 17). This is the United States' national challenge, not its crisis.

I first became aware of the U.S. public's preoccupation with a national "reading crisis" in the 1960s as an undergraduate education major. One of the assigned readings in my educational foundations course was Rudolf Flesch's 1955 bestseller, *Why Johnny Can't Read—And What You Can Do About It*. Although Flesch was not considered a reading professional or an "expert" in the field, he wrote a stinging commentary on the "whole-word method" of teaching reading, also commonly known as the "look-say" method. *Why Johnny Can't Read*, to my knowledge, was the first book on reading to have a major impact on the public's perception of how reading is taught in U.S. schools. Not only was it on *The New York Times* bestseller list for 37 weeks, but it also rekindled the controversy on how children should be taught to read.

Flesch's book made an impassioned plea for an emphasis on phonics in the teaching of reading. However, he allowed his emotional appeal in favor of phonics to go too far, "and his book was discounted among reading professionals as the work of a crank" (Yarrington, 1978, p. 7). Nevertheless, *Why Johnny Can't Read* brought the teaching of reading into the public consciousness in a way that had not been done before. For the first time in U.S. history, a popular book on reading practices in schools was read by a mass audience and was widely covered by the print media. The *Saturday Review*, for example, featured Flesch's beliefs about teaching reading and suggested that his book "may be ranked as the most important contribution to the betterment of public-school teaching methods in the past two decades" (Morris, 1955, p. 21).

Flesch's book had little, if any, substantive impact on the work of reading professionals. Because it was dismissed by the educational establishment as the emotional rants of a malcontent, the controversy over how to teach reading soon faded from the public's eye. Not until Jeanne Chall, a much respected Harvard University educator and member of the reading establishment, wrote *Learning to Read: The Great Debate* (1967) did the controversy over how to teach children to read surface again. Although Chall's book had a major impact on the field of reading and led to some changes in the development of basal reading materials, the controversy over how to teach reading was confined primarily to the world of academe. Much has occurred in the field of reading since I first read Flesch's *Why Johnny Can't Read* as an undergraduate, and later, Chall's *Learning to Read: The Great Debate*. Yet the controversy first kindled by these two books, and more recently flamed by misinterpretation of the NAEP, has developed into the "Reading Wars" as we know it today.

The so-called Reading Wars is a media-driven phenomenon. Although the wars have been waged along several battlefronts—in the media, in legislatures, and in school districts—newspaper and magazine coverage, in particular, has characterized the Reading Wars as a bloody conflagration between the proponents of phonics and whole language. But instead, Flippo (1999) explains that "some politicians, aided by the media's need for sensational news and topics, have kept the reading wars going" and that these wars are not really between reading researchers but "against the reading-research community" (p. 38). Flippo (1997) expresses the concern of most reading professionals about the message being delivered in the media to the U.S. public about reading and learning to read. She cites the ill-effects of sensationalism in numerous headlines that have appeared in newspapers and magazines throughout the country when news coverage of the Reading Wars reached its peak in the mid-1990s:

> "As Reading Scores Plummet, States Get Hooked on Phonics" (*Christian Science Monitor*, 18 April 1996)
>
> "Parents Report on America's Reading Crisis: Why the Whole Language Approach to Teaching Has Failed Millions of Children" (*Parents Magazine*, October 1996)
>
> "Why Kids Can't Read in California" (*San Francisco Chronicle*, 12 January 1996)
>
> "Phonics Boom: Proponents Say Any Other Approach to Reading Only Spells Trouble" (*Washington Post*, 15 November 1996)
>
> (Flippo, 1997, p. 301)

The message being delivered, of course, is that whole language practices contribute to reading failure. In 1995, the headline on the front page of a Los Angeles newspaper proclaimed the end of an "educational fad" (whole language) as state legislators voted to approve a new instructional framework for teaching reading in California schools. The article (Robinson, 1995) accompanying the headline described the "failure" of the whole language movement and championed the return of phonics in the teaching of reading. What was troublesome for me was the simplistic pitting of an important philosophy of literacy learning (whole language) against an important instructional tool in learning to read and spell (phonics). The sidebar to the article, however, crystallized the sensationalism and misinformed stance that exists over instructional practices related to the teaching of reading and writing today.

The sidebar to the news story showed the writing of a first grader in response to having heard the story *Jack and the Beanstalk* read aloud by the teacher. The title of the sidebar, in big bold letters, read, "**DOOMED KIDS?**" The child's writing illustrated the use of invented spelling in learning to read and write. What alarmed me about the sidebar was the insinuation that young children who use invented spelling in their writing may somehow be "doomed" as literacy learners despite three decades of research on the importance of invented spelling in children's development as spellers and readers (Bear & Templeton, 1998).

At the height of the Reading Wars, I had the good fortune to serve as the 42nd president of the International Reading Association (IRA). My presidential term coincided with the 1996 presidential election that resulted in the re-election of William Jefferson Clinton as the 42nd president of the United States. As amused as I was that both IRA and the United States were being served by 42nd presidents (a numerical oddity that will never occur again), I found it supremely ironic that Clinton identified reading as the centerpiece of his education policy and reform proposals. As a reading educator, I sat glued to my chair in amazement as I watched him on television delivering his State of the Union address to the U.S. Congress. In that address, Clinton promoted the importance of reading and learning to read as the foundation for educational, economic, and social success in the United States. Before that, never in the history of the country had a U.S. president even mentioned the word *reading* in a State of the Union address, let alone devoted extended time to creating a national conversation on its importance to the well-being of U.S. citizens and the general welfare of the nation as a whole.

In the 1996 presidential campaign, education was THE major domestic concern on the minds of most U.S. citizens, and reading became the "poster child" for educational reform. As IRA's president, I received numerous calls from newspaper reporters as well as "talk radio" show hosts throughout the United States asking me to comment on issues and concerns related to reading and learning to read. In the wake of highly publicized state reading initiatives and reform efforts in California and Texas, these media interviews often re-volved around two questions: (1) Why the decline in reading achievement among U.S. school children? and (2) Is phonics better than whole language as an approach to teaching reading? My attempts to explain the myths and mis-perceptions associated with the first question and the theoretical and practical complexities inherent in the second question often were sidestepped by re-porters and radio commentators. For example, I would be careful to explain that it is unfair to teachers and children to pit phonics and whole language against one another. Whereas phonics is an important tool for beginning read-ers to learn and use, whole language represents a set of beliefs that results in teachers using multiple approaches and strategies for learning to read, includ-ing phonics. Often, follow-up queries to my explanation of the differences be-tween whole language and phonics included questions such as, "Then why aren't teachers today teaching phonics?" Usually my response to the question was an exaggerated, "Who says so?" followed by a description of a federally funded large-scale research project conducted at the National Reading Research Center. This study, which surveyed teachers of beginning readers throughout the United States, provides overwhelming evidence that virtually all primary teachers in U.S. schools teach phonics on a day-to-day basis (Baumann, Hoffman, Moon, & Duffy, 1997).

My sense is that most of the reporters with whom I talked in the media were more concerned with short, terse statements—"sound bites"—than in-volved explanations. Some, I feared, already had developed a "story angle" based on personal bias, preconceived notions, or limited research on reading and learning to read. Call me paranoid, but in many of these media-related interviews, I felt that reporters around the United States were reading one or two articles on the World Wide Web and essentially recycling the ideas they encountered for their local newspaper audiences. The legendary "legwork" and rigor that news reporters put into a story seemed to be missing. In only one instance out of many did a reporter call me more than once to "try and get it right" as she grappled with the complexities of the issues related to her subject (in this case, the neglect of adolescent readers).

As a reading professional in a university context, I was often put in the position of attempting to simplify responses to media-related questions while trying to represent complex ideas accurately. During my presidency, IRA hired a nationally recognized media consultant to work with the Board of Directors on how to respond to the questions from the media. The media consultant put the Board through a variety of simulations so that we would be comfortable at creating the much-sought-after "sound bite" without sacrificing content. Maybe the 30-second sound bite works well for politicians, but as an educator, I of-ten wondered whether I was advancing the state of reading, informing the pub-lic about the verities of reading and learning to read, or making a difference in the lives of literacy learners. More often than not, I felt that the "quick quip" or "memorable moment" response to a question resulted in a web of superficiality that would result in more harm than good. Nevertheless, I remain hopeful that reading professionals have much to contribute to the educational policy process. Two research-inspired directions in the 1990s, discussed in the next section, are cause for optimism and serve as rallying points for reading professionals in an era of policy-driven literacy practices.

Rallying Points for Reading Professionals

In Ohio, where I work, teachers I have interviewed are frustrated and discouraged because teaching and learning comes to a virtual standstill by March of the school year as they prepare students at all grade levels to take state proficiency tests in reading and other subject areas. Primary-level students, for example, are taking "off-year" proficiency tests in reading to prepare them for the "make-or-break" fourth-grade proficiency test, where the threat of retention looms large for children. Teachers of first and second graders report the inordinate stress and duress that children experience in preparation for, and during the actual taking of, a high-stakes reading assessment. Some children cry during testing. Others claim that they hate reading. Still others have resigned themselves to failure and have given up in the face of external pressure placed on them by politicians and state education officials. One cannot help but question the developmental inappropriateness of policy instruments, such as assessment and the threat of retention, that put such stress and strain on children and adolescents.

Nevertheless, there are at least two rallying points that have emerged during an era of systemic reform that reading professionals can use to their advantage as they attempt to influence educational policy from the bottom up and meet the challenges inherent in the development of high-level literacy programs. The first rallying point revolves around the findings of the Expert Study (Flippo, 1998) reported in Chapter 1 of this volume. These findings make clear that the field of reading is not as fractious as it has been reported in the media. The findings serve to identify a set of core literacy practices that would tend to make learning to read difficult for students, and a set of core literacy practices that would tend to facilitate learning to read. Why are the points of agreement by reading experts important to the work of reading professionals? Flippo (1997) responds to the question this way:

> We must use our expertise and the findings of research...to shape the public's understandings. Educational philosophies, in any area of the curriculum, should not become the scapegoats for our politicians' inability to solve the economic and sociocultural problems of our states. Nor can we simply shed our belief systems in order to "fit in" with a more currently acceptable political viewpoint. (p. 304)

A second rallying point for reading professionals involves one of the most dramatic outcomes to emerge from the insidious portrayal of the Reading Wars in the media—namely, an emphasis on balance in the teaching of reading. The search for balance in literacy programs is critical to reading professionals but must be approached with caution. In several states, for example, legislators and policy makers have called for balanced literacy programs as a means of ensuring that children receive systematic instruction in the "basic skills" associated with reading and writing. Balanced instruction, as viewed from this narrow perspective, is an extension of the "back to basics" movement. This movement, which champions the return to direct and intensive instruction in the teaching of skills such as phonics and spelling, is a knee-jerk response to whole language practices. Proponents of a return to basic instruction contend that as reading professionals widely embraced whole language practices, there has been a decline in reading achievement as measured by student performance on large-scale assessments such as statewide proficiency tests, national assessment surveys, or school district-wide standardized tests. As a result, a narrow view of balanced instruction has been linked politically and educationally to *accountability* in the wake of systemic reform efforts (Johns & Elish-Piper, 1997).

Dorothy Strickland (1996), former president of both the International Reading Association and the National Council of Teachers of English, warns reading professionals against a narrow view of balanced instruction:

> Achieving balance in our literacy programs is not meant to imply that there is one specific Balanced Approach. Nor should it suggest a sampling method in which a little of this and a little of that are mixed together to form a grouping of disparate approaches.... Finally, balance does not mean having two very distinct, parallel approaches coexisting in a single classroom in the name of "playing it safe"—for example, literature-based instruction on Mondays and Wednesdays and skills worksheets the remainder of the week. (p. 32)

Combining explicit strategy instruction with literature and language-rich activities calls for a mix of different instructional approaches in a balanced literacy program. The combination of instructional methods and approaches, often called *eclectic instruction,* is supported by one of the most influential and ambitious undertakings in reading research during the 20th century: The United States Cooperative First-Grade Studies (Bond & Dykstra, 1967). The First-Grade Studies compiled data from 27 individual research projects examining the effects of instructional approaches on beginning reading and spelling achievement. The First-Grade Studies found that *no instructional approach was superior to the others* for students at either high or low levels of readiness. Instead, the findings suggest that "although no single method proved best, combinations of methods were associated with the highest achievement" (Shanahan & Neuman, 1997, p. 643).

The First-Grade Studies, more than anything else, underscored the importance of the "teacher variable" in children's reading achievement. Teachers make a difference. The more informed and knowledgeable the reading professional, the more influential he or she will be in dealing with the complexities of learning to read. Highly effective classroom teachers and reading specialists weave approaches and strategies into a seamless pattern of instruction.

A recent research project supports the notion that highly effective teachers are an informative source of knowledge about exemplary literacy practices (Pressley, Rankin, & Yokoi, 1996; Pressley, Wharton-McDonald, Rankin, Yokoi, & Ettenberger, 1996). The project, conducted by a team of researchers from the National Reading Research Center, investigated the nature of outstanding literacy instruction in primary classrooms. In a series of studies, the research team conducted surveys, interviews, and extensive observations of primary teachers who were considered by their supervisors to be outstanding teachers of literacy. As a result of the project, the researchers determined that highly effective first-grade teachers strike a balance between children's immersion in literacy experiences and explicit instruction. The characteristics of highly effective literacy teachers include the thorough integration of reading and writing activities and the extensive use of instructional scaffolding to support the development of children's literacy skills and strategies.

Concluding Comment

Systemic reform efforts are a political response to an educational issue. Because assessment and literacy standards are policy tools that have emerged primarily from a political context, a growing number of reading professionals feel their discretionary instructional powers slipping away in the wake of systemic reform. Some have even bought into the notion that there is a national "reading crisis" in the United States and that schools are responsible for the failure of students to achieve high levels of literacy.

The media no doubt will continue to play an influential role in shaping the perceptions (and misperceptions) of the public toward education generally and reading specifically. In turn, U.S. politicians at national, state, and local levels, as witnessed in the 1990s, will continue to respond to educational issues through legislative action in the name of systemic reform. All of this, of course, affects practice and the work of reading professionals. As Flippo (1997) suggests, reading professionals often find themselves at the mercy of the policy makers who control legislation and the purse strings that keep schools and colleges operating. As reading professionals, we must understand and embrace our roles as policy makers. We must use our expertise and knowledge to shape the public's perceptions of the work we do and to inform policy discussions and debates. And, as Flippo (1999) has suggested, we must all be more politically aware and attuned to how our debates *inside* the profession have been used by some on *the outside* for their own purposes; otherwise, as she warns, "the children who are now being taught as if there is only one way to teach reading" will be the real losers (p. 39).

REFERENCES

Baumann, J.F., Hoffman, J.V., Moon, J., & Duffy, A.M. (1997). *It's not whole language versus phonics but a matter of balance, eclecticism, and common sense: Results from a survey of U.S. elementary teachers.* Athens, GA: National Reading Research Center.

Bear, D.A., & Templeton, S. (1998). Explorations in development spelling: Foundations for learning and teaching phonics, spelling, and vocabulary. *The Reading Teacher, 52,* 222–242.

Berliner, D.C., & Biddle, B.J. (1995). *The manufactured crisis: Myths, fraud, and the attack on America's public schools.* New York: Addison-Wesley.

Bond, G., & Dykstra, R. (1967). The cooperative research program in first-grade reading instruction. *Reading Research Quarterly, 2,* 135–142.

Bracy, G.W. (1997). A nation of learners: Nostalgia and amnesia. *Educational Leadership, 54,* 53–57.

Chall, J. (1967). *Learning to read: The great debate.* New York: McGraw-Hill.

Cunningham, P.M., & Allington, R.L. (1999). *Classrooms that work: They can all read and write* (2nd ed.). New York: Addison-Wesley Longman.

Elam, S.M., Rose, L.C., & Gallup, A.M. (1996). The 28th annual Phi Delta Kappa/Gallup poll of the public's attitudes toward the public schools. *Phi Delta Kappan, 78,* 41–59.

Flesch, R. (1955). *Why Johnny can't read—And what you can do about it.* New York: Harper & Brothers.

Flippo, R.F. (1997). Sensationalism, politics, and literacy: What's going on? *Phi Delta Kappan, 79,* 301–304.

Flippo, R.F. (1998). Points of agreement: A display of professional unity in our field. *The Reading Teacher, 52,* 30–40.

Flippo, R.F. (1999). Redefining the Reading Wars: The war against reading researchers. *Educational Leadership, 57,* 38–41.

Fraatz, J.M.B. (1987). *The politics of reading: Power, opportunity, and prospects for change in America's public schools.* New York: Teachers College Press.

Johns, J.L., & Elish-Piper, L. (1997). *Balanced reading instruction: Teachers' visions and voices.* Dubuque, IA: Kendall-Hunt.

Morris, W. (1955). Teaching Johnny to read. *Saturday Review, 38,* p. 21.

National Commission on Excellence in Education (1983). *A nation at risk: The imperatives for education reform.* Washington, DC: U.S. Office of Education.

Pressley, M., Rankin, J., & Yokoi, L. (1996). A survey of instructional practices of primary grade teachers nominated as effective in promoting literacy. *The Elementary School Journal, 96,* 363–384.

Pressley, M., Wharton-McDonald, R., Rankin, J., Yokoi, L., & Ettenberger, S. (1996). The nature of outstanding primary grade literacy instruction. In E. McIntyre & M. Pressley (Eds.), *Balanced instruction: Strategies and skills in whole language* (pp. 251–276). Norwood, MA: Christopher-Gordon.

Robinson, M. (1995, December 12). Last rites for an educational fad. *Los Angeles Times,* p. 1.

Shanahan, T., & Neuman, S.B. (1997). Literacy research that makes a difference. *Reading Research Quarterly, 32,* 636–647.

Strickland, D.S. (1996). In search of balance: Restructuring our literacy programs. *Reading Today, 14*, p. 32.

Valencia, S.W., & Wixson, K.K. (1999). *Policy-oriented research on literacy standards and assessment.* Ann Arbor, MI: Center for the Improvement of Early Reading Achievement.

Yarrington, D.J. (1978). *The great American reading machine.* Rochelle Park, NJ: Hayden.

CHAPTER 19

The "Real" Common Ground: Pulling the Threads Together

Rona F. Flippo

ave we found some "real" common ground? Yes, I believe we have. Does this common ground provide all the answers to the questions that parents, teachers, and other concerned stakeholders have about reading development and instruction? No, of course it does not. Will the field of reading education ever have all the answers? Probably not. So, what is the real common ground and what good is it? What purpose does it serve and why bother reflecting on it? And finally, where do we go from here? These are the main topics of this summary chapter.

The "Real" Common Ground

The real common ground may already be obvious to you. At least it jumps out at me as I reread and reflect on the experts' points of view and the chapters by the other distinguished researchers who have contributed to this volume. This common ground encompasses so much more than just the lists of experts' agreements displayed in Chapter 1 of this book (also see Flippo, 1998), although they are certainly a part of it. It is so much more than the discussions and research cited throughout this volume that support these experts' agreements. It is bigger than all of these combined findings and the combined wisdom of all who have participated. And yet, even though it seems so obvious and big, this common ground can be elusive to those who do not know what to look for, or to those who are seeking simple answers.

The real common ground includes the common understanding that reading is not simple, and there are no simple answers or solutions that can be applied to all children and situations: Instead of simplistic answers, solutions, and one-way-only approaches, the common wisdom of the field points to the need to allow teachers the flexibility to select the methods, approaches, and materials to fit the particular child and situation. Reading development and instruction is far too complex and involves far too many variables to try to simplify and prescribe it for all children in all situations (see Flippo, 1999a).

As Diane DeFord articulates in her chapter on Jerry Harste, "There are no formulas or magic combinations." Rather, the teacher "actively orchestrates and negotiates a complex set of materials, professional knowledge, knowledge of students, interests, social interactions, and instructional decisions."

This common wisdom is exemplified when Brian Cambourne says, "Teaching literacy is a lot more complex than I ever imagined"; when Edward Fry says, "There is not any best method of teaching reading"; when Scott Paris says, "There is no panacea in the methods or materials"; when Jane Hansen says, "We never get it to work all the time"; and when Richard Robinson interprets and restates George Spache's assertion that, based on Spache's lifetime of research and experience in the field of reading, "No single approach to reading was clearly superior to all others." Another thread of this common understanding becomes obvious when Rand Spiro points out, "It all depends."

Yes, we do know that reading development is generally enhanced and hindered by certain contexts and practices, but we also agree that there are always exceptions, and the teacher and child as they work together are ultimately in the best position to figure out what is helpful (and when) and what is not. Because it does "all depend." The summation of all these understandings, then, is our *real* common ground.

More Threads That Bind

Throughout this volume, reviews of research and discussions from numerous areas and avenues relevant to the experts' agreements are shared. Kathryn Au documents a number of rich examples to show that the experts' agreements are supported by what is known about multicultural education and work with students of diverse backgrounds. Victoria Purcell-Gates provides examples to highlight that her research and work with struggling readers of various age groups supports the findings from the Expert Study. Linda Gambrell thoroughly reviews the research on motivation and provides insights about its relationship to reading achievement. She documents many of the experts' agreements that relate to motivation and has indicated that "if we can find ways of increasing motivation and the amount of effort that young children expend on literacy learning, the impact on reading achievement would be significant."

Jay Campbell discusses the similarities between the experts' agreements and the perspective of the National Assessment of Educational Progress (NAEP), and indicates that this further reinforces the notion of a common ground of agreement among *most* reading educators. His chapter also implies that the findings of the NAEP assessment may have been misunderstood by some policy makers. The NAEP is intended to measure comprehension, not phonics skills: "It would be inappropriate to infer directly from the NAEP reading results that students who scored low on the assessment were necessarily deficient in phonics or phonemic awareness skills."

Timothy Rasinski strongly suggests that the findings from the Expert Study should be shared with parents. Many of the findings, he believes, could be useful to parents and community members to reinforce developing readers. Timothy points out that schools of education and reading professionals must get much more involved and provide parents and the public with the information they want and need.

Finally, Richard Vacca suggests that the agreements that have been uncovered from the Expert Study findings are "a rallying point" that could and should be used to share our common ground publicly; he wants us to use our collective expertise to shape the public's perceptions and to affect policy decisions. He also warns us not to confuse "balance," which he sees as combining explicit strategy instruction with literature and language-rich activities and which he sees as desirable, with the recently politicized and narrow interpretation of the "balanced approach," which is being used by some to "candy-coat" (my word, not his) the *new* "back to basics" movement in the United States and forced educational accountability. How many more children will have to cry during testing, as Richard describes in his chapter, before we (reading professionals, parents, communities, other education stakeholders, and even policy makers) say, "No more!"?

What Purpose Does All of This Serve?

What good can it do to know there is a common ground among different reading researchers, whose agreements on many contexts and practices for teaching reading include an acknowledgment that *no answers fit all situations*? And that likewise, because of this understanding, there can be no one best way to teach reading to all children? Knowing that diverse reading researchers do share this common ground could begin to benefit the future decisions of policy makers. All too often in recent years we have witnessed policy makers and other concerned leaders looking for simple solutions regarding reading instruction. Such an awareness of the collaborative wisdom of the reading field, which indicates these simple solutions are neither good nor appropriate for children's reading development (and in fact, certain agreements even point to harming and making reading difficult for children), might help policy makers redirect their efforts.

As Scott Paris points out, "Teachers who know the diversity of individual problems in learning to read do not expect researchers or legislators to derive a single-minded approach to teach reading to all children." If we can convince policy makers that this search for simple solutions and "the one best method" goes against everything that we (classroom teachers and other reading professionals) know, and against the real common ground that we do share, maybe we can stop the destruction we have all been witnessing. Certainly I agree with David Pearson when he suggests that if the present situation continues "unbridled by saner heads," the real disaster will be victory for one side or the other. David, as well as all the other experts and contributors to this volume, knows that *a one-way-only approach to instruction is just not right*. As I have indicated elsewhere (Flippo, 1999a), when the pendulum swings again—and it will if we cannot end this quest for "the best way"—there may be other winners and losers, but the saddest outcome is that the children are always among the losers when our policy makers become so focused on *only* one way.

Why Is Common Ground Important?

Without an awareness of this common ground, it is far too easy for concerned citizens and politicians to jump on every bandwagon and research finding that comes forward. It is far too easy to look for simple solutions to very complex problems. It is far too easy for many to throw out the research and collaborative knowledge of decades of reading research and reinvent the wheel periodically, irreverently searching for the *nonexistent* one best approach. Missing from these misguided searches is an awareness that it is the teacher, not the method, that makes the difference; see Duffy and Hoffman (1999) for their take on these "flawed searches for a perfect method."

Why Should We Continue to Reflect on This Common Ground?

We should continue to think about and reflect on the common understandings of the field in order to provide the necessary expertise and leadership for future policy decisions and for future conversations and discussions with new as well as experienced teachers and other researchers. The field of reading, within the broader field of literacy, just like other fields of expertise, does have a common ground. If we do not remember to reflect on it and nurture its continued development over time, we will again be at the mercy of those who lack this expertise and wish to make changes none of us would agree to, individually or collectively. We have seen it happen before as well as now, and like all things documented in history, it can happen again.

A new teacher, responding to the survey for school professionals that appears in my book *What Do the Experts Say?* (Flippo, 1999b), shared the following: "I think the idea of establishing a common ground among reading teachers and researchers is an incredibly practical idea, particularly for beginning teachers like me who seek a foundation grounded in research from which to build and create our own hypotheses about how children become able readers" (personal communication). Responses from other school professionals have been similar—all have seen the value of common ground, particularly in the present highly politicized environment. Teachers as well as parents and, of course, the children themselves, are all important to our common ground understandings. As Yetta Goodman suggests, we must have high regard for their roles and their work.

I urge and invite all teachers and other school practitioners to take the next necessary step and see what they too can agree on (see Flippo, 1999b). Then we will have further evidence of and refinements to the common ground we need to continue cultivating in order to influence policy decisions, to help inform the general public, to answer parents' questions, and to professionalize the decisions made about reading instruction in our schools.

Lest we forget, as some of the experts have reminded us, we must all "continue to search for gaps where our knowledge needs to be deepened and extended" (Linda Fielding speaking for Richard Anderson). We must continue our inquiry. Even though we have learned a great deal, David Pearson tells us that "we can do better." Our agreements will mean very little, says Yetta Goodman, without "professional elementary and secondary teachers who understand what they do in classrooms and why." And Robert Rude, in his point-of-view chapter on Wayne Otto, urges, "May we all change...and continue to do so...so our students become the benefactors of our wisdom and change."

I suggest that continued consideration of and reflection on our common understandings can help us identify areas of needed research, can help us do better, and can help us continue to learn and grow. I concur also with Jay Campbell, who indicates that our common ground includes very specific contexts and practices, activities, and uses of materials that have direct implication for classroom practice and policy setting *today*. I believe strongly that these common understandings must not be brushed off or ignored. As reading professionals and others concerned with educational opportunities, development, and outcomes, we would be negligent if we did not share the common ground revealed by this study and by the distinguished contributors to this volume with the general public, politicians, parents, and communities with which we interact. Failing this, I fear we will continue to see more evidence of inattention to what we know are important areas in the teaching of reading—like comprehension, word knowledge/vocabulary, and strategy instruction (for examples see Cassidy & Wenrich, 1997, 1998/1999; Cassidy & Cassidy, 2000/2001)—and more and more inappropriate interpretations like those that have promoted the current phonics-first-and-foremost curriculum decisions throughout the United States.

What Can Happen? A Caveat From Recent History

As we finalized the manuscript for this book, I reread Richard Vacca's description, written in mid-1999, of his amazement and also obvious delight when in the 1996 election year the incumbent U.S. President (Bill Clinton) made "reading" the centerpiece of his education policy and reform proposals. Yes, I agree *it was significant* that in 1996, for the first time in U.S. history, reading education was actually part of a presidential platform and presidential interest. Yet, even more recently, as the 2000 election campaign reflects, not only was reading education a part of George W. Bush's platform for president, but he went much further, letting it be known *how* he thought reading should be taught—with an emphasis on phonics.

We should all be truly astounded: This is an instance of what can happen when we have failed to make known the common ground understandings of the field of reading.

Further Support for the Real Common Ground

On the other hand, new support for many of the experts' agreements and for the common-ground understandings that have been intertwined throughout this volume is increasingly evident. For example, the International Reading Association's (IRA) position statement "Making a Difference Means Making It Different: Honoring Children's Rights to Excellent Reading Instruction" (2000b), highlights the importance of motivation, reading a wide variety of materials and texts, and use of flexible grouping; the statement also emphasizes that "no single method or single combination of methods can successfully teach children to read" (p. 3). Another IRA position statement on "Excellent Reading Teachers" (2000a) emphasizes that teachers make the difference and lists many qualities of excellent classroom teachers that clearly overlap with many of the experts' agreements and common-ground understandings. Furthermore, the position statement recommends that *it is important that children value reading* and have many opportunities to read, and that legislators and policy makers *should not impose one-size-fits-all mandates.*

These position statements, reached by the consensus of the IRA Board of Directors (comprised of diverse representatives of the field of reading and representing a membership of approximately 90,000), clearly lend their support to many of the findings of the Expert Study as well as to the common ground shared in this volume.

Where Do We Go From Here? An Encouraging Word

I hope that where we go from here is back to our communities, colleagues, constituents, and the parents, classrooms, and students with whom many of us work; I hope, too, that we share and reflect on the agreements and the threads of wisdom from the common ground in the field of reading. Asking questions, and discussing and sharing ideas, will help each of us continue to refine and shape our own common understandings—common understandings that will help all of us provide better reading development environments and opportunities for all children with their diverse and various needs and motivations.

Thus, as you can see, in spite of everything that has happened in the current political environment, I remain an optimist. The knowledge I have gained from the Expert Study and as editor of this volume has further reinforced my belief that the field of reading education does share a common denominator of agreements based on solid research and classroom practice. We owe it to our children to keep these agreements and the real common ground revealed here in the forefront of decisions about reading instruction, to continue to reflect on them and refine them as we learn more, and to always keep parents, the public, and policy makers fully informed.

REFERENCES

Cassidy, J., & Cassidy, D. (2000/2001, December/January). What's hot, what's not for 2001. *Reading Today, 18*, pp. 1, 18.

Cassidy, J., & Wenrich, J.K. (1997, February/March). What's hot, what's not for 1997. *Reading Today, 14*, p. 34.

Cassidy, J., & Wenrich, J.K. (1998/1999). Literacy research and practice: What's hot, what's not, and why. *The Reading Teacher, 52*, 402–406.

Duffy, G.G., & Hoffman, J.V. (1999). In pursuit of an illusion: The flawed search for a perfect method. *The Reading Teacher, 53*, 10–16.

Flippo, R.F. (1998). Points of agreement: A display of professional unity in our field. *The Reading Teacher, 52*, 30–40.

Flippo, R.F. (1999a). Redefining the Reading Wars: The war against reading researchers. *Educational Leadership, 57*, 38–41.

Flippo, R.F. (1999b). *What do the experts say? Helping children learn to read.* Portsmouth, NH: Heinemann.

International Reading Association. (2000a). *Excellent reading teachers: A position statement of the International Reading Association* [Brochure]. Newark, DE: Author.

International Reading Association. (2000b). *Making a difference means making it different: Honoring children's rights to excellent reading instruction: A position statement of the International Reading Association* [Brochure]. Newark, DE: Author.

INDEX

FAWSON, P.C., 134
FELTOVICH, P.J., 10, 92–95
FIELDING, L.G., 22–27, 108, 129
FIT: Paris on, 74–75
FITZGERALD, J., 111
FLAVELL, J.H., 69
FLECK, L., 55
FLESCH, R., 146, 169
FLEXIBILITY: Spiro on, 92–97
FLIPPO, R.F., 1, 5–21, 23–26, 28, 39, 41, 53, 55, 70–72, 81, 84, 93, 99, 103, 127, 129, 136, 138, 145–148, 163, 170, 173, 175, 178, 181
FORD, M.E., 134–135
FRAATZ, J.M.B., 167
FREPPON, P.A., 137
FREQUENCY: Fry on, 37–38
FRY, EDWARD, 35–40; background of, 10; philosophy of literacy development, 17f
FRYE, B.J., 129
FUNCTIONAL SYSTEMIC LINGUISTIC THEORY, 29, 32–3
FUTTERMAN, R.B., 131
FUTURE OF READING RESEARCH AND INSTRUCTION, 181–184; Anderson on, 26; Pearson on, 82

G
GADSDEN, V., 73
GALLUP, A.M., 168
GAMBRELL, L.B., 129, 131, 134–138
GEORGE, J.C., 49
GLOVER, J.A., 133
GOAL ORIENTATION THEORY, 132
GOALS: focus on, 122–123; personal, 134–135
GOLLNICK, D.M., 102
GOODMAN, K.S., 79, 113
GOODMAN, YETTA M., 41–48, 63; background of, 10, 41–42, 47; philosophy of literacy development, 17f
GRAHAME, K., 37
GRAVES, D., 10, 50–52, 63–64
GREENE, D., 133
GRIFFIN, P., 82, 106, 128
GROLNICK, W., 133, 137
GROUPING: Hansen on, 50–51
GUTHRIE, J.T., 126, 129–130, 134, 136–138, 156

H

HABITS OF MIND: Spiro on, 95

HALLIDAY, M.A.K., 29, 32

HANNA, J.S., 38

HANNA, P.R., 38

HANSEN, JANE, 49–54, 64, 73; background of, 10, 49–50; philosophy of literacy development, 17f

HAROLD, R., 130, 135

HARRIS, K., 136, 138

HARRIS, V.J., 113

HARRISON, C., 73

HARSTE, JEROME C., 33, 55–60; background of, 10; philosophy of literacy development, 18f

HEATH, S.B., 107, 110

HEFFERNAN, HELEN, 42

HERMAN, P.A., 22

HIEBERT, E.H., 2, 10, 23–25, 63

HODELL, M., 132

HODGES, R.E., 38

HOFFMAN, J.V., 73, 145, 172, 181

HOLDAWAY, D., 32, 110

HOME-SCHOOL CONNECTIONS, 159–166

HOOKED ON PHONICS, 160–161

HOWARD, D., 164

HOYLE, R.H., 132

HUMPHRIES, C., 159

HYPERMEDIA: Spiro on, 95

I

IDEOLOGY: Pearson on, 82; and reading instruction, 30–31, 31f, 31–32

INDEPENDENT READING: and diverse learners, 108–109; and motivation, 137–138; for students with learning disabilities, 120

INDIVIDUALIZED READING: Spache on, 85

INFLEXIBILITY: Spache on, 89

INITIAL TEACHING ALPHABET, 39

INSTANT WORDS, 37–38

INTEGRATION OF READING INSTRUCTION: Anderson on, 24; for diverse learners, 103–106; Yetta Goodman on, 42; Hansen on, 53; Harste on, 55–56; NAEP on, 150; Otto on, 63–64; Paris on, 70–71; Pearson on, 80; points of agreement on, 12f; Spache on, 85

INTERACTIVE APPROACH, 8–9, 11; Pearson on, 79

INTERNATIONAL READING ASSOCIATION (IRA), 93, 163–164, 171, 183

J

Jacobs, L.B., 88
Jacobs, V.A., 161
Jacobson, M.J., 94–95
Jehng, J.C., 92–93, 95
Jenkins, M., 88
Johns, J.L., 174
Johnston, P., 73, 125
Junt, B., 129, 137

K

Kaczala, C.M., 131
Kamil, M.L., 9–10
Karelitz, E.B., 50–52
Karnoil, R., 133
Kear, D.J., 135
kidwatching: Yetta Goodman on, 44
Klare, G.R., 37
knowledge: and reading instruction, 30–31, 31f, 32–33
Koestner, R., 133
Koff, S.B., 131
Korkeamaki, R.L., 135
Krashen, S.D., 32
Kuhl, J., 130

L

Lafave, C., 131, 135–136
language acquisition: conditions for, 29–30; teachers on, 32–33
language experience approach, 39. *See also* whole language approach
Lawton, T.A., 73
learning: by the side of the pool, 123–126; teachers and, 32–33, 41
learning disabilities: and reading instruction, 118–128
Lepper, M.R., 132–133
Levine, A., 7, 16
linguistic data pool, 33, 33f
linguistic theories, 29, 32–33
Linnakyla, P., 137
Linstone, H.A., 8
Lipson, M.Y., 70, 124
literacy: effective, 30–34; roots of, 46
literacy development: conditions for, 29–30, 73–75. *See also* reading instruction
literacy standards: and policy, 168

READING INSTRUCTION: Anderson on, 25–26; Cambourne on, 30–31; closed versus open-ended activities in, 71; complexity of, ix, 30–34, 74, 93–94, 178–179; for diverse learners, 101–117; freedom in, 19–20, 39–40, 44, 74–75; Harste on, 58–59; learning disabilities and, 118–128; NAEP on, 151; Otto on, 66; Paris on, 74; Pearson on, 80; philosophies of, 17f–18f; points of agreement on, 13f–14f; Spache on, 90–91

READING PROCESS: Pearson on, 79–80

READING PROFESSIONALS: media and, 170–171; and policy, 167–177; rallying points for, 173–175

READING RECOVERY, 24, 62

READING RESEARCH: future of, 26, 82, 181–184; Yetta Goodman on, 44–47; on motivation, 130–135; Pearson on, 81–82

READING WARS, 6, 84; Fry on, 39; media and, 170–171; and parents' views, 159–160; Paris on, 75; Pearson on, 81

REESE, C.M., 150–151, 155, 161

REINKING, D., 126

RETROSPECTIVE MISCUE ANALYSIS, 44–47, 63, 79

RICE, M.E., 129, 137

RICHMAN, B., 37

ROAMING THE KNOWN, 62

ROBINSON, M., 171

ROBINSON, R.D., 1, 84–91

ROESER, R.W., 131

ROSE, L.C., 168

ROSEMOND, J., 159

ROSKOS, K.A., 137

ROSS, K.N., 162

ROSS, M., 133

ROTH, J.L., 73

RUDE, R.T., 61–69

RUDORF, E.H., JR., 38

RUMELHART, D.E., 122

RUSSELL, D.H., 87

RYAN, R.M., 132–133, 137–138

S

SAMARAPUNGAVAN, A., 92–95

SAMUELSON, R., 163

SANTA, C.S., 73

SCHAFER, W., 138

SCHEU, J., 101–102, 114

SCHIEFELE, U., 137

SCHMITZ, J., 92–95

SCHUNK, D., 131, 135, 138
SCIBIOR, O.S., 59
SCOTT, J.A., 2, 10, 23–25, 63
SELF–IMAGE: and motivation, 138–139; Spache on, 86
SELF-PERCEPTION: and students with learning disabilities, 126–127
SELF-SELECTION: and motivation, 137–138
SEUSS, DR., 110
SHANAHAN, T., 174
SHANNON, P., 73, 109
SHERMAN, B., 45
SHIREY, L., 22, 24–25
SHORT, K.G., 10, 56–59
SIDE-OF-THE-POOL ACTIVITIES, 124–125
SILENT READING: Anderson on, 25
SILVER, S.H., 73
SKILL INSTRUCTION: and diverse learners, 111–112; Pearson on, 80; for students
    with learning disabilities, 120
SKINNER, B.F., 133
SKINNER, E.A., 137
SLAVIN, R.E., 138
SLOBODKINA, E., 49
SMITH-BURKE, T.M., 129
SMITH, F., 8–9, 28, 63
SMITH LIST, 8, 9f, 63; Cambourne on, 28
SNOW, C.E., 82, 106, 128
SOCIAL CONSTRUCTIVISM, 16
SOCIAL INTERACTION: and motivation, 138; Paris on, 70–71
SPACHE, E.B., 84, 90–91
SPACHE, GEORGE D., 20, 84–91; BACKGROUND OF, 10; PHILOSOPHY OF LITERACY DE-
    VELOPMENT, 18f
SPAULDING, C.L., 137–138
SPEARS-BUNTON, L.A., 114
SPINDLER, G., 113
SPINDLER, L., 113
SPIRO, RAND J., 15; background of, 10; philosophy of literacy development,
    18f
STANOVICH, K.E., 126
STEVENS, J.R., 138
STIPEK, D.J., 135
STRATEGIES, 15; and diverse learners, 110; Harste on, 58–59; Paris on, 74;
    Pearson on, 80
STRICKLAND, D.S., 174